PRAISE FOR *LINCOLN'S LIE*

"Elizabeth Mitchell has woven together some of my favorite subjects— nineteenth-century New York City, early newspapermen, the Civil War, secrets, gold, America's iffy history with alternative facts—into a riveting and delicious work of nonfiction that could pass for a novel. Its contemporary resonances are remarkable." —KURT ANDERSEN, author of *Fantasyland: How America Went Haywire: A 500-Year History*

"*Lincoln's Lie* exemplifies the very best of narrative nonfiction: an intriguing, long-forgotten slice of Civil War history, a rogue's gallery of devious characters, meticulous research and dazzling prose, and a stranger-than-fiction tale that will stay with you long after you turn the last page. Elizabeth Mitchell has written a classic that will appeal to history buffs and fiction fans alike. I couldn't put it down." —KAREN ABBOTT, *New York Times* bestselling author of *The Ghosts of Eden Park*

"In this meticulously researched and carefully argued study, Elizabeth Mitchell makes a strong case [about the culprit] behind one of the greatest hoaxes of the Civil War—the publication of a bogus presidential proclamation that rocked the North . . . Vividly and thoroughly described." —MICHAEL BURLINGAME, author of *Abraham Lincoln: A Life* and *The Inner World of Abraham Lincoln*

"*Lincoln's Lie* is a delicious, suspenseful, exquisitely well-researched, and cleverly written romp through a dramatic and forgotten moment of American history. Mitchell's thorough examination of a strange example of nineteenth-century 'fake news' brings Lincoln back to life in all his subtlety, contradictions, and savvy. This is a wonderful read, as well as a fascinating history lesson. I loved it." —ELIZABETH GILBERT, author of *City of Girls* and *The Signature of All Things*

LINCOLN'S LIE

LINCOLN'S LIE

A TRUE CIVIL WAR CAPER THROUGH
FAKE NEWS, WALL STREET, AND
THE WHITE HOUSE

Elizabeth Mitchell

COUNTERPOINT
Berkeley, California

Lincoln's Lie

Copyright © 2020 by Elizabeth Mitchell
First hardcover edition: 2020

Library of Congress Cataloging-in-Publication Data
Names: Mitchell, Elizabeth, 1966– author.
Title: Lincoln's lie : a true Civil War caper through fake news, Wall street, and the White House / Elizabeth Mitchell.
Other titles: True Civil War caper through fake news, Wall street, and the White House
Description: First hardcover edition. | Berkeley, California : Counterpoint, 2020.
Identifiers: LCCN 2020006260 | ISBN 9781640092822 (hardcover) | ISBN 9781640092839 (ebook)
Subjects: LCSH: Lincoln, Abraham, 1809–1865—Relations with journalists. | United States—History—Civil War, 1861–1865—Censorship. | Presidents—Press coverage—United States. | Journalism—United States—History—19th century. | Press and politics—United States—History—19th century. | United States—History—Civil War, 1861–1865—Journalists. | United States—History—Civil War, 1861–1865—Press coverage.
Classification: LCC E457.2 .M67 2020 | DDC 973.7092—dc23
LC record available at https://lccn.loc.gov/2020006260

Jacket design by Donna Cheng
Book design by Jordan Koluch

COUNTERPOINT
2560 Ninth Street, Suite 318
Berkeley, CA 94710
www.counterpointpress.com

Printed in the United States of America

10 9 8 7 6 5 4 3 2 1

To Al and Liz,
favorite journalists,

and to

all reporters, past and present, who witness

Truth is generally the best vindication against slander.

—ABRAHAM LINCOLN

Contents

LINCOLN'S LIE

1

THE BOMBSHELL

[New York, N.Y. – May 18, 1864]

I t was just after three o'clock in the dark early morning hours of May 18, 1864, when the footsteps of a seventeen-year-old boy broke the near silence around New York's Printing House Square. The newspaper editors had all closed up shop for the night, having received the Associated Press's "all-in" alert, meaning that every bit of breaking news had been delivered to the papers' offices for the day and, therefore, the morning editions could go to print. Editors Horace Greeley of the *New-York Tribune*, James Gordon Bennett of *The New York Herald*, and Henry Raymond of *The New York Times*—the three most powerful people in the press business—had already headed home or to social events. Lower-ranking editors had departed thereafter. Only the foremen and night managers stayed on, monitoring the churning high-powered, steam-driven presses as they rolled over the newsprint paper, preparing the news to send far and wide.

In his hands as he ran through the dark, the harried boy held fluttering copies of an Associated Press report. He ran from building to building along the edge of City Hall Park, visiting each of the city's biggest papers, pounding on doors. At *The New York Times*, he discovered an open door and hurried into the business office. He threw three pages down on the desk and rushed out. Then he ran to the *Daily News* and *The New York Herald*. At each paper, he barely paused to deposit the manifold pages, delivered without an envelope and in full view of anyone who picked them up.

Having visited the Associated Press member newspapers near Park Row, the boy raced all the way down the cobblestone streets to the *Journal of Commerce* at the end of Wall Street, near the banks of the East River. He knocked at the newspaper office door. No one answered. A copyholder who had just been fired for incompetence as the proofreader's second set of eyes sulked nearby, out of view, but he heard the commotion and called out. The boy hurried over and thrust the tissue-thin manifold sheets into the copyholder's hand. Only a crucially important story would be delivered at this strange hour. Glancing at the familiar format and handwriting of the Associated Press's small team of copyists, the copyholder struggled to read the text in the dark but realized the piece was long. He carried it inside.

It had been thirty-seven months of carnage since the American Civil War began. A couple of weeks earlier, Union General Ulysses S. Grant initiated his Overland Campaign, with the aim of destroying Confederate General Robert E. Lee's army between the Rapidan River in north central Virginia and the capital of the Confederacy in Richmond. At the start of the month, the most gruesome firefight of them all, the Battle of the Wilderness, had left the Union forces battling nearly blind for two days in the dense, dark thickets of Northern Virginia. Soldiers could only detect the enemy approach by ear, only determine the battle line from smoke rising above the trees, the flash of gunfire illuminating the bramble. "There is something horrible, yet fascinating, in the mystery shrouding this strangest of battles ever fought," an eyewitness reported.[1] The final casualty tally in eight days: 29,800.

After the Battle of the Wilderness, the Union army had moved south toward Spotsylvania, clearer ground. Over two days, Union forces inflicted high losses on the Confederates, including about ten thousand killed, wounded, or captured. Union losses were high as well. Assistant Secretary of War Charles A. Dana, formerly a journalist for the *New-York Tribune*, remembered surveying the wreckage, with night coming on: "The silence was intense; nothing broke it but distant and occasional firing or the low groans of the wounded. I remember that as I stood there I was almost startled to hear a bird twittering in a tree. All around us the underbrush and trees, which were just beginning to be green, had been riddled and burnt. The ground was thick with dead and wounded men, among whom the relief corps was at work. The earth, which was soft from the heavy rains . . . had been trampled by the fighting of the thousands of men until it was soft, like thin hasty pudding. Over the fence against which we leaned lay a great pool of this mud, its surface as smooth as that of a pond.

"As we stood there, looking silently down at it, of a sudden the leg of a man was lifted up from the pool and the mud dripped off his boot. It was so unexpected, so horrible, that for a moment we were stunned. Then we pulled ourselves together and called to some soldiers near by to rescue the owner of the leg."[2]

The armies moved into new positions starting on May 13, but torrential rain starting on the fifteenth had stopped the fighting for three days. In that pause, Grant looked over the tally of thirty-three thousand men killed, injured, or missing from the Union side. He expressed regret to Major General George C. Meade, head of the Army of the Potomac, who stood with him. Meade remarked, "Well, General, we can't do these little tricks without losses."[3]

Newspapers in New York braced for reports of these clashes. Under the printing room's oil lamp, the copyholder skimmed the lines of the Associated Press piece the delivery boy had just brought in. It was a nine-paragraph proclamation from President Abraham Lincoln, countersigned by Secretary of State William H. Seward. Just a week earlier, on May 10, the president had pushed an optimistic "Call to Thanksgiving" to the newspapers, asking everyone to thank God for the victories, bloody as they were, leading up to the Battle of the Wilderness.

But now, in passionate, foreboding prose, Lincoln said the nation needed to "meekly implore forgiveness."[4] He reported that the recent battles at Spotsylvania had gone worse than expected. "In view . . . of the situation in Virginia, the disaster at Red River, the delay at Charleston and the general state of the country," Lincoln confessed he possessed a heavy heart and requested a solemn day of fasting, humiliation, and prayer.

The previous year, he had also called for "prayer and humiliation," at the urging of Congress. That proclamation, too, had been countersigned by the secretary of state. Lincoln then begged the people "to confess their sins and transgressions in humble sorrow."

In this new proclamation, Lincoln tied his plea more closely to the recent events. While expressing faith in Grant and the damage he had caused the Rebel forces, Lincoln lamented the nation's role as the "monumental sufferer of the 19th century." But most terrifyingly, a desperate President Lincoln called for 400,000 more Union men, ages eighteen to forty-five, to sign up for the army immediately and report to the front. If he did not get his full quota, the compulsory draft would commence after June 15.

Every New Yorker was sure to tremble at a renewal of the draft, given that Lincoln's first draft, less than a year before, had turned New York's streets into blood-soaked, charred avenues of terror when the citizenry rebelled. Lincoln had been forced to temporarily suspend the conscription. In March, just two months earlier, Lincoln had put out a call for 500,000 men, as young as twenty years old, then found his demand reduced dramatically when various states argued that their previous volunteers counted against the quotas. Now Lincoln would require even more bodies, including those of men as young as eighteen.

The foreman faced a costly decision. His editors were gone. Only four men labored over the churning presses. The *Journal of Commerce* offices lay so far from the other newspapers that the foreman dared not spare a man to run all those blocks back to Printing House Square to check what the other newspapers made of this proclamation and return before the paper needed to be printed. Was the story so important that the presses should grind to a halt? Should he remove a story to make space for the president's horrific call?

His options were limited. He could decide to hold the report until the editors arrived mid-morning.[5] But by doing so, the *Journal of Commerce* might miss the enormous and dire story of the state of the Union cause and end up humiliated. His newspaper prided itself on its immediacy. It had been one of the first newspapers in pre-telegraph years to buy a schooner to snag the news arriving from Europe before the competition's rowboats could reach the ships finishing their transatlantic journeys. The foreman also risked the ire of his boss, William C. Prime, if the *Journal of Commerce* lagged behind all the other papers. On the other hand, many editors insisted that absolutely nothing should be accepted in the columns without one of the editors present.

In the end, the foreman decided the paper could not afford to be scooped. He quickly put his assistants to work. He ripped the proclamation into strips, each of the men taking a section to set into type. They hurried so quickly that no one stopped to read the final version in its entirety before the ink slicked the letters and the paper rolled through the muscle of the press. By morning, the daily edition would hit New York streets, and the newsboys would scream the headlines about the need for hundreds of thousands of more bodies. Other copies would be sped by trains to cities across the United States and journey farther still by boat to the trading floors of Europe. International bankers would then read the level of desperation of this news, helping them decide if the United States should be, once and for all, considered two nations.[6]

2

A LAUGHING STOCK

[Cincinnati, Ohio – February 12, 1861]

A train whistle blast sounded through the Ohio Valley. It was 1861, and twenty-seven-year-old *New York Times* star reporter Joseph Howard Jr. brightened at the sound. His time for charming and cajoling had arrived. President-elect Abraham Lincoln would soon appear through a veil of locomotive smoke and amid the vast sea of Cincinnati citizenry that had gathered to cheer his arrival. To be chosen from the throng of reporters to accompany Lincoln on his two-week train trip toward his inaugural in Washington, D.C., would take all of Howard's wiles.

Despite the revelry of the some 100,000 supporters gathered, the journey ahead threatened to be more sinister than celebratory. Even as Lincoln set off to the White House, the United States of America was splintering around him. Just that day, the front page of Howard's paper, *The New York Times*, had reported the activities at the Convention of Secessionist States in Montgomery, Alabama.[1] Representatives of the six rebel states, forging the floods of a near monsoon, had named their own government officers, established their own constitution, and chosen their own president, Jefferson Davis. In a series of highly secretive meetings, they had "dissolved all the political association which connected them with the Government of the United States," as the convention's chairman declared. "The separation is perfect, complete and perpetual."[2]

Under the circumstances, Lincoln's dark pilgrimage to claim the governance of a suddenly much smaller nation was obviously a story of wide interest, and, not surprisingly, Howard wished to make it his own. He won his position at the *Times* by covering smaller episodes of American life with style and wit and had graduated to serving as special correspondent at the presidential political conventions the previous year. With his pen put to this task, he might even supplant *The New York Herald*'s correspondent, Henry Villard, who had become the season's most influential journalist by tracking Lincoln's every move from the election onward.

Certainly, Howard was popular in New York, from the theater district to the pews of the packed Plymouth Church in Brooklyn Heights, from City Hall to Wall Street. Everyone knew his jet-black mustache, spectacles, and near-uniform of crisp, black broadcloth suit and slouched, brimmed hat, as well as his reputation as an infamous flirt who preferred ladies whose dresses, as one colleague said, "ended not too early or too late."[3] Howard's wit drew fellow journalists into his circle, with whom his gregarious, excitable manner spun so high that, on occasion, it even expressed itself in facial twitches.

Lincoln's notoriety was, of course, far greater. He possessed "fame as wide as the continent," as his former law partner noted.[4] This was the soon-to-be president of the United States, a man whose bold condemnation of slavery and vow to keep the nation united had cleaved the country in two. A man Turkish reporters oddly insisted was the tallest man in America, though "slovenly."[5] A man the majority of American voters had rejected and yet who the *Cincinnati Daily Press* argued would, by some miracle, deliver the people from the "treachery, imbecility and rascality" of the Confederates who had "disgraced this great people in the eyes of the whole world."[6] A man whom Howard had heard praised many a Sunday from the lips of perhaps the second most famous man in the country, his dear friend and mentor, the abolitionist preacher in Brooklyn, Reverend Henry Ward Beecher. Now Howard would get his chance to inscribe his portrait of the president-elect into the columns of the most influential newspaper of the time, *The New York Times*.

Lincoln had won Ohio by a hearty 51 to 43, and on this February day, it was touching to see the display of patriotism and support, or as Howard would write, "insanity," among the Porkopalians—his term for the citizenry of Cincinnati, a city internationally known as Porkopolis due to its abundance of pig butchery. In a spirit of national unity, the Democratic mayor had granted his people the day off. Unusual weather patterns delivered gorgeous hours in which they could wait. And the buntings and flags and banners bestowed gladness on every inch of the city's grand broad streets, which had been embellished through the years by the riches of pork and beer.

Howard jotted his notes amid the elbowing. *Tall, gaunt, uncut-haired men.* Women bound breathless in holiday dress. *Germans, Irishmen, Africans. Tired offspring. Flashily-attired damsels* and a man *without a cent in his pocket or a hat upon his head* side by side with men whose pockets held thousands. Rich and poor shoved for space. Giddy women leaned from windows. Men paced the roofs in search of a better view. The platform for the dignitaries sagged with the weight of what seemed like every chairman and subcommittee member and would-be subcommittee member the city could dredge up.[7]

So far, the only reporters traveling with the president-elect were Henry Smith of the *Chicago Tribune*, Edward Baker of the *Illinois State Journal*, and the aforementioned *New York Herald* correspondent, Henry Villard. The latter, a German immigrant a year younger than Howard, had written only in his mother tongue until two years prior when he rapidly taught himself English, so as to cover the groundbreaking debates between Lincoln and his Senate rival Stephen Douglas. Those debates had focused on the most heated issue of the day, the expansion of slavery.

Once Lincoln won the presidency this past November, Villard, as the correspondent for the Associated Press, set up residence in Lincoln's hometown of Springfield, Illinois, tracking the comings and goings of cabinet hopefuls and legislators.

Howard hungered for such proximity. His job now was to charm the impresario of this journey, William S. Wood, a self-important former hotel and railroad man who controlled which reporters could travel with the president-elect on this thirteen-day-long press marathon on wheels. The train was slated to roll from Illinois to Indiana to Ohio, then dip into Pennsylvania through the deep blue smoke of Pittsburgh, then back to Ohio, and up along the Great Lakes to upstate New York. There, the Presidential Special would pause in most any metropolis of size in that state. The mapped route would plummet south from Troy, down through New York City, New Jersey, and Pennsylvania again.

Only after Harrisburg, Pennsylvania, on day thirteen, would Lincoln dare work his way into Maryland, the first state on the junket that he had lost, and by a wide margin, having earned only a thin 2.5 percent of the residents' vote. From there, he would forge on to the White House, buried in the slave-owning territories. Danger might crop up at any time. As Howard informed his readers the next day, Lincoln's life had been threatened by packages of poisoned honey (the unpoisoned kind being the president-elect's favorite vice) and anonymous letters.

A cannon boomed. The presidential train sped into view, unfurling its ribbon of steam through its great canonical stack. The crowd roared so loudly that the slave owners across the river in Kentucky likely heard it.

No one knew what Lincoln's demeanor would be upon his arrival. The news had been so gloomy. The Cincinnati newspapers that very morning reported that during Lincoln's departure from his hometown of Springfield, he had sobbed. If that hadn't heralded an impending national horror—the president-elect weeping as he set off to claim the White House—then what could? Lincoln had removed his old, worn hat and stood silent on a dingy platform in the snow and rain, his chest shaking under his thin overcoat. Some wondered if he could speak at all. Tears ran the hollows of his cheeks. "I know not how soon I shall see you again," he had said. "I go to assume a task more difficult than that which has devolved upon any other man since the days of Washington." The eyes of many listeners welled up and they turned away with emotion. The *Daily Illinois State Journal* would later agree with Lincoln's assessment.[8]

His daunting task had been growing ever clearer since November. The divisions between the states erupted quicker than the *Times* could fully cover and appeared as mere headlines, sometimes with an additional sentence, on the front page. Rumors swirled that, within the week, the Confederates would attack the Union bulwark, Fort Sumter, in Charleston. The state of Louisiana had seized the federal mint. In New York, weapons headed to the South had been confiscated, and now it was said that more than eight New York ships would be boarded and chained down South in retaliation. Southern congressmen on their way out of Washington, headed back to secessionist territories, had even tucked valuable volumes from the Library of Congress into their cloaks—whether as first contributions to a Confederate Library of Congress or as personal souvenirs from a time when that Library of Congress had served all of the thirty-four states. And Lincoln was still two weeks out from his oath of office.

The president-elect's train slowed, inching its cowcatcher into the throngs that considered it somehow wise to stand on the train rails in anticipation. Howard could now take in the magnificent sight of the Presidential Special's black steam engine, draped with little flags and pulling four well-furnished bright yellow cars—one with compartments for the Lincolns and their friends, and one for assorted committee members—plus the luggage car set up with refreshments.

Standing on the platform with the city's mayor, city council, committees, and subcommittees, not to mention reporters, Howard strained to get the best view.

"The press is a magic word," a contemporary journalist and lecturer, Matthew Hale Smith, would write about the era. "It runs the guard. It breaks through the lines of police. It ascends platforms and scaffolds. It opens places of amusement and galleries of art. It commands a plate at a twenty-dollar dinner. It brings obsequious authors and proud capitalists into its dingy sanctum. It invades the privacy of aristocratic life . . . To one fairly entitled to it the New York Press will carry a man round the globe."[9]

Howard's reports already reached an astounding fifty thousand people directly each time they ran—more if the Associated Press picked up his columns and spread them to the papers in its member group. Newspaper owners and investors had amassed muscle in the last quarter century. In those last decades, print circulation had risen thirty-fold to 300,000. New York papers returned 75 percent on investment. What journalists said mattered.

As police bludgeoned through the crowd, opening up space for the train to reach the platform, a roar went up. Howard caught his first glimpse of fifty-two-year-old Lincoln, who had just turned fifty-two that day. While a city dignitary immediately set to "boring [Lincoln] with an interminable address," Howard took the opportunity to jot his other first impressions. The next day, the *Cincinnati Daily Press* would suggest that Lincoln sue all newspapers for libel, given that he was far more handsome than previous coverage had suggested.[10] Howard, however, precisely and meticulously recorded the president-elect's appearance as if judging a prize-winning pig. According to Howard, Lincoln stood six foot, four inches tall and possessed a "large head, with a very high, shelving forehead; thick, bushy, dark hair; a keen, bright, piercing, indeterminable colored eye; a prominent, thin-nostriled nose; a large, well bowed mouth; a round, pretty chin; a first crop of darkish whiskers; a clean, well built neck; more back than chest; a long, lank trunk; limbs of good shape and extreme longitude; arms ditto, with hands and feet symmetrical but naturally large. He wore a black silk hat, (plug,) a dress coat, and pants of sombre hue; a turn over collar, and (I presume) other garments, such as usually are found upon gentlemen who enjoy an annual income of at least $25,000."[11] That was the official salary for the president—enough to buy twenty-five three-story brick houses in Philadelphia should the spirit move him.

He was joined by Mrs. Lincoln; their sons, seventeen-year-old Robert and seven-year-old Tad (eleven-year-old Willie would arrive before departure from the city; their son Edward had died at age three in Springfield eleven years earlier); a military escort that included Colonel Edwin Vose Sumner, a white-haired cavalry commander; Ward Lamon, his bodyguard; his business manager; and "diverse friends of no particular account," as Howard would put it.

When the public official finished his welcome, the crowd hurrahed, cannons blasted, and Lincoln climbed onto a carriage drawn by six white horses, which would eventually convey him a short distance up the hill to the well-appointed Burnet House, the grandest of the city's hotels. The procession, led by officials and uniformed soldiers, crept for two and a half torturous hours to the site where Lincoln would speak briefly, be feted, be serenaded by two thousand German workers—they being the dominant immigrant group of the area—and lay his thick, bushy-haired head for the night.

In his public remarks from the Burnet House balcony, Lincoln noted how much more important government institutions were than party identity in securing the rights of men. Such a bipartisan celebration as the inauguration of a president every four years, he remarked, would be impossible without those institutions. Earlier in the day, in Indiana, he had also emphasized the importance of the people in maintaining an honest Republic, fighting for the rights inscribed in the Constitution. "I have been selected to fill an important office for a brief period, and am now, in your eyes, invested with an influence which will soon pass away," he had said, "but should my administration prove to be a very wicked one, or what is more probable, a very foolish one, if you, the PEOPLE, are but true to yourselves and to the Constitution, there is but little harm I can do, thank God!"

At the reception that evening, Howard watched as well-wishers glad-handed, back-slapped, complimented, and lobbied the weary president-elect. "He was recommended to the Divine blessing about six hundred and fifty times, and urged to 'take care of yourself old man,' on at least three hundred and seventy occasions," Howard would report. In moments of quiet, Lincoln's face would darken, his brow furrow, and his mouth slacken to an expression of utter melancholy. But when inspired into renditions of his long, rambling anecdotes—many of them fictions—he would burst back to life again, squealing with laughter more raucous than that of his listeners.

In the very long, large, and wide hotel dining room, decorated with American flags, police struggled to create order around the president-elect's platform, as well-wishers streamed by. But as the clock struck ten o'clock, a weary Lincoln could bear the harangue no longer and said his goodnights. Already he must have been regretting that he had agreed to travel this convoluted route to Washington instead of going directly to the capital. He showed his fatigue even one day in. Within the hour, one of the reporters noted that a pair of long, large calf-skin boots had been placed outside the president-elect's door, a sure sign he was done for the day.

The policemen waved everyone off. The reporters closed shop. And then Howard got his wish: Woods stopped him on his way to bed to pass along an engraved card.

SIR—You are respectfully invited to participate in the courtesies extended to Hon. ABRAHAM LINCOLN, President elect, by the several Railway Companies, from Springfield to Washington.

Howard had won his prize: an invitation to continue with the president-elect toward his destiny on March 4, when Lincoln would be sworn in as president of the United States on the Capitol's steps.

Truly, Howard should not have been surprised that he had been chosen for the honor of covering the president. Within eight months of his first dispatch a year earlier, the *New York Illustrated News* reported that Howard's posts "have excited more general interest than any letters of a similar character which have been published in this country."[12]

This achievement could be considered doubly outstanding since Howard hadn't primed to be a reporter but instead stumbled into his career. Trained as an engineer at Rensselaer Polytechnic Institute in Troy, New York, he had been on a pleasure trip in California when he detoured away from his homeward journey after learning of a shoemakers' strike in Lynn, Massachusetts.

Lynn was not a normal vacation spot for anyone, nor a shoe strike the normal interest of an engineer, but it spoke to Howard's unquenchable curiosity and taste for adventure. He determined to have a look "to see the fun."

Shoes fascinated him for a number of reasons, as he pointed out in his subsequent writings about the strike: everyone wore shoes, in fact, usually two. Shoes were necessary from toddlerhood to death, which he knew all too well since he had at home "a lovely wife and three responsibilities." Thirty million people in the United States, Howard estimated, went through three pairs of shoes each year.[13]

On Howard's first night in a hotel near the strike activities, as he registered in the logbook, he noticed a reporter guest had preceded him who listed his affiliation as "New York Herald." Howard drew inspiration and penned in his own name with the added and fictitious affiliation "New York Times."

Having written the words, Howard proceeded to behave as if they were true. He reported his journey on "the top of a rickety omni bus . . . and fifteen cents' worth of ride over ruts and through mud to [Lynn's] Liberty Hall."[14] There the female stitchers barred his entrance to a strategy session, excluding all males but their chairman. To cover the real action, Howard knew he would need to sit shoulder to shoulder with these workers. From atop a table, he began pleading his case, then "while talking, . . . worked and worked," until he found himself in, "on condition we would tell the whole truth and nothing but the truth, leaving out what nonsense might be uttered on the spur of the moment." Loyal now to his new fake profession, Howard begged for his "colleagues" from the *Herald* and *Journal* to be granted his same freedom and won their admission as well.

In Lynn, he observed the action so keenly and wrote a record so frank and droll that when he sent his uninvited report to the editor of *The New York Times*, Henry Raymond, the editor was so impressed, he hired "Howard"—his official signoff on each column—on the spot. Howard proceeded to report regularly from Lynn for the next five weeks.

Howard's culminating dispatch from Lynn established values that he would hold close through his subsequent journalism career. He declared, "I will hide nothing for charity's sake but give all I can—good, bad, and indifferent."[15] He believed outside forces had manipulated the men and women in Lynn. He described how the factory owners realized they had manufactured too many shoes, more shoes than feet in the market. Smart and heartless businessmen would have stopped production altogether and sold out the stock in the warehouses to the bare shelves. But such a decision would throw much of the city out of work. Alternately, the factory owners could soften their hearts and continue production but at a reduced pay rate for the workers. That's what they did, and all progressed relatively smoothly until, as Howard saw it, interlopers arrived to tell the workers that they should never stand for being paid so little. The workers struck. But with no other means of income, they not only suffered in the present but also anticipated the future agony of nonexistent savings.

Republicans at the time were known to favor pro-business views, ones that melded the interests of owners with workers. Howard was not apolitical, but, in fact, so staunchly Republican that he had been the first chairman of the Republican Association of Brooklyn. Howard absorbed those views from his father, John Tasker Howard, one of the four founders of the famous Plymouth Church in Brooklyn Heights. In that two-story, vast blank ark of a building on Orange Street, the highly articulate and supremely popular Western transplant preacher, Reverend Henry Ward Beecher, espoused abolitionist sentiment twice every Sunday. And Beecher did not rely on words alone. He often employed dramatic tactics to press his agenda, such as raising funds to buy enslaved people and granting them their freedom, or sending Sharps rifles to the Kansas abolitionists as they confronted the first rumblings of the civil rift.

In power structures of that time, Beecher's seductive reach rivaled that of the press, and, in fact, Howard had not only served as Beecher's private secretary when he was fourteen, but also helped ensure that each of Beecher's sermons were printed in one of the dailies to expand their influence. "In an age in which pulpit eloquence has again and again been demonstrated to have gone obsolete, superceded by the more frequent, the more persistent, and the easier vehicle of the press, [Beecher] has come to possess such a power in the land as no journalist in it," a *World* editorial stated.[16]

"There are dramatic preachers but none so finely or largely dramatic as he," a *Brooklyn Eagle* editorial explained. "There are word painters, but their brushes are brooms compared with his. There are tumultuous thunderers 'gainst wrongs but none storm so vehemently as he. There are men who play upon the feelings of audiences as Rubenstein on the keys of a piano, but none elicit such harmonies as he . . . What he does not know of human nature is hardly worth learning. The flowers talk to him as to no other student of their secrets."

Penitents, particularly wealthy and powerful ones, packed his pews each weekend. Leading up to the 1860 elections, *The New York Times* reported that a "pushing, wriggling, tip-toeing crush of humanity" occupied even the outside window ledges on Sundays, and the throngs on the sidewalks populated so far out they could neither see nor hear, but they at least satisfied themselves by hovering in proximity to the pulpit where Beecher might offer a word of support for Lincoln.

Lincoln had called on Beecher for advice starting a year before his election, and once Lincoln won his presidential victory in November 1860, Beecher had advised him on policy, his platform, and his cabinet appointments. In fact, Howard thought that had it not been for Beecher, the fifty-thousand-some-odd New York votes that had won Lincoln the state might have gone otherwise or never been cast.

Lincoln knew he had a loyal friend in Beecher. Howard did, too. Beecher had mentored Howard from an early age and graced him with his reflected glow as well as his powerful connections. In fact, it was quite possible that Lincoln himself had helped select Howard for the assignment of the inaugural trip. During the campaign season, Lincoln was painted a "man of the people," with, as Villard would tell his daily readers, "an embarrassed air . . . like a country clodhopper appearing in fashionable society."[17] Lincoln, however, demonstrated a savvy understanding of the press, one that might rival that of any Manhattan socialite. His relationship with Raymond, Howard's editor at the *Times*, went back at least eight years to when the two served together on the national Whig Party committee. Raymond had been elected lieutenant governor of New York in 1854 while advocating a strong anti-slavery position. In 1856, Raymond helped draft the charter of the party that Lincoln now represented, earning Raymond the moniker the "godfather of the Republican party."

In May 1860, *The New York Times* ran a column on Lincoln so honeyed it virtually endorsed Lincoln for the upcoming party nomination at which Raymond served as the party committee's vice president. Then the

Times pushed Lincoln's candidacy through the general election. Raymond even stumped for Lincoln.[18] Lincoln, therefore, would have good reason to believe that any *New York Times* coverage of his inaugural train trip would be glowing.

Lincoln had also shown particular ingenuity in guaranteeing positive reports in other newspapers. For example, before the election, his press aide, John Hay, had written letters about him for the *Providence Journal* and the *Missouri Democrat* under the pen name Escartes. On this train trip, in addition to his usual duties, Hay was also working as the special correspondent for *The World*. Writing for the paper anonymously, Hay reported, "No one could witness this frank, hearty display of enthusiasm and affection on the one side, and cordial, generous fraternity on the other, without recognizing in the tall, stalwart Illinoisan the genuine Son of the West, as perfectly *en rapport* with its people now, with his purple honors and his imperial cares upon him, as when he was the simple advocate, the kindly neighbor, the beloved and respected citizen."[19]

Lincoln had in fact been playing the press for a quarter century. As far back as 1837, he wrote letters under the pen name Sampson's Ghost to the local newspaper, the *Sangamo Journal*, run by his friend, Simeon Francis. In those published letters, Lincoln attacked a judicial candidate, the defendant in a land-theft case he was prosecuting. Under his anonymous disguise, he pushed his prosecutorial view, going so far as to accuse the candidate of "fraud" and "forgery." Both claims he presented no evidence to support. Had he written under his own byline, readers would have rightly understood that he was simultaneously prosecuting the target in court. By hiding his identity and, in effect, lying about his involvement, Lincoln was able to make the subject of his attacks look worse and to allow himself a forum that legal protocol would otherwise not allow.

Interestingly enough, Lincoln's letters did little good. The defendant won his election, the public apparently convinced that the anonymous attacks had unfairly persecuted the judicial candidate.

In 1840, while backing the Whig candidate, William Henry Harrison, for the presidency, Lincoln financed a newspaper, the *Old Soldier*, which promoted Harrison and savaged the Democrat candidate, President Martin van Buren. Here, his tactics paid off and Harrison won.

Two years later, Lincoln engaged in a public dispute with Illinois's auditor, Democrat James Shields, over the state's refusal to accept taxes paid in bank notes after the state bank crashed, instead insisting on payment in gold and silver. For several years, Lincoln had been positioning himself as a strong supporter of a federal banking system and now condemned the state's practice as hypocritical, illogical, and cruel. The state had forced paper money on the people, and now it refused to accept its own creation.

Lincoln delivered a scathing letter to the editor of the *Sangamo Journal*, employing the pseudonym Rebecca. Lincoln's letter described in the vernacular how this Rebecca had come across a wheat farmer neighbor, Jeff, griping over the payment policy. The piece, with its false identity, pointedly insulted the auditor: "Shields is a fool as well as a liar. With him, truth is out of the question." "Rebecca" went further with "her" attack, describing Shields attending "a gatherin . . . All the galls about town was there, and all the handsome widows, and married women, finickin about, trying to look like galls, tied as tight in the middle, and puffed out at both ends like bundles of fodder that hadn't been stacked yet, but wanted stackin pretty bad."[20] Shields put down money for privileges, the piece's author alleged. "He was paying his money to this one and that one, and tother one," but since he doled out paper money, he was getting less than he wanted. "His very features, in the exstatic agony of his soul, spoke audibly and distinctly."[21]

The newspaper printed the piece Lincoln delivered instantly. Mary Todd, Lincoln's sweetheart whom he had just lured away from his political rival, Stephen Douglas, was thrilled at its publication and secretly crafted an insulting poem to run a few days later, adding more references to Shields's womanizing.[22]

After enduring this barrage, Shields went to see Francis at the *Sangamo* newspaper office and insisted he reveal the identity of the letter's author. Francis relented after Lincoln told him to confess that it was him. Shields wrote Lincoln a letter demanding "a full, positive and absolute retraction of all offensive allusions," marveling at Lincoln's "secret hostility."[23]

Lincoln refused and found himself challenged to a duel. Given the opportunity to select the weapon, Lincoln picked broadswords, due to the advantage he would gain from his long arms. On the banks of a river, readying for the battle, Lincoln slashed at high branches above his head, as if testing his weapon, but Shields would not back down and the situation looked dire. Finally, Lincoln stared at Shields and said, "Shields, do you want to know who wrote that article?"

"Did you do it?" asked Shields.

Lincoln smiled. "No, Mary Todd wrote it."[24]

The circle of friends in attendance burst into laughter, and so did Lincoln. Eventually, Shields did the only thing he could in the circumstances—he backed down, canceling the duel. But had Mary Todd really been the author of the original letter? Before the duel, Lincoln had signed a letter to Shields that detailed his authorship, and certainly the printed attack bore Lincoln's obsession with banking and politics. Yet, here with his life at stake, Lincoln named his sweetheart Mary Todd as the article's author, making her not just the co-conspirator but the sole culprit.

Lincoln failed to truly suffer for his falsehoods. His scurrilous fiction, which included not just disguising his identity but inventing fake witnesses and fake dialogue and libeling Shields by calling him a liar and a fool, remained in print uncorrected.

Seventeen years later, Lincoln knew still better how to manipulate the press. He served as an anonymous contributing editor to the *Illinois State Journal*, again run by Francis. At that paper, Lincoln wrote anonymous editorials, and when he later moved on to the presidency, the paper rewarded him with reviews that allowed no room for dissent: "True patriots of every name rally around the President."[25] He also collaborated with his own correspondent to cover his famous debates with his rival, Douglas, creating a scrapbook of events that appeared in the *Chicago Tribune*, and which was reprinted as a special edition, with no suggestion that its contents had been overseen by Lincoln.

But Lincoln went even further. Realizing that the German American vote would count heavily in the 1860 election, in which he was the Republican candidate, Lincoln secretly purchased the new German-language *Illinois Staats-Anzeiger* (a paper that also occasionally printed its pages in English). To do so, he appealed to the Republican State Central Committee for the funds. The committee members, however, shied from what could be considered an unseemly manipulation of the free press and denied him any money.[26]

His law partner, William Herndon, claimed Lincoln covered the cost of the paper with a filched split fee from their firm: "Herndon, I gave the Germans $250 of yours the other day," Lincoln had casually remarked.[27] To publicly disguise his purchase, he then asked a friend to deliver the funds on his behalf and pose as the purchaser. He himself drew up the contract. Lincoln would take no profit from the paper but would demand absolute loyalty. The paper would not "depart from the Philadelphia and Illinois Republican platforms." If the paper printed anything "opposed to, or designed to injure the Republican party, said Lincoln may, at his option, at once take possession of said press, types, &c and deal with them as his own."[28]

The contract stipulated the paper was to operate under these rules until after the presidential election of 1860, at which time the paper's property would revert to the editor, but, again, under the stipulation that the newspaper would never print anything against the Republican Party nor move the paper out of Springfield without Lincoln's consent. The readers knew nothing of these hush-hush deals. Further, powerful Republicans received free copies from Lincoln with notes praising the newspaper, without revealing he was the owner.[29]

Aware of the potential influence of this inaugural train ride on public opinion, the president-elect had decided to put aside his desire to speed to the capital. He would wield a unique tool on the winding journey—the ability to woo local reporters and the traveling New York press. (By the fifth day, that pool included Villard, Howard, and reporters for the *New-York Tribune*, *Frank Leslie's Illustrated Newspaper*, *Chicago Tribune*, *Philadelphia Inquirer*, *Cincinnati Gazette*, and the Associated Press.) Lincoln hoped to receive a few weeks of happy coverage and to convey a few patriotic words, but nothing controversial or truly newsworthy, so as to save substantive press attention for the inaugural itself. In addition, he wanted the public to see him in the flesh to make their own judgments, uncolored by the biases of journalists. That said, he was not above bolstering the press's fond sentiments for him. His boyish press aide, John Hay, used one of his anonymous dispatches for *The World* to openly explain the press strategy of the long train journey: "The devotion which men in general feel for their government is a rather vague and shadowy emotion. This will be intensified, and will receive form and coloring, by personal interviews of the people themselves with their constitutional head."[30]

The risks of this elongated journey to D.C. quickly became evident, however. As the train left Cincinnati, Lincoln's aides discovered a bag in his car with a ticking time bomb inside set to detonate fifteen minutes from departure.[31] They quickly diffused it, but the terror remained.

With tensions high, the days flowed by in a ritual of whistle stops and starts, speeches, and songs. Lincoln drew ever closer to the moment he would breach the slave-state line. As Howard observed, even among friendly folk up north, the pauses in the small towns could become "crazy." Take, for example, the train's entrance during the first days into tiny Xenia, population 472, at one o'clock in the afternoon: the excited citizens swarmed the car, climbed on the roof, crawled into the windows, shoved at the doors to get near their hero, and devoured the lunch that had been laid out on the long tables for the official retinue.

Lincoln responded to the disappointment of his empty belly with his favorite recourse: falling asleep. The presidential car remained open to the press, and so Howard found himself able to note for his readers that Lincoln did not engage in such unattractive activities as snoring, drooling, or snoozing open-mouthed, which Howard deemed a real positive in a president, given Lincoln's inability to escape the scrutiny of the press and public.

Lincoln's stupor also allowed Howard to more directly observe Mary Todd and inventory the admirable qualities that had earned her the president-elect's heart more than twenty years earlier. Replacing James Buchanan's beautiful orphan niece, Harriet Lane, as first lady would be no easy task for Mary Todd. The young Lane had become the darling of journalists for her charm. As one journalist would describe her at her final party at the White House while dressed in pure white, Lane was "blonde with deep violet eyes, golden hair, classic features, and bright expression, and a mouth of peculiar beauty. Her form had a statuesque majesty, and every moment was grace."[32]

Mary Todd, well educated, older, and raised in a political family, was less beloved for being more outspoken. Passionate about her husband and his values, she did not shy from voicing her political opinions or from fighting on his behalf, winning her few admirers. She drew fire from the press for her extravagant shopping sprees, including one to New York just before the train journey. But Howard declared the accusations against her in many press accounts false: she "does not chew snuff, does not dress in outré style . . . does not use profane language, nor does she on any occasion, public or private, kick up shindies." According to Howard, her new admirer, she had luxurious hair, a large head with broad forehead, and clear, blue intelligent eyes. He admitted: "Her nose is—well, not to put too fine a point on it—is not Grecian."[33] He insisted on reporting so meticulously he even approved of her hands and feet, "which are really beautiful," as well as the shape of her ear. Most importantly, he liked the fact that she had fallen in love with Abraham Lincoln when he seemed to hold no great future.

In Albany, on the eighth day of the journey, twenty-one-year-old *New York Herald* reporter Stephen Fiske, whom Howard had encountered when covering the eighteen-week North American visit of the Prince of Wales the previous autumn, joined the entourage, replacing Villard, who had grown bored of the speeches and buntings and would get off at New York City. Fiske had not yet graduated from Rutgers University but had deep journalistic experience from having worked as a newspaper columnist since the age of twelve and having served as an editor of the *New Brunswick Daily Times* from the age of sixteen. Howard and Fiske became roommates for the rest of the trip.

What might have been merely a historic celebration like that of the Prince of Wales's visit grew more anxious with every turn of the Presidential Special's enormous wheels. With each stop, reporters began noticing crowd tensions growing—not just enthusiasm now, but chaos. A few days earlier, at a stop in Alliance, Ohio, the blast from a cannon, fired in salute, shattered the window by Mrs. Lincoln's dining table, causing her to bolt from her seat amid a shower of glass. In Buffalo, Lincoln's bodyguards fought off ruffians who surged toward Lincoln with a bewildering mix of passions that ultimately dislocated the shoulder of one of the president-elect's men. In Philadelphia, people shouted and jostled Lincoln's carriage as he moved through the streets, and Howard reported the throngs swarming through the entourage's hotel. Howard and the other journalists wondered how anyone could keep the president-elect safe.

By this point, a significant security detail had joined the train ride, including not only Colonel Sumner and bodyguard Ward Lamon, who was carrying two revolvers, two derringers, brass knuckles, and a large bowie knife, but also George H. Burns, attaché of the American Telegraph Company and agent of E. S. Sanford, Esq., rumored to be connected to the Pinkerton detective agency.

In Washington, Democrats had introduced a bill to end federal taxation on the Southern states and demand that the federal government withdraw from all forts, handing the property over to the Confederacy. With that tension awaiting him, Lincoln's train pulled into Harrisburg, the last stop before crossing the slave-owning line. One reporter noted that not one member of the gathered crowd cheered the president-elect, which seemed disturbing. Perhaps people had come purely for the spectacle. Or, perhaps, they wished the president-elect to register the suspicion in their eyes.

At the four-story Jones Hotel, Howard realized that the agitation of the masses had become a riot. Other journalists feared Confederate spies mingled with the crowd, stirring up trouble and picking up details to send to conspirators closer to Washington. The military on hand responded with force. Wrote Howard, "Dragoons flourished swords, and their horses plunged most violently; militia men plunged their bayonets and their victims yelled most wildly."[34] The entire scene descended into chaos.

Lincoln was preparing to speak outside to the hordes after a banquet dinner, but the "eager, impulsive, and thoughtless" people, as Howard called them, surged in through the doors and foyer, filling every hall and passageway. Howard would report: "The 'Jones House' may well be considered the ne plus ultra of all that is noisy. On the 22nd day of February, 1861, the proprietor thereof, agitated beyond computation by the presence of Mr. LINCOLN, grew pale with anxiety. He knew not whether he was man or skyrocket; he flew here, there and everywhere, like a chestnut in a hot pot; he ran up stairs and down . . . It was dreadful and fearful to behold."

Given the mayhem, the press pool was not greatly surprised when partway through the dinner, Pennsylvania governor Andrew Curtin rose from his seat to announce the president suffered a headache and would retire early. He led Lincoln by the arm through the dining room and into the halls. Lincoln had already spoken fifty times in the first week alone.

The next day, tensions mounted: the train was scheduled to travel to Baltimore, the first city on the itinerary in a slave state, and the first city in which Lincoln had not been invited to speak. Due to the lack of track connection between the east–west and north–south lines, the president's locomotive would have to be removed from the rails, drawn by horse for a mile through the city, and then reinstalled on the track headed south. The prospect terrified Lincoln's staff and reporters alike. Confederates lay in wait.

With Lincoln in bed for the evening, Howard and Fiske retired to their elegant hotel room in Harrisburg, which they had been lucky enough to procure in the scramble for lodging. The two had just settled to work on their dispatches back to New York when the bedroom door flew open. Burns, the young telegraph agent, rumored to be connected to the Pinkerton detective agency, burst into the room and locked the door behind him. A flabbergasted Howard demanded an explanation for his sudden arrival and their sudden imprisonment.[35]

Burns refused to explain. He insisted for the safety of the president-elect, he needed to keep the reporters locked up throughout the night.

Howard rejected that reply. His livelihood and reputation depended on his telling the most urgent stories, and anything involving the president's safety could clearly be described as urgent. He began fighting and cajoling, as he had done successfully back at the strikes in Lynn. He heatedly explained that his entire reporting success depended on his being able to send his account to the telegraph that night for the newspaper the next morning. If he failed to file promptly, his editor would suspect more dissolute reasons. But Burns assured Howard and Fiske that Lincoln's men had restrained every reporter, eliminating competition, and that their imprisonment was crucial to the public good.

The men argued. Burns parried. Finally, worn down, Burns declared that he would reveal the full reason for their captivity if both reporters promised not to file details until the following day when the president had safely reached Washington.

The tale Burns told was strange and ominous: it turned out, as far back as Cincinnati, the president (whom Burns referred to as "Nuts" in coded telegrams) had been alerted to a plot to assassinate him. Agents had discovered that murderers planned to blast the train off its rails as it rolled toward Baltimore or, after it had arrived, shoot the president or plunge a stiletto into his heart.

At first Lincoln had resisted his aides' advice to change his plans to save his life, but in Philadelphia, he had been rousted from his room with the message that a stranger wished to speak to him about a matter of life and death. A third source had confirmed the report. He agreed to alter course.

After Lincoln had exited the Harrisburg banquet dining room on the arm of Pennsylvania governor Andrew Curtin, he had walked straight to a waiting carriage in which his bodyguard, Lamon, had come to escort him to a special, unlit train.

Whether the threat had been real and fatal could not be known for sure, but one of Lincoln's companions so believed its power that he drew up his own will in case the president continued with his planned public itinerary. Burns told Howard that when Lincoln had left Harrisburg, "no one would recognize Mr. Lincoln at night." Those words stuck with Howard.

Left with no choice, Howard and Fiske used their captivity to complete their dispatches. In his report, Howard emphasized how reluctant Lincoln had been to flee, but that he had finally agreed with Mrs. Lincoln; his friend and campaign advisor, Illinois state senator Norman Judd; and the informant who had provided the original information. Howard claimed that "statesmen laid the plan, bankers indorsed it, and adventurers were to carry it into effect."

Unaccustomed to writing with so few visual cues, Howard stretched beyond the facts provided to imagine what Burns had meant when he said "no
one would recognize" the president-elect. Howard summoned a description
from what he would later call "his mind's eye," attempting to consider "what
disguise Lincoln or any other man could obtain in the little town of Harrisburg at nine o'clock in the evening in the year of our Lord 1861."[36] Howard
considered what Lincoln's outer garment might look like, and the first attire
that came to him was the cape worn by Lincoln's companion on the trip,
the refined cavalry commander Sumner. Howard also knew that Lincoln
carried a small traveling cap, but Howard considered it insufficiently "pic-
turesque," so imagined the opposite of the tall silk hat that Lincoln usually
wore, and, as he would later recall, "jauntily placed" a "Scotch cap . . . upon
[Lincoln's] dear old head."

While newspaper editors of the time accepted the inevitability of political partisanship, they also highly valued accuracy, scoops, access, timeliness,
and style. Howard seemed to respect the last four attributes while disregard-
ing the first.

At one o'clock in the morning, Burns released the two journalists to the
hotel's empty halls. They trawled for reportable details but found little, and
no messages could be sent until eight o'clock in the morning because, in
fact, outside Philadelphia, Burns had personally gone two miles beyond city
limits with his most trusted linesman to climb the poles and place copper
stops. He had tested the system by sending a message along the line and
been gratified to find it failed to complete.

At eight o'clock on Saturday morning, February 23, *The New York Times*'s
day editor received Howard's filing just as he got to his desk. His first thought
was, "Well, this is a pretty time of day for Howard's dispatch to arrive."[37]

He glanced at the first sentence: "Abraham Lincoln, the President-Elect
of the United States, is safe in the capital of the nation." That got his at-

tention. The president-elect had been threatened? The day editor knew instantly that a story so dramatic demanded to be sent out as an extra. Deeper into the story, the day editor read the detail that, according to Howard, the president-elect had not only changed his schedule to avoid assassins but also had actually donned a ridiculous costume to sneak to the most important office in the land. A president in disguise?

Within hours, hundreds of newsboys hawking papers in the streets of New York City stunned passersby with the news brought from the imagination of Howard, that Lincoln, already ready for bed, had grown fearful and, under cover of night, dashed to Washington in a ludicrous, even comic, state of dress. "What a farce! What a coward!" a letter to the editor of the *Cincinnati Daily Enquirer* exclaimed.[38]

At nine o'clock in the morning, the soot-black presidential train, its flags near rags, carried toward Baltimore a grumpy and anxious Mary Todd, the dignitaries (many of whom to Howard amusingly seemed at a "boil like effervescing soda" about being left behind), and the journalists, with no Abraham Lincoln onboard. Along the line, at regular intervals, fifteen thousand sober-faced flagmen each held a white pennant aloft. They also clutched a lowered red flag should they need to signal that an armed killer lurked ahead. Nearly all the passengers feared that they would still be targeted since no conspirator would know Lincoln had left their midst.

In Baltimore, hoodlums hammered at the car, sticking their faces through the windows and hollering, "Trot him out! Let's have him! We'll give you hell! You bloody Black Republicans!"[39] They streamed in through the doors and packed the journalists' car until the reporters found themselves backed up against the sides. A few men even burst into Mrs. Lincoln's car and aides forced them out. All the while the conductor bellowed that the president-elect was not on board.

If anyone had wondered at the sagacity of the president's decision to leave undercover the previous night, it would have been answered then. After a half hour of terror, Mrs. Lincoln and the other women in the procession were ferried away to a different train. Still, one dignitary in Philadelphia insisted to Woods that it was shameful that Lincoln had denied a glimpse of himself to men who had risked their lives to vote for him.

As this scuffle unfolded, Howard's imagined costume continued tarnishing the president-elect's reputation. No reporter could dispute the accuracy of the description because only Ward Lamon had seen the president. Newspapers that had not received the costume detail from their own reporters recalled their papers to correct the visual and send out fresh editions. The famous cartoonist Thomas Nast, who had joined the train in New York City, found that his work had been reconfigured in the newsroom to reflect the theatric buffoonery as described by Howard.[40]

Some editorialists used the opportunity of the camouflage to vent their own prejudices. The *Dallas Herald* asked not just about the Scotch cap, but "did [Lincoln] borrow that old military Cloak from a nigger . . . did he have his face blacked *a la mode?*"[41] *The Anderson Intelligencer* of South Carolina jokingly claimed that the commissioner of patents had swiftly enlarged the glass case that contained General Washington's regimental suit to now also house the long military cloak and Scotch cap that had saved Lincoln's life on the way to Washington.[42]

The *Brooklyn Eagle* called the assassination plot "a fabrication" and particularly criticized the claim printed by Howard that statesmen, bankers, and politicians had been party to the plot's design. But the *Eagle*, which claimed the highest circulation of any evening paper in the United States, went on to declare that Lincoln, for sneaking to the capital in disguise, deserved the "deepest disgrace that the crushing indignation of a whole people can inflict."[43]

In the days following Lincoln's inaugural, the newspapers continued to mock his costume, a disguise entirely fabricated by Howard. A *Vanity Fair* cartoonist crafted a vision of a towering Lincoln wrapped head-to-toe

in the cape and cap, titling it "The New President of the United States —
From a Fugitive Sketch."[44] The magazine ridiculed him in a separate article: "The President-elect disguises himself after the manner of heroes in
two-shilling novels, and rides secretly, in the deep night, from Harrisburg
to Washington."[45]

In the years that followed, Lincoln's bodyguard Lamon would say that
Lincoln's great shame and regret in his presidency was that he had taken
flight, which allowed him to be made a target for the fabrication.[46] It had
tainted his administration before it even began. With all the pomp above
the slave line, intended to please the press and secure political allies, Lincoln
would appear to be a president only of the North. Up there, above the segre-
gation line, he had bands and buntings at every stop, and he had popped up
at each one to wave and smile to the citizens. But, as soon as he crossed the
line to the segregated South, he had stolen away like a thief, like a coward.
Mary Todd deeply regretted the choice, too. Even a home state newspaper
excoriated him. "People now marvel how it came to pass that Mr. Lincoln
should have been selected as the representative man of any party," read an
editorial in the *Salem Weekly Advocate* in Illinois. "His weak, wishy-washy,
namby-pamby efforts, imbecile in matter, disgusting in manner, have made
us the laughing stock of the whole world. The European powers will despise
us because we have no better material out of which to make a President."[47]

What made the damaging fabrication so strange was that Howard, having been around Lincoln almost continually for two weeks, had come to
sincerely admire the man. Howard wrote: "I am satisfied that Mr. Lincoln
is far above the ordinary standard of human capabilities. His mind works
clearly, quickly, and with great directness. He is a shrewd judge of character . . . He has brought to the present exigency one of the most unprejudiced,
calm, philosophical and vigorous minds to be found in the country . . . Physically, he is a remarkable person."[48] Yet through a few words plucked from
his imagination, Howard had managed to make Lincoln not the country's
hero, but its buffoon.

Why had Howard stooped so low? Had he so given in to the drama of the event that he lost sight of his reporter's role and embellished the journalistic account to make a better tale? Was he seeking to pay back Burns for blocking him from covering the greatest escape in presidential history with a barbed swipe at Burns's charge? Or was he a writer not dissimilar to Lincoln himself, who, while composing as Rebecca, vented emotions through the medium of fictitious details, in Howard's case, a distaste for Lincoln's abrupt departure from plan?

In fact, when Lincoln escaped through the night to Washington, he had worn his own bob-tailed overcoat and a soft wool hat that a friend had given him in New York City. Lincoln apparently never publicly scolded Howard about the lie. He let the incident fester, for the moment, unresolved.

And so it was that Abraham Lincoln came to claim his presidency, the last man to slowly climb down from an emptied train onto a Washington platform, a lonely figure emerging with his bodyguard and the detective Pinkerton to a gray day without family or advisors, his wife arriving later, the newspapers soon to fill with mocking caricatures, all based on the brief, fictitious description that flowed from one supposedly friendly journalist's pen.

And those journalists still possessed the power to craft the story every day, each hour of Lincoln's trying and fatal presidency.

3

THE CRIME

[New York, N.Y. – May 18, 1864]

T he bells of Trinity Church, at Broadway and Wall Street, let loose a glorious peal.[1] It was eight o'clock in the morning. For the past three years, two months, and two weeks, Lincoln had occupied the White House. Civil war had raged only one month and eight days short of that.

In a dingy, carpet-less headquarters, up seventy-eight dimly lit stairs at 145 Broadway, an Associated Press operator reviewed the morning newspapers. Nearly every day, the papers included official death lists. So many sons gone forever, identified only by their rank and division. Lately, those lists had grown horrifically long. An estimated forty thousand Union casualties, including the missing, had amassed in the last few weeks.

A few days before, torrential rain stalled the main battles around the courthouse in Spotsylvania, Virginia. But that delay only heightened tensions. "The intense anxiety is oppressive, and almost unfits the mind for mental activity," Navy Secretary Gideon Welles wrote in his diary. "We know it cannot be long before one or more bloody battles will take place in which not only many dear friends will be slaughtered but probably the Civil War will be decided as to its continuance, or termination."[2]

More dead men meant more volunteers needed to fight. But New York was in no mood to send them. Twelve thousand armed soldiers, police, and volunteers had been required to stop the rioting after last year's summer draft. Hooligans in the city had burned buildings, looted, and fatally beat and lynched anyone who came across their path, particularly black people.

Adding to the political pressure was the impending Republication nomination. In three weeks, the party would decide if it should keep Lincoln as its presidential candidate for the November election.[3] Lincoln's chances were uncertain. Multiple rivals had already made themselves known. Even Thaddeus Stevens, chair of the House Ways and Means Committee, expressed doubts about Lincoln's potential abilities to defeat his challengers. The previous November, the president excused himself from a cabinet meeting to attend the dedication of the cemetery at Gettysburg. Someone asked Stevens the whereabouts of the president and secretary of state, and he told the questioner the trip caused their absence: "Let the dead bury the dead."[4] Lincoln later related this story at a cabinet meeting, as if amused.[5] He would close those dedication proceedings with his Gettysburg Address.

Of the Republican-leaning newspapermen, most preferred secretary of the treasury Salmon Chase for the nomination. In fact, James M. Winchell, a popular *New York Times* reporter, simultaneously served as secretary of the Chase for President National Committee. A confidential letter he printed and circulated in February, later known as the Pomeroy Circular, promoted the Chase candidacy. But even the flattered and deeply ambitious Chase realized how unseemly it was to run against the president he served. He wrote a letter to Lincoln disavowing prior knowledge of the Pomeroy Circular. Lincoln accepted the excuse and allowed him to stay, though a seed of distrust had been planted.

Republican abolitionists harbored hopes that General John C. Fremont, an 1856 Republican presidential candidate, would enter the race. As commander of the Department of the West early in the war, Fremont, without consulting Lincoln, took the bold step of declaring all slaves in his territory free. Lincoln reversed the order and fired him for his presumption of power.

As the Associated Press operator scanned the pages of *The World*, he read the president's astounding proclamation. In it, Lincoln lamented the disasters of the war and called on the people to participate in an upcoming day of fasting, humiliation, and prayer. But most horrifying, he called for a draft of 400,000 citizens, ages eighteen to forty-five, to go to the front.

Understanding the import of these words, the Associated Press operator keyed the story over the wires to newspapers "east and west."[6] Almost instantly, the telegraph operators across the country picked up the clack of dots and dashes, sending the information into the columns of local newspapers. As *The New York Times* pointed out, through the telegraph, a public figure like Lincoln possessed unprecedented power: "The telegraph gives the speaker . . . an audience as wide as the Union. He is talking to all America . . . immediately, and literally with the emphasis of lightning."[7]

After the Associated Press operator telegraphed *The World*'s story, D. H. Craig, the AP's lead agent, tapped out a message to Washington. His goal: to check the proclamation's veracity.[8]

Uptown, at his elegant townhouse on East Twenty-Third Street, thirty-nine-year-old William C. Prime, editor in chief of the *Journal of Commerce*, woke up, having enjoyed a rare good night's sleep. His wife of thirteen years, Mary, was in Hartford, Connecticut, on a family visit. He missed her terribly. But he felt somewhat relieved that she would be far from New York City that day, out of reach of the war's breaking news, including a horrific body count of three hundred Union men two nights before near Spotsylvania.

Two days earlier, Prime wrote Mary, "I find the state of feeling here deeply depressed," more depressed than he had expected, given recent trends. "The news I have from Washington is also depressing . . . As nearly as the truth can be come at, Lee has only changed position—is probably as strong as Grant today."[9] Will and Mary Prime were true intellectual equals, both authors of well-respected books about their adventures together throughout Egypt and the Holy Land. "You know Scott who was assistant secretary of war," he went on. "He is a strong Republican and on best terms for information of anyone. He told a friend of mine this evening, confidentially, that there was no prospect in his opinion of Grant going to Richmond. That he and his friends regard the news as all bad. That our losses thus far are not less than forty thousand, not counting prisoners taken by Lee."

Six days earlier, Prime had dined at the home of Samuel Barlow, the investor and business manager of *The World*, the most popular newspaper in the country. They had been joined there by *The World*'s editor, Manton Marble. Prime and Marble were both members of the Peace party, seeking to end the war at all costs; in particular, they were both members of the publication committee. *The New York Times* accused the committee of trying to turn the army into a "Peace Machine," by sending thousands upon thousands of pamphlets to the Army of the Potomac, "where like the beaver of which we have read," they had succeeded in stirring up doubts among the troops. A "let-me-go-home desire [is] creeping upon the ranks."[10]

The anonymous *New York Times* reporter went on to say that the "circulation of certain New-York dailies in the camps" had contributed to the desertion rate, which stood on the Union side at two hundred soldiers a day. "Whole brigades are discontented; rank insubordination stares the Generals in the face; utter impotence will soon be the fate of the Commanding-General."

Prime and Marble did not consider themselves anti-government radicals so much as pro-Constitution patriots. A *World* editorial, "Why the North Abandoned Slavery," made clear Marble considered slavery morally wrong, but he had failed to strike on a legal reason for why the North could force the South to agree.[11] He believed Lincoln had become a danger by claiming his power not from written law but from a vague appeal to a "higher authority." A lapsed Baptist, Marble felt suspicious of human interpretations of what God would want. Even the Emancipation Proclamation, in Marble's mind, allowed the federal government to interfere in the "domestic institutions" of the country without a legal basis.[12]

Lincoln worried Marble further by a series of authoritarian acts launched in his first days in office. Just over a month after Confederates fired on Fort Sumter, Lincoln's administration had simultaneously seized all New York telegraphic messages at all telegraph offices sent for the entire past year, starting May 1, 1860.[13]

Within weeks of that first Confederate military action, Lincoln told his generals that they could consider the right of habeas corpus—a citizen's right to a fair trial—suspended in the territory between Annapolis, Maryland; Philadelphia, Pennsylvania; and Washington, D.C. According to Lincoln's declaration, the military officers could lock up anyone who interfered in military movements toward the South without proving guilt.

When asked to review the case of a Maryland secessionist, John Merryman, imprisoned without trial, a judge on the U.S. Supreme Court's state circuit swiftly declared Lincoln's order unconstitutional. Only Congress could authorize the suspension of citizens' specific constitutional rights. Lincoln ignored the ruling. Merryman remained behind bars, while Lincoln pushed Congress to pass a law to his liking. As he wrote in his July 4, 1861, message to Congress, he felt the secession crisis forced his action: "Are all the laws, but one, to go unexecuted, and the government itself go to pieces, lest that one be violated?"[14] He also claimed authority from a section of the Constitution that allowed habeas corpus to be suspended during a rebellion if necessary for the "public safety." He took that to mean a kind of general safety, not necessarily a specific physical safety, such as avoiding travel to a courtroom while bullets flew.

The issue of whether or not to let Lincoln suspend habeas corpus was so controversial, Congress introduced a bill in its next session to give him the right, debated it hotly, and failed to pass it. Over the next years, in various parts of the country, Republican officials requested the right to shut down dissent or arrest draft dodgers without warrant or trial, and the Lincoln administration approved, but again, without legal authority.

In August 1862, the War Department issued an order by "direction of the President of the United States" forbidding foreign travel or travel to another state when a draft was pending. The order suspended habeas corpus for anyone arrested under this order and further "all persons arrested for disloyal practices."[15] Secretary of War Edwin Stanton immediately released a second order, going even further, that all U.S. marshals and chiefs of police anywhere in the country were authorized "to arrest and imprison" anyone who discouraged volunteer enlistment or gave "aid and comfort to the enemy" or for "any other disloyal practice against the United States."

Marble weighed in heavily against these broad, punitive edicts. In a *World* editorial in the fall of 1862, he reported that highly placed Lincoln officials threatened "that if we continue this sort of comment, it will be at our peril."[16]

And indeed, *The World* noticed signs of harassment. In early 1863, the Senate passed a bill—after the failure of a Democratic filibuster on a technicality—granting Lincoln the power to suspend habeas corpus, saying any of the president's Civil War orders "shall be a defense in all courts to any action or prosecution—civil or criminal, pending or to be commenced—for any search, seizure, arrest, or imprisonment."[17] But Congress also kept a significant protection for detainees: the right to a trial before a grand jury. The law's constitutional validity had yet to be tested in the U.S. Supreme Court.

A potential test case cropped up almost immediately. In May 1863, General Ambrose E. Burnside, head of the Department of the Ohio for the Union army, ordered the arrest of a fiery former congressman, Clement Vallandigham, after he delivered a speech denouncing what he called "a war for the freedom of blacks and the enslavement of whites" and "for the purpose of crushing out liberty and erecting a despotism."[18] *The World* defended Vallandigham's right to free speech.[19]

On June 1 that year, Marble received a letter from S. S. (Samuel Sullivan "Sunset") Cox, a Democratic congressman from Ohio, who served as a friendly sounding board to the paper: "Your *World* stopped here [Columbus, Ohio] at our P.O. today," Cox wrote, meaning that the newspapers had been blocked from circulation. "[Burnside] owed you something and he paid it but it won't hurt in the end. My wife said . . . she would rather Burnside would confiscate all the strawberries of the season than the *World*. I have made a private agreement with an insider to beat them and get my *World* anyhow. They give them away as waste paper."[20]

"We made the most of what we had and had a nice time," Prime further reported to Mary about the dinner at Barlow's, "though gloomy and sad about . . . the war . . . The carnage is awful . . . It is impossible to see the end."[21]

Prime's dear friend, retired Major General George McClellan, the front-runner for the Democratic presidential nomination, and his wife also attended that dinner party. Early in the war, McClellan had been the darling of the press, the army, and the public for winning the first, albeit minor, victories for the Union forces. He understood the power of the press. He had not only brought portable printing presses to the battlefield but also directed that all military telegraph wires go through his offices.

But Lincoln fired McClellan in November 1862 for what the president saw as his maddening reluctance to engage in combat. In February 1864, just three months before this dinner party, the government printing office put out McClellan's official war report, justifying his military decisions and essentially critiquing the Lincoln administration.[22] Now he was the clear front-runner for the Democratic Party.

Over 115 miles north, Mary was experiencing her own trials. A staunch Democrat, she found her stay in her Connecticut hometown particularly difficult due to the Republican ferocity of her family and social circle—

including her father, who held state office. Her relatives insulted her for her Democratic views, calling her a "traitor," which provoked a fierce headache.

The night of May 17, though, her concerns focused on her husband's well-being. She wrote him, urging him to leave his desk at a reasonable hour—surely his health would suffer if he kept toiling every day late into the night. And she confessed her deep grief at the state of the country: "It is a sad age of the world in which we live—joy does not live in these days . . . Perhaps when the storm is over we may see why we have been tried so fearfully . . . These terrible anxieties, this desolation of our land—the bloody fields where our dead are being piled—is it not fearful? When will it come to an end?"[23]

Will Prime had no answers for her. He could do nothing but keep covering the news however it unfolded. Down at the newspaper district near City Hall Park, deliverymen even now loaded the strapped bales of newspapers onto trains to ship across the country.[24] Delivery boys hollered the headlines on street corners. Most importantly, workers hauled the newspapers to the harbor where they would be taken down the bay to the *Scotia*, the vessel headed to Europe that very day at noon.

That bright and balmy morning of May 18, Prime went as usual to his stoop for his copy of his own newspaper. It was missing. In all the years, the boy had never failed to deliver his copy to him. Why, of all days, in a time when news was crucial, would the delivery fail? He set about getting himself out the door and to the office.

At ten o'clock in the morning, M. S. Roberts, the New York manager of the American Telegraph Company, who happened to be in Boston, read the president's proclamation in *The World* and sent a telegram to his military superior in Washington, thirty-eight-year-old assistant superintendent military telegraph officer Thomas Eckert.

Eckert never seemed to leave his desk and was the person most likely to see President Lincoln first each day.[25]

Over the last thirty years, the telegraph had knit the states together in fifty thousand miles of cable. Clerks tapped out the code created by telegraph inventor Samuel Morse, which transcribers on the other end took down in dots and dashes and gave to another operator for translation. Soon that extra step of translation became unnecessary. As operators sat all day listening to its rhythms, their thinking changed. In the clickety-clack, they began to hear stories, ideas, and congratulations translated instinctively to words, the Morse code becoming like a mother tongue.

Through the efforts of industrialists, the telegraph had become "a common necessity like Croton water, the express, and the post office," one journalist observed, bringing the cost within "every man's means" and bringing "a wire to every man's door."[26] A wife struck by the flu telegraphed her husband to fetch a doctor. A businessman needing his carpetbag for an impromptu trip to Europe telegraphed his maid to bring it to the dock. A planned night at the theater could be switched that very day to a frolic at a costume ball. "Contracts are made, money paid, the payment of checks stopped . . . and millions of stocks change hands through the subtle agency of the wire. The General Superintendent of Police sits in his office and converses with his captains thirty miles away."

When Morse introduced his invention, he thought it would bind Americans closer together. But its use, in fact, did the opposite. Once Americans possessed a clear lens into the specifics of regional opinions, they came to understand their glaring differences.

Alarmed at the unearthed divisiveness, back in March 1861, Morse formed the American Society for Promoting National Unity. While the sentiment was welcome, the group held stern views. They stood opposed to abolitionism, woman's rights, free-love, spiritualism, socialism, agrarianism, and all other "visionary schemes" by which people "vainly think to inaugurate a millennium of bliss, by their imaginary reign of liberty and equality."²⁷ In other words, the way to have unity would be to quash individual rights.

Three main companies served most of the country. Western Union sent information west, as far as the Mississippi River and from the Great Lakes to the Ohio River. The new Independent Telegraph Company, at Twenty-Eight Nassau Street, capitalized on Wall Street traders' need for instant news, setting up a branch on the trading floor of Gilpin's Exchange, at the corner of William Street and Exchange Place, partitioned off from the main gold trading floor.²⁸ The most dominant telegraph company, with three-quarters of all transmissions, eight hundred offices, and two thousand employees, was the American Telegraph, with a headquarters at Broadway and Liberty streets.²⁹ "The headquarters smack of mystery," wrote journalist Matthew Hale Smith. "Everything is systematized and order and quiet rule. The endless click of a hundred instruments sounds like a distant cotton factory."³⁰

Lincoln's announcements usually went out over the American Telegraph, so it was odd that Roberts hadn't seen the message before the Associated Press had. Attaching the long proclamation text for reference, Roberts tapped out a message to Eckert: "The following is taken from the New York World of this morning. Is it genuine?"

Down in Washington, Eckert read Roberts's message. Eckert hadn't telegraphed the president's proclamation, and if he hadn't, who had the president trusted in the middle of the night to key this in?

Lincoln had grown obsessed with the telegraphic messages that flowed through the War Department. At the time he took office, the technology was so new, sending or receiving a telegram meant he had to dispatch a messenger to the private telegraph office in the city, where the messenger would stand in line, the president's note in hand. Due to that awkward arrangement, Lincoln tended to send only one or two messages a month.

Within weeks of taking over as secretary of war in early 1862, Stanton issued an order from Lincoln that "from and after the 26th day of February, the President . . . takes military possession of all the telegraph lines in the United States." The order specified that the president did not intend to disrupt "private business," but every message could potentially be monitored by the government.[31]

Lincoln then invited the president of the American Telegraph, Colonel Edward S. Sanford, to serve as the government's military telegraphic censor, which meant every message on that main line was monitored. This arrangement made official and perpetual Lincoln's keen desire for surveillance.[32]

When Stanton in early 1862 directed all military telegraphic wires through his offices, Lincoln found the telegraph's new proximity invaluable. With the War Department on the White House grounds, only yards away, Lincoln's passionate interest in the candid and immediate flood of information racing over the lines became nearly all-consuming. He even slept in the telegraph office during important battles so as to track each pulse of the troops. The communication was so immediate, he might even track frequent two-hour strategy sessions between Ulysses S. Grant and Stanton or jump in himself to message a colonel during a firefight.[33]

If Lincoln headed to the War Department, his friend and looming bodyguard Ward Lamon was supposed to accompany him, to fend off passersby who traveled the paths outside the White House unchecked. On nights Lincoln went alone, Mary Todd insisted he carry a stick. But Lincoln rarely invited Lamon nor carried a stick.[34] He was so open to strangers, he would stop to hear out anyone who even jumped from behind a tree to vent.

He mingled so openly that early in his presidency an onlooker might barely notice him. As Benjamin Brown French, soon to be the commissioner of public buildings, wrote in his diary: "I staid about the War Department perhaps an hour, saw President Lincoln pass through the lower passage, which was crowded with people. He was dressed in a common linen coat, had on a straw hat, & pushed along through the crowd without looking to the right or left, and no one seemed to know who he was . . . I was somewhat amused to see with what earnestness he pushed his way along & to observe his exceedingly ordinary appearance."[35]

On his arrival each day in that building, Lincoln chatted briefly with the cipher operators of whom he seemed fond. He trusted many of them implicitly, particularly Thomas Eckert, whose desk he used as a writing retreat when he penned the Emancipation Proclamation.[36] Lincoln was a good listener, and when he responded, "his face would lighten up with its homely, rugged smile, and he would run his fingers through his bristly black hair, which would stand out in every direction like that of an electric experiment doll," remembered journalist Benjamin Perley Poore.[37]

Each day, many times a day, Lincoln opened Eckert's desk drawer, which contained the latest decoded telegrams, and read them all—no matter to whom they were addressed. Eventually, Lincoln got to a point when he said, "Well, boys, I am down to raisins."[38] And that was the sign that he was entirely up to date.

Mystified by the expression, the cipher operators asked its origin and learned that Lincoln had once heard long ago of a little girl allowed to eat anything she wished on her birthday. She later became violently ill. Hours into her vomiting, the doctor assured her worried parents that she would be fine, as she was "down to raisins."

With access to all those telegrams, Lincoln could read messages meant for others—often without their knowledge. Only the sheer abundance kept him from monitoring absolutely everything that raced across the wires. He often picked up actionable tidbits: in the weeks after the Battle of Antietam in 1862, for example, Lincoln noticed that in a message to other officers, McClellan blamed the fatigued state of his horses for his lack of fight. Lincoln intervened, sending a caustic question as to why the horses were worn out, given they had been put to no use. Two weeks later, Lincoln fired McClellan.

McClellan once sent a telegram to Stanton that read: "If I save this Army now I tell you plainly that I owe no thanks to you or to any other persons in Washington. You have done your best to sacrifice this army."[39] That insult never made its way to Lincoln because Colonel Sanford, head of the American line and military censor, confiscated it before Stanton had the chance to see it.

Now Eckert read this proclamation, which seemed to have burst to life in New York City. Could it be a fraud? If so, the damage would shake the nation. A few decades earlier, a bit of false information might creep slowly into public view and be killed in minutes, leaving no trace. But the past decade had seen such a widespread uptake of telegraph technology, information now traveled almost at the speed of light. Not only could the railroads deliver the newspaper bales up and down the coast and much farther west this very day, the telegraph spread news in minutes. A fraudulent message could proliferate until the whole world believed a lie.

Eckert assessed the necessary deadlines for correcting the possible falsehood.

In New York, the mail going to the *Scotia*, the vessel that conveyed information once a week to Europe, closed at 10:30 a.m.

That mighty four-hundred-foot-long, iron-hulled beast lay at anchor, ready to board five hundred passengers and crew this very morning, load crates of gold bullion to pay overseas import bills, and carry the reports of the horrendous war. At noon, fifty short, half-dead men, sustained by oatmeal and grog, would stoke the furnaces twenty feet below the waterline, which would pump the steam that turned the forty-foot paddle wheels through the ten-day journey, through calm seas or stormy to Liverpool.[40]

What news went to Europe mattered dearly. A year earlier, with Lincoln's hopes and fears riding on the outcome, Reverend Henry Ward Beecher hurried there to employ his famous rhetorical skills to convince France and Britain not to recognize the Confederacy as an official nation. Now, those same European governments waited for the kind of news to change their minds. If the Union seemed to be losing, France, Britain, and other nations wanted to launch economic relations as quickly as possible with the two newly separated countries, divided forever.

If a correction did not get to the post office by 10:30 a.m., the newspapers already loaded into the holds, with the proclamation in their columns, would dominate news overseas. European households, offices, and the hallowed arcade of British Parliament would begin to buzz. The London trading floors would shake with the prediction of the final Union defeat.

If the president hadn't sent this proclamation and wished to block its dissemination, he needed to do so immediately.

4

A HOT DAY
ON WALL STREET

[New York, N.Y. – May 18, 1864]

N
ew York began to hum as the sun climbed in the sky. Steamboats
lumbered up the grand Hudson River, headed to the state capital in
Albany, where Governor Horatio Seymour, sworn in the year before,
struggled to hold the Democratic line against the Republican president's
agenda. Twelve grand avenues fanned north past hotels and eateries, past
silk hat finishers and watchmakers, through the filthy, putrid bone-boiling
establishments at West Thirty-Ninth Street to the last paved blocks at Forty-
Fourth Street.[1] Nearly twenty thousand carriages and wagons would race
and collide in the streets over the course of the day.

As Will Prime's carriage carried him downtown to his *Journal of
Commerce* office, he passed between Ninth and Tenth Streets, where the
renowned retailer A. T. Stewart had recently inaugurated another giddy
department store on Broadway. For the society lady, Stewart's reigned supreme. The "Cast-Iron Palace" soared up six tiers, overlooking a bustling

central foyer lit by gilded chandeliers and windows softened by blue shades.[2] New Yorkers had engaged in an orgy of consumption since the war began, particularly of foreign fashion luxuries. Mary Todd Lincoln, trying to keep up with the society set, indulged herself in Stewart's stores.

Much of New York blossomed with signs of the excessive wealth created by the war for merchants, manufacturers, and stockbrokers. "New York never exhibited such wide-spread evidences of prosperity," James K. Medbery, a journalist covering the scene, wrote. "Broadway was lined with carriages. The fashionable milliners, dressmakers, and jewelers reaped golden harvests. The pageant of Fifth Avenue on Sunday, and of Central Park during week-days, was *bizarre*, gorgeous, wonderful! Never were such dinners, such receptions, such balls. Vanity Fair was no longer a dream."[3]

Meanwhile, inflation caused by that trading and the increased release of paper money caused deep suffering in the working classes. "There can be no question but that the tendencies of these times are for the elevation of the few and degredation and humiliation of the many—the poor," an editorial writer in Pittsburgh's *Daily Post* opined early that year. "The extravagant inflation of the money market, consequent upon the ocean of paper money with which our country is flooded, and the almost total absence of gold, will tend strongly to the one inevitable result of making the poor poorer, and the rich, richer."[4]

Out on the New York streets, brass bands wandered in search of coins. Wagons, covered in advertising placards, grazed the cobblestones, trying to coax a sale for a city store or service. Barefoot homeless children wandered the streets, searching for coins.[5] Telescope men set up their devices to let paying viewers glimpse Venus or the mountains of the moon as evening came on.

In the shadow of towering Trinity Church, the streets grew more turbulent. The territory from Wall Street to Chamber Street, from Broadway to the East River, encompassed the power centers: the politics of City Hall, the newspapers of Printing House Square, and the dealmaking of Wall Street.

The newspaper industry had grown at lightning speed since Lincoln's election, and now approximately fifteen newspapers clustered in a four-block radius on the western edge of City Hall Park, churning out some 140,000 copies daily on powerful steam-driven presses.[6]

"Public sentiment is everything," Lincoln acknowledged in his 1858 notes for his famous Senate debates with Stephen Douglas. "With it, nothing can fail; against it, nothing can succeed. Whoever moulds public sentiment, goes deeper than he who enacts statutes or pronounces judicial decisions. He makes the enforcement of these else impossible."[7] Across the country, more than 3,725 different American newspapers circulated.

Having graduated from writing his letters to the editor as Rebecca to having secretly bought the German-language newspaper that would help win him the election, President Lincoln now either ghostwrote or directly fed stories to the *Philadelphia Press* under the "Occasional" column. In an August 1861 letter from the newspaper's editor, John Forney, to then Secretary of War Simon Cameron, Forney helpfully attached an "Occasional" column, offering: "Lest you not see the President's article in the *Press* today, I enclose it to you."[8] The War Department also paid large sums to Forney's publication for advertising.

Lincoln also encouraged members of his staff to write favorable pieces anonymously for the press, including John Hay, as mentioned earlier, and presidential secretary William O. Stoddard, who wrote under the pen name Illinois for the *New York Examiner*.[9] This young confidant to both President Lincoln and to Mary Todd, as the aide whom she asked to open her mail, wrote pieces praising the Lincolns, Stanton, and Grant, passing on D.C. updates, and mocking Lincoln's political rival, McClellan. Under the title "Our Noble President," the anonymous correspondent pondered: "Did you ever try to realize the idea of losing our good Chief Magistrate? Perhaps not, but suppose you try, and then look around you in imagination for the man whom you could trust . . . to take the reins from *his* dead hand. The fact is, that at present the country has entire confidence in no one else, and we might almost say, 'after him the deluge.'"[10] Readers would have believed they were getting the review of an unbiased reporter, not a paid assistant.

No matter the number of challengers, or the violence of press opinions, the people in general liked their president. By February 1864, city and state legislators endorsed him. As Horace Greeley said: "The People think of [Lincoln] by night and by day & *pray* for him & *their hearts* are where they have made so heavy investments."[11]

Lincoln had risen to popularity by speaking in relatively plain language—an orator who could address the biggest issues of the day, leavening his speeches with jokes and self-deprecations. His inaugural trip, which attracted large and wild crowds in even the sleepiest towns, gave the people direct memories of their excitement that, in turn, had connected them to their leader. In the years that followed, he coaxed, or through aides planted, favorable stories about him or his policies, so the people came to believe that even caustic journalists shared their fondness for him. But perhaps most importantly, Lincoln now personified the Union and the war effort. The citizens had bequeathed their sons and fathers to him. They felt a deep tie to the man who mourned with them and now held their loved ones' lives in his hands.

Within the news center of New York, Lincoln favored *The New York Times*, Henry Raymond's paper. It operated from a five-story, six-year-old stone and iron skyscraper on the south edge of Printing House Square. Up in the editorial floors, above the powerful Hoe lightning press, the forty-four-year-old Raymond could claim to be the most influential man in publishing, due to his paper's foreign and domestic reach. He also held social status, driving a well-turned-out team of bays and enjoying a hearty social life with younger men.[12] The paper prided itself on what it considered neutrality—at turns conservative or radical as Raymond felt the occasion required. Luckily for Lincoln, he continued to enjoy the *Times*'s support through the first three years of his presidency. Raymond planned to publish his own epic assessment of Lincoln, including his speeches and correspondence, timed to arrive just before the Republican convention in June. Its printing had been delayed by the unexpected release of a competitor's *Old Abe's Jokes*.[13]

In the building catty-corner to *The New York Times*, Horace Greeley, a former congressman known as the "Old Philosopher," played kingmaker and political executioner through the pages of his *New-York Tribune*. Greeley was an unusual-looking man, ghostly pale, with a head of near-perfect roundness, whiskers sprouting not so much on his chin as on his neckline, and with a preference for the fashion of small round spectacles and a string necktie. In 1860, he helped Lincoln win the Republican nomination mainly to foil Greeley's former ally, William H. Seward. (Now, Seward served as secretary of state.) But Lincoln had disappointed Greeley with what the editor considered the president's slow disavowal of slavery and lugubrious conduct of the war. In August 1862, Greeley published "The Prayer of Twenty Million," expressing what he believed to be the entire Union citizenry's point of view. At the time, Lincoln had not yet released his Emancipation Proclamation. "We think you are strangely and disastrously remiss in the discharge of your official and imperative duty with regard to the emancipating provisions of the new Confiscation Act," Greeley wrote. Lincoln had required Congress to create extra explanations of the legality and long-term application of this law, which would free slaves as confiscated property. Greeley saw this as hesitancy. "Those provisions were designed to fight Slavery with Liberty. They prescribe that men loyal to the Union, and willing to shed their blood in her behalf, shall no longer be held, with the Nation's consent, in bondage to persistent, malignant traitors, who for twenty years have been plotting and for sixteen months have been fighting to divide and destroy our country. Why these traitors should be treated with tenderness by you, to the prejudice of the dearest rights of loyal men, We cannot conceive."[14]

"What is he wrath-y about?" Lincoln questioned an intermediary.[15]

Now, in 1864, Greeley opposed Lincoln's nomination for a second term. Two blocks south, at the corner of Fulton and Nassau, *The New York Herald*'s James Gordon Bennett, a Scotsman otherwise known to his newspaper rivals as "His Satanic Majesty," put a premium on breaking news, gossip, and intrigue. "It is the mouthpiece of the mob and as we all know, the mob is king in the United States," a British journalist assessed Bennett's product in 1863. "He has pandered to the vitiate tastes of the hordes of lazy, grumbling Irishmen and the ignorant bigoted rowdies of New York who find their chief gratification in vomiting their rancid disaffection upon this earth."[16] Twice, Bennett found himself beaten with a cane by a former colleague he attacked in his pages. He came away with a slashed forehead and an unbowed determination to continue printing viciousness.[17]

On the southern edge of the same block as the *Times*, at Park Row and the corner of Beekman, sat the upstart *World*. Financial stress had caused its handsome and charismatic bachelor editor, Manton Marble, to become one of Lincoln's most vociferous critics.

Two years earlier, Marble had been excited to take over what was then a failing religious paper, but he rapidly drained his own and his friends' finances. Desperate for backers, he approached Republican investors, offering to transform *The World* into a politically conservative paper. Unfortunately for him, plenty of talented journalists working throughout the city favored Republican views. Republican partisans didn't need to finance a house organ, and a risky one at that.

He then approached Samuel Barlow, a rich lawyer, who believed Democrats required a soapbox to marshal their dissipated strengths. Within a half hour of talk, Barlow agreed to back *The World*, restoring Marble, in his own words, to "peace and salvation."[18] Wrote Barlow of the explicit quid pro quo, "I aided you to form a company with sufficient capital . . . You agreed to support Governor Seymour's [1862] election."[19]

And so Marble was catapulted into the arms of Democrats.[20] While hated in Washington, *The World*, by the end of 1863, boasted three times the circulation of any other newspaper, that is, a full half a million readers across the country.

The journalists at all the newspapers possessed a certain glamor to readers, but not to their investor employers. Scribbling their reports under lamps with green shades burned through with holes and surrounded by dusty plaster or boarded walls and windows so dirty they could only kindly be called translucent, the reporters constantly absorbed an understanding of how despised they could be in the pursuit of the true details of events.[21]

An editorial writer of the time pointed out how the ugliness of their offices—up many exhausting flights of stairs, cluttered with old furniture, tables amassed with paper, broken and sludged pens and inks, and pigeonhole cupboards so stuffed with notes they defied a stranger to interpret the system of organization—had shaped their mindset. "It is known that the corollary of an empty stomach is an ugly disposition and that if a man be shut out of doors on a cold night he will feel malicious towards the whole race," the writer noted.[22]

The writer believed Horace Greeley's vicious editorials came into being because "even abstracted as he is known to be while working, a casual glance around the room suddenly smites his mind with such a sense of poverty, bareness and general lack of satisfaction in all the uses of the world" that he strikes out. "Why should an editor who is nevertheless a man be forced to do his work in a place which would be a dungeon if it only had a bolt on the door?"

Prime's carriage moved farther south until it came to the traffic coursing to the "seething, whirling, roaring maelstrom" of Wall Street, where it was said one could "read the heart of man better than in books."[23]

Pickpockets roamed. *The New York Herald* reported that week: "No one should enter this dangerous locality without having all his senses about him. It is one of those places in which a man would be sure to leave his skin if there was anything to be got by the flaying of him."[24]

Soon the market gamblers would hurry to their grand office buildings. The most refined brokers—those who paid for the privilege to trade in stocks and futures—would duck from the street's sunlight, through labyrinthine tunnels, up and down murky staircases, all heading toward the coliseum roar of the elegant official trading floor.[25] During the war the army's requisition of goods had built the "futures" trade. Military purchases, set to be filled months ahead, meant that large quantities of goods were bought, sometimes at a price vastly different than the price upon delivery, depending on, say, the health of harvests or calving. In the big-city commodities markets, wool, hay, whiskey, tallow, and freights would go up for sale.[26] The livestock market would sell cows and sheep.[27] The produce exchange would market fruits and corn.

A mania for stock and commodities trading had gripped the country during these war years, and had hit fever pitch starting in September 1863, the previous year. At least $100 million had exchanged hands from then until the end of the prior month, April 1864. Brokers were earning from $800 to $10,000 a day. Warrens of brokerage offices cropped up as if burrowed into every Wall Street nook, some in dank underground cellars, some in attics reached by creaky, groaning staircases.[28] The biggest names in brokerage could be found working out of these rat holes from noon to three o'clock in the afternoon, placing the buys of the nation's most powerful money men, who were capable of acquiring whole railroads in an instant or destroying the stock prices of a brewery in seconds.[29]

Gloomy as those broker cells were, there was one trading area more disturbing to passersby than all the others: the Gold Room in Gilpin's News Room at Twenty-Six Exchange Place at William Street. It was impossible to miss, with a "clock" hanging high outside that marked the movement of gold prices from minute to minute.[30] From ten o'clock in the morning until four thirty in the afternoon, men and boys raced up and down the stairs. Somewhere, a cutthroat investor waited. A roar surged into the street, as traders responded to the rise and fall of one preeminent commodity: gold. At noon, messenger boys ran back and forth between the buildings, delivering sacks of gold, each holding up to five thousand coins, marking the transactions. A respectable messenger could carry one bag in each hand, but banks sought men or boys who could carry two in each fist.

Then there was the fourth tier of the trading: on the cobblestones themselves, curbstone brokers clasping books and pencils bought and sold stocks after the close of the official markets. Deep into the dark evening, hordes of people—lawyers, shopkeepers, judges, theater impresarios—bargained. This particular day, the turbulent neighborhood seemed in even greater commotion.

On May 18, the day the president's proclamation ran, the stock exchange opened at 10:00 a.m., as usual, but for some unknown reason, the Gold Room had opened early. It was not known who had allowed transactions before the usual bell, but the activity inside was frantic. Gold had been active the previous day. The British market listed it at 109 ¾, but it had ended at a dizzying 177 in New York. That meant someone buying the previous day in England could sell even one increment of gold in New York at a profit equal to more than eleven weeks of a New England teacher's salary. And traders tended to sell in bulk, one hundred thousand dollars' worth of gold at a time. Now the sidewalks outside on William and Beaver Streets, too, were thronged with eager curbstone brokers shouting their bids.

At the official exchange opening, gold listed at 184, which meant that the Gold Room action had increased in value by seven dollars per $100 worth of gold before the market could even officially begin.

Gold prices began a volatile swing as investors tried to dump the government bonds and Northern securities, accepting even the lowest prices in favor of gold. Only gold would outlast the Union. Nothing but gold would translate into value overseas. Gold rose by 5 percent.[31] Traders placing their bets from afar over the telegraph to their brokers became millionaires almost instantly.

As gold rose, the cost of all goods soared, including petroleum and cotton, because it would take more and more greenbacks to purchase each.[32]

Railroad stocks sold rapidly. Ferocious traders, passionate to make a profit out of this harrowing piece of news, let their roars echo out to the streets.

Prime noticed that his *Journal of Commerce* building at 91 Wall Street near the East River seemed a particular focus of furor. A large agitated crowd had formed outside with people holding copies of his newspaper. As he made his way through the crowd, he saw the alarming story, a dire demand from the president. FOUR HUNDRED THOUSAND TROOPS.

Prime could not believe this sudden news. Back in February, Lincoln had issued an order for 500,000 men to serve for three years starting in March. States had begun negotiating down the demands by counting up their previous volunteers. Rumors circulated of another draft coming in April or May. Here now, all of Will and Mary Prime's fears were being realized. The battles in Spotsylvania had been so devastating, Lincoln needed 400,000 more bodies just a month and a half later to feed the war machine.

Prime hurried up to the editorial rooms. The manifold copy of the Associated Press dispatch looked to be in the syndicate's usual handwriting and format.[33] As president of the board of the Associated Press, Prime knew its features well. From 11:00 a.m. until 2:00 a.m., six copyists at the AP handwrote the news that came over the telegraph wire. Debates in Congress, European dispatches, and tales of a Brooklyn murder ticked out in Morse code. By using a sharp stylus in lieu of a pen, the copyists duplicated their transcriptions to ten to twelve manifold sheets, then two or three sleepy adolescent messenger boys ran the copies through the city, braving rain or hail, hustling to scale the mountains of staircases at the AP's member newspapers—the *Journal of Commerce, Tribune, Express, World, New York Times, Herald,* and *Sun.* The afternoon news went out at one o'clock in the afternoon, and the morning papers received their news reports starting at ten o'clock at night.

Late in the night, or sometimes even in the early morning hours, the

Associated Press manager would send a final "all-in" confirmation, the sign that the gathering of the news was done for the day.

Prime grabbed his competitors' newspapers to check how they had covered this astounding late proclamation. Scanning the first pages, he found that most of his competitors had missed the story entirely. *The New York Times* led with the standoff in Spotsylvania. *The New York Herald* screamed "GRANT!" in big type over a report from their special correspondent at the front. The only other paper to run the story was Marble and Barlow's *World*. The lack of coverage from the other newspapers disturbed Prime.

The crowd outside the building now included irate merchants and Wall Street bankers who were getting killed on the market. Investments that had been tracking upward from earlier in the month based on relatively positive news from the front now crashed with the proclamation's arrival. The bettors claimed to have proof the *Journal of Commerce* had been duped and wanted the correction that would also correct the market values. Mr. Wade from Grinnell, Minturn & Co., with a delegation of other merchants, showed the *Journal* editors a telegram sent from Washington to the Board of Brokers, declaring the proclamation false.[34] Prime and the editors looked the telegram over but could not determine if it was true or a fraud. They needed the State Department to weigh in one way or another with official word, and so far their telegram had not been answered.[35]

Just as Prime worried over what to do, McClellan arrived at the *Journal of Commerce* office. Now Prime would at least have a vent to his confusion. He sent out a messenger to gather the reasons why the other papers had missed the astounding story.

Joseph Howard arrived at his office at the usual hour that morning, complaining of fatigue and the hazards of having shared a champagne-soaked evening with editor Henry Raymond. Unfortunately, Raymond was not at that moment Howard's editor, although Howard wished he were. The *Times* had fired Howard two years earlier.

Howard was now working for the *Brooklyn Eagle*, at Thirty-Two Fulton Street, down near the ferry, a mile across the East River from the power centers of Printing House Square and Wall Street. For Howard, this was a kind of exile, a newsman's purgatory. Over the past three years, since writing of that Scotch cap and cloak, he had ridden the highs and lows of the news business. In May 1864, he happened to be in a professional low. Nothing, it seemed, could undo his personal fame. He still appeared to know every powerful or pretty person in New York. Readers loved his witty, candid takes on the news. Walt Whitman considered him a social friend. But he had lost the power of his *New York Times* platform. Now he served as city editor of the *Brooklyn Eagle*, which was not a member of the Associated Press and therefore did not have the same national reach.

Some said Howard had tested the *Times* editor's patience before the Scotch cap incident by ringing up $7,000 in telegraph bills when covering the Prince of Wales's visit to the United States; to block his competitors' access to the wire, he had hired an underling to dictate the genealogy of Jesus.

But that hadn't caused an actual break in relations. After all, the editors had sent him to cover the president's inaugural train ride.

His creative fiction about the president's inaugural train ride costume hadn't destroyed his status either. Perhaps his editors never realized that their star reporter had made up key facts. The story received such wide pickup, perhaps they had remained ignorant of the fiction at that time. Raymond had earlier received complaints from a host on the Prince of Wales's itinerary who said Howard had mocked him for social blunders he hadn't perpetrated, but Raymond must have gotten those sorts of letters from disgruntled subjects all the time. The editors happily put Howard to work covering the president on other occasions, including leading up to the inaugural in Washington, the inauguration speech, and the president and first lady's first formal reception.

Lincoln certainly knew what he wore on that night journey and let Howard into the White House again. Not only did he accept Howard's presence as a representative of the press, Lincoln had, according to Howard, personally written a substantial response to Howard's query that spring about whether or not Lincoln would appoint his former political (and romantic when it came to Mary Todd) rival Stephen Douglas to be brigadier general: "No, sir, I have not done so," Lincoln allegedly responded, "nor had I thought of doing so until tonight, when I saw it suggested in the paper. I have no reason to believe Mr. Douglas would accept it." He went on to praise Douglas as highly qualified, so much so that Douglas once, according to Lincoln, took out a map and showed Lincoln the problems the troops would have getting through Baltimore.[36]

Lincoln may have felt too beholden to *The New York Times* and Raymond to keep Howard at a distance.

Howard also received prestigious beats at the *Times* on the frontlines for important battles, including the Battle of Ball's Bluff. The Lincoln administration heavily censored all journalists in the war zone to project the best news possible, so Howard had focused on the scene between engagements. "The near white tents of the various regiments dotted at intervals the beautiful camp grounds, while all about them were seen the weary soldiers resting, cleaning their arms, playing ball, or going monotonously through the everlasting drill, while the overcoated, muddy-shoed sentry uselessly stalked up and down, up and down like an old-fashioned pendulum, whose working gear is rusty, and whose period of usefulness is about played out." Howard praised the colonel in charge for his "wholesome disregard for the gentleman of the Press" but revealed he had talked the man into giving him his list of the missing, the wounded, and those killed—a list, printed in full, of 384 casualties.[37] It was easy to imagine the thirst for such information back at home and how much pain it could generate in readers, who would see the name of their son or husband in black and white.

Howard's personal style made it seem as if he were writing a letter to friends, but it demonstrated a strain of narcissism. Just before closing with the list of dead men, he complained that his stirrup buckles had been hurting him. In another column, he joked about his desire to choose sleep over breaking news. "Last night about 12 o'clock, I heard some twelve or fifteen heavy reports in this direction," he wrote, "and though the claims of a good night's rest seemed very strong, and were urged by weary eyelids and chafed limbs with great force, I remembered the hundred thousand readers of the TIMES, and called out to my venerable colored attendant to saddle my slab-sided nag as quickly as possible, while I bundled up in the best possible manner, took a long swig of 'Old Rye,' and shortly after cantered down the road from Poolesville."[38]

When, in June 1862, Lincoln went on a secretive mission to West Point to seek strategic military wisdom from General Winfield Scott, a hero of the Mexican-American War, Howard won close access over several days. On a steamboat taking the general and the president on a tour of the area, Howard reported from the president's elbow, "The President chatted familiarly with one and all; formed the centre of an attentive circle, who listened with pleasure to a story about a shark which swallowed a red-hot harpoon; asked about all points of interest, and pointed out to the party the target at which, on Tuesday, the shells were thrown from the Parrot guns."[39]

That harpoon story might have contained "mature" content. Howard liked to relate off-color stories in social circles that he claimed to have heard from the president directly.

He also recorded a moment when Lincoln gaily referred to Secretary of War Stanton's iron-fisted control over news leaks. "The Secretary of War, you know, holds a pretty tight rein on the Press, so that they shall not tell more than they ought to, and I'm afraid that if I blab too much, he might draw a tight rein on me," the president said. Listeners roared with laughter and loudly applauded as Lincoln retreated to his train car.

All of this proximity meant that Howard held favor with the *Times* at least through that West Point visit. His dismissal from the *Times* allegedly was due a few months later to his desire to land a scoop covering the funeral of Brigadier General Philip Kearny, a disabled Union commander famous for his brash fearlessness (he once, for example, cheered his troops into battle with "I'm a one-armed Jersey son-of-a-gun, follow me!"). Kearny's family barred the press from traveling from the church to the burial, perhaps as retribution for the *Washington Post*'s traumatizing them by attending and covering in detail the brigadier general's embalming, including the removal of his eyeballs.[40] Howard, though, could not bear to be excluded from a story that would surely garner a wide readership. When the funeral procession returned from the graveyard, the other reporters on the beat noticed a robed Howard in the row of clerics, marching solemnly, holding a copy of the burial program. That sacrilege was too much for the *Times*.

After his firing, Howard moved from paper to paper, generally loved by readers for his witty, candid coverage, including his reports from the society event, the Sanitary Fair at the Academy of Music, which he detailed under the pen name Dead Beat.

He had also been in the center of the city's most terrifying uprising when he covered the New York City draft riots in July 1863. That summer, fury boiled over when Lincoln abandoned his reliance on an all-volunteer army to force inscription of men twenty to forty-five in preparation for future drafts. The Lincoln administration assigned New York a heavy quota, and Governor Seymour warned Lincoln that his oversized demand created an unconstitutional burden on that one state. New York's working men not only resisted being sent to the frontlines, they grew incensed at the additional loophole that allowed a man to pay for his own replacement, a setup that clearly favored the rich. The white working men took their wrath and racism out on the black population, whom they saw as competitors for paying work and whose freedom they had never intended to help gain.

Over several brutal, bloody days, gangs of drunken, unhinged men and boys with clubs and women with sticks rushed through the streets from City Hall to Central Park and down to Gramercy Park, looting and burning property, including police stations and newspaper offices. They clubbed police and killed civilians, focusing their violence particularly on black men, women, and children. "There were probably not less than a dozen negroes beaten to death in different parts of the City during the day," *The New York Times* reported on July 14, the second day of rioting. The *Times*'s report continued:

> Among the most diabolical of these outrages . . . is that of a negro cartman living in Carmine-street. About 8 o'clock in the evening, as he was coming [from] having put up his horse, he was attacked by a crowd of about 400 men and boys, who beat him with clubs and paving-stones till he was lifeless, and then hung him to a tree opposite the burying-ground. Not being yet satisfied with their devilish work, they set fire to his clothes and danced and yelled and swore horrid oaths around his burning corpse. The charred body of the poor victim was still hanging upon the tree at a late hour last evening.[41]

That same day, the rioters came across Howard on Forty-Sixth Street. They attempted to pick his pocket, which Howard prevented, saying, "I reckon this will do."

They could not be brushed aside. They slapped his face, kicked his shins, yanked his hair, and punched him in the ribs, cursing him as a "damned abolitionist" and a Lincoln spy. They started up chants to hang him. Hundreds of onlookers rushed to Howard's side, but only to take part in the beating. They pulled him up and down and kicked him. As Howard's hanging grew more likely, a group of firefighters came to his rescue by pulling him inside their station house.

Badly cut on his lip, bruised, bloody from neck to waist, and scalped in patches, bereft of his gold watch and chain, breast pin, pocketbook, and hat and cane, Howard relied on a disguise from a firefighter to get downtown. Unfortunately, his anonymous rescuer met a similar fate, owing to the confusion of identity. The firefighter dressed in Howard's clothes "was stigmatized as a Lincoln spy, to his great annoyance. Boys attacked him and screaming women punched him repeatedly with short pieces of telegraph wire that had been ripped down."[42]

That incident had been nearly a year earlier and Howard had recovered from the altercation. He since had suffered bruises to his ego from being slighted in his career pursuits. When a new Republican publication was starting up in Brooklyn, Howard considered himself the obvious choice to serve as editor. After he was passed over, he approached its competitor, the *Eagle*, with the goal of burying the other publication from his role as the *Eagle*'s city editor.

The *Brooklyn Eagle* boasted a large enough readership—it claimed the largest circulation of any evening paper in the country. But morning papers held more sway over financial markets, as well as the day's agenda in D.C. The *Eagle*'s serious content was slim compared to its Manhattan competitors: most editions of the *Eagle* ran only four pages, of which half were advertisements. As a staunchly Democrat publication, the paper lacked the direct White House access and influence that Raymond's *Times* enjoyed, although Howard himself boasted in social settings that he personally enjoyed favor in D.C., and another reporter said he was "on intimate terms with the practical joker in the White House."[43]

At the *Eagle*, he found himself devising ways to amuse himself—enjoying hypocrisy and subterfuge with a wink and a nod by savaging a fellow theater critic for his "dirty tricks," which Howard complained included writing a negative review under a pen name, while he himself wrote his critique under the pen name Jacques.[44]

Howard believed journalism to be the greatest calling, "an active, pushing, steam-enginery kind of gait, which keeps abreast of the age and enables one to see and know and be part and parcel of all there is to appreciate."[45] Writing underhanded theater criticism did not fit the bill.

Howard's idling inspired him to reach out to Manton Marble of *The*

World, begging for a chance to return to New York City proper. Two years earlier, he had petitioned Marble to hire him.

The World's ideology directly opposed his Republican views, but then so did the *Eagle*'s. He was a Unionist, the first president of the Republican Association in Brooklyn. He had been elected a few months earlier to head the Young Men's Republican Committee, and he had started the year in a cloud of cigar smoke at the Republican General Committee meeting.[46] But *The World* had more than half a million readers.

On May 3, Howard wrote Marble again. "As you are aware I have long sought a connection with the *World*. I now desire it earnestly. I am doing well here, have entire control of inside matters and am pecuniarily satisfied. But—the Presidential excitement approaches and this mill pond is excessively small. I would like exceedingly such a position as I formerly held on the *Times* . . . May I be permitted to follow in your train of constant success?"[47]

Marble denied him a second time.

That left Howard in the position of having to discover and report the most important news of the day from his remote perch as city editor of the *Eagle*. And that news could come at all hours.

Now this day, the astounding story of the president's dire proclamation calling for four hundred thousand more men appeared in *The World*. The *Eagle* editors needed to decide what to do with this new information, to print an extra to cover this monumental story or ignore it and wait for confirmation. A fellow editor asked Howard what he thought of the piece.

Howard lifted his glasses and examined it. Then he observed: "It's not Lincoln's style. It may not be genuine."

He took another moment and peered at the text more carefully. "I guess it's all right," he demurred, "but it seems premature."[48]

5

A WARNING FROM WASHINGTON

[Washington, D.C. – May 18, 1864]

F rancis F. Browne, an artist granted six months to follow Lincoln about his daily life in preparation for a portrait, recalled witnessing a man in misery that month of May. Lincoln had previously wrestled with black moods. Before marrying Mary Todd, he had faced a depression so severe a friend had intervened, recalling, we "had to remove razors from his room—take away all Knives and other dangerous things. It was terrible."[1] The friend had taken him home for several months until he seemed stable. In February 1864, Lincoln observed: "This war is eating my life out; I have a strong impression I shall not live to see the end."[2] His tears had flowed at his departure from the Springfield depot on his way to the presidency three years earlier, and each year had gotten worse. Now the week's frontline reports ravaged him.

"I intently studied every line and shade of expression in that furrowed face," the resident artist recorded. "In repose it was the saddest face I ever knew. There were days when I could scarcely look into it without crying. During the first week of the battles of the Wilderness he scarcely slept at all. Passing through the main hall of the domestic apartment on one of these days, I met him clad in a long morning wrapper pacing back and forth a narrow passage leading to one of the windows, his hands behind him, great black rings under his eyes, his head bent forward upon his breast,— altogether such a picture of the effects of sorrow, care, and anxiety as would have melted the hearts of the worst of his adversaries."[3]

No matter Lincoln's mood, early every morning, and multiple times a day, he set off for the War Department, about two hundred yards west of the White House.[4] In that building, at least, he could feel that the dire circumstances of the war were being addressed by a team of busy officials. Assistant Secretary of War Dana stated that from June 1863 to June 1864, the purchases alone totaled $285 million in services and goods, from fuel to coffins, as well as three million pairs of trousers, five million flannel shirts and drawers, seven million pairs of stockings, 325,000 mess pans, 207,000 kettles, and over 13,000 drums and 14,830 fifes.[5]

Back in the White House, Lincoln left his wife, Mary Todd, wracked with anxieties. The Republican convention loomed in June with all its attendant press scrutiny on her wardrobe and social niceties. Beyond that hovered the terrifying question of whether or not her husband would win reelection. Everywhere, it seemed, enemies and fake allies lurked, bound to trouble him.

Known by White House staff as "the hellcat" and "Her Satanic Majesty," she ruled, according to a staff member, the domain from the entrance to the first floor to "the upper floor west of the folding doors and across the hall at the head of the stair."[6] There she vented her grievances over many of Lincoln's cabinet members and key appointments, including Seward, Chase, and Grant. The latter, she told Lincoln, was "a butcher, and is not fit to be at the head of an army."[7]

Lincoln tried to tease her out of her opinions. Would she like her own army? he joked. But she refused to be cajoled. Mary Todd had regularly visited the hospital wards to comfort Union solders torn by battle, sitting with the men, reading to them, and taking dictation from those who had lost use of their hands. Grant's apparent carelessness tortured her. "He has no management, no regard for life," she said. He lost two men for every Confederate and considered those slaughters successes.

Mary Todd developed an unremitting loathing as well for Secretary of the Treasury Chase, partly due to jealousy caused by the attention paid to Chase's beautiful, fashionable daughter, and mostly for Chase's unrelenting presidential ambitions. She warned her husband, "He is anything for Chase. If he thought he could make anything by it, he would betray you to-morrow."[8]

Her husband protested that he had received similar warnings, but only from people with political motivations.

"You will find out some day," she retorted, "if you live long enough, that I have read the man correctly. I only hope that your eyes may not be opened to the truth when it is too late."[9] Spotting Chase's name, along with that of his daughter, on the guest list of a White House event in January 1864, Mary Todd let loose her temper in front of the lively, charming, twenty-nine-year-old William Stoddard, an assistant secretary to her husband who handled her personal correspondence, a man she otherwise liked. According to John George Nicolay, Lincoln's private secretary, Stoddard "fairly cowered at the volume of the storm, and I think for the first time begins to appreciate the awful sublimities of Nature."[10]

Mary Todd's critics argued that she trusted the wrong people; for example, she chose as her confidant Chevalier Henry Wikoff, a social advisor who *The New York Herald* described as "contemptuous."[11] He would lounge around the White House, smoking and gossiping. Their carriage rides together gave much material to Washington tattlers.

Worst of all, he appeared to get her into trouble. In 1861, Wikoff faced accusations of leaking excerpts of Lincoln's State of the Union to *The New*

York Herald hours before Lincoln officially submitted it to the Senate. Wikoff had secretly served as a correspondent to the newspaper.

In a House Judiciary Committee investigation in early 1862, Wikoff refused to testify, so as to protect what were said to be his "female sources." He was thrown into the basement of the Old Capitol Prison, where he contended with rats and roaches. The *New York Herald* reporter, who had vetted the State of the Union excerpt for publication, admitted that Wikoff had told him his source was Mary Todd. *The New York Times* reported:

> Chevalier WIKOFF, of the New-York Herald, seized to-day for contempt of the House, is sent to jail to-night. He refuses to testify from whom he obtained, surreptitiously, extracts from the President's Message . . . to be telegraphed to the Herald in advance of its delivery. He affected at first to have obtained it through female agency, thus reflecting on the ladies of the White House, in revenge, it is said, for having been forbidden to visit there.[12]

The New York Times said that Wikoff's leaked information had a singular purpose:

> The private knowledge of important Government papers, obtained by WIKOFF for the Herald, was doubtless used first for stock-jobbing swindles.

A second report in *The New York Times*, by a correspondent going by the sign-off of X.Y.Z., said that Wikoff had gotten his information from women with access to the administration's most coveted secrets.

> The Judiciary Committee of the House have been pressing WIKOFF to tell how he obtained the quotation from the message, and the rumor in the city is that he has refused to tell, but appeals for protection

to the chivalry (!) of his nature that will not allow him to expose his female friends![13]

These allusions became more specific. The *Herald*'s correspondent testified that Wikoff told him "that he got it from Mrs. Lincoln . . . I would have not had sent it unless I thought he had obtained it from such a responsible source."[14]

Given all the evidence pointing to her, Mary Todd Lincoln would have been fully investigated, but as the inquiry unfolded, the Lincoln's eleven-year-old son, Willie, lay wasting in a feverish delirium, caused by what was likely typhoid. As pressure bore down on Mary Todd to leave her brutal vigil with her son and report to the Hill for questioning, the president made a sudden appearance in a Capitol Hill conference room where senators were discussing the investigation.[15]

The senators looked up to find the president before them, hat in hand. "The pathos written upon his face, the almost unhuman sadness in his eyes . . . and above all an indescribable sense of complete isolation" overwhelmed them. He began to speak: "I, Abraham Lincoln, President of the United States, appear of my own volition to say that I 'of my own knowledge,' know that it is untrue that any of my family hold treasonable communication with the enemy." Lincoln likely suspected Mary Todd played a role. He probably thought he was parsing the truth in front of the Senate investigation because he said that no one in his family was involved in treasonous activities. He was separating the act of leaking the fragments of the State of the Union address from the charge of treason; it was more innocent than that. But he had still attempted to cover up the truth—albeit for compassionate reasons—and shut down the investigation.

Lincoln's sorrowful and unprompted testimony was enough for the senators, who dropped all allegations against the poor grieving woman and adjourned for the day. Six days later, Willie Lincoln died.

Ultimately, the White House gardener, who had served multiple presidents, came forward after Lincoln's visit to say he had found the draft speech, memorized sections, and leaked the material . . . After he confessed, he was promptly forgiven of the charges and received a sinecure position with the U.S. Patent Office. Observers at the time believed he had only taken the fall to protect the first lady. To help bury her complicity, Congress agreed not to publish testimony relating to the first family.

Ever since Lincoln's election, the first lady had tried so hard to fit in, traveling to the fashion houses in Washington and New York, constantly agonizing over the White House refurbishment. Only three years had passed since Joseph Howard Jr., then at *The New York Times*, had written rapturously about Mary Todd's mind and manner. Despite having injured the president's reputation with his fictitious cape and Scotch cap, Howard had returned to the White House to cover a March 1861 reception. "Had the mistress of the White House been born and bred at Washington, accustomed from childhood to the surroundings of the most prominent positions, she could not have exhibited, outwardly, less anxiety, less embarrassment, or more entire *savoir faire*," he wrote about her first public appearance as First Lady. "Do not misunderstand me. Mrs. LINCOLN has three characteristics, which, when given to an American woman, will sustain her under any circumstances, and enable her to bear up against any pressure. They are common sense, self-confidence, and tact . . . in addition to these, she has a naturally pleasing manner, an open heart, and a working brain. Her dress will command itself to all who admire simple elegance."[16]

Mary Todd appreciated flatterers because she was so desperately insecure—and, indeed, Joseph Howard was said to rival Wikoff as her confidant, which would make sense since like Wikoff he was handsome, charming, and full of energy and gossip.[17] He also had the power of the pen. In the autumn of 1861, Mary Todd had written to James Gordon Bennett of *The New York Herald*, "My own nature is very sensitive; [I] have always tried to secure the best wishes of all, with whom through life, I have been associated;

need I repeat to you, my thanks . . . when I meet, in the columns of your paper, a kind reply, to some uncalled for attack, upon one so *little desirous* of newspaper notoriety, as my inoffensive self."[18]

In late April, she and her son Tad had taken the night train to New York so that she might replenish the props of gowns and decorations that would see her through the season's festivities—most importantly, the Republican convention coming up in June.

Bennett's *New York Herald* reported that "from the early hours . . . until late in the evening, Mrs. Lincoln ransacked the treasures of the Broadway dry goods stores. The evenings were spent in company of a few private friends."[19]

But that was then. Now, Mary Todd knew her husband faced colossal losses, both of the war and the Republican nomination within the same months. While interested in the outcome, the president wondered at his wife's excessive anxieties over his reelection. He felt less concerned about winning than she did. In a state of torment, she quizzed her seamstress as to what she considered her husband's chances of victory. The seamstress, Elizabeth Keckley, an African American woman formerly enslaved, reassured her that the public appreciated his decency.

Mary Todd brightened at the news but otherwise issued a dire prediction: "If he should be defeated," she said, "I do not know what would become of us all. To me, to him, there is more at stake in this election than he dreams of."[20]

Back at the *Journal of Commerce* on Wall Street, with crowds still demanding a retraction of the day's story about the president's proclamation, Will Prime continued trying to sort out the stakes for his newspaper this May 18. The messengers he had sent out to check with his competitors began returning with their responses. Of the seven newspapers in the AP, only the *Tribune* had not received the proclamation. Others had rejected the report because it arrived without an envelope. Only *The World*, edited by Prime's friend Marble, appeared to have trusted its veracity.

At *The New York Times*, the mysterious boy had thrown down the tissuey pages and run out. The *Times*'s business room clerk then sent the sheets to the editorial room. The former war correspondent Lorenzo L. Crounse, the lone editor on duty in New York at that dark hour of early morning, examined them and wondered at the unfamiliar handwriting. He also puzzled as to why the item had followed the Associated Press's all-in note by fifteen minutes. Surely, someone at the AP would have noticed a scribe at work making copies of such a significant proclamation. But he couldn't ignore such a big story. He began the process of setting the proclamation into type just in case.[21]

As he began that procedure, he asked the business office why they hadn't forwarded the report in the usual AP envelope and was told the message had none. This concerned him. He sent a runner the few blocks to the Associated Press office on Broadway, copy in hand.

Meanwhile, a messenger arrived from the *Daily News*, which had recently begun picking up AP stories, asking if Crounse had received the proclamation. The *Daily News*, it seemed, was equally suspicious. The *Times* sent back a message to the *Daily News* that it was surely a forgery and the *Times* would not be running the piece. The *News* also decided not to publish it.[22]

The messenger returned to the *Times* with a response from the Associated Press:

DEAR SIR: The "Proclamation" is "false as hell," and was not promulgated through this office. The handwriting is not familiar.[23]

The *Brooklyn Eagle*, where Howard served as city editor, would later point out how helpful it would have been had *The New York Times* passed along its "false as hell" report to its rivals.[24]

The editors at *The New York Herald*, at Nassau and Fulton Street, were shocked when they received the proclamation. They typeset the piece and began running it through the press. But after churning out some twenty-five thousand copies and sending them in their wagons for delivery, the night manager saw the first editions of the *Times* and *Tribune*, both without any mention of the massive story. He halted the presses and destroyed the issues that he was able to call back, even as the staff marveled at the precision of the dupe.

At *The World*, on Park Row and the corner of Beekman, the clerk had chastised the delivery boy—whom he took for the news messenger from Brooklyn—for his late arrival. "This is a pretty time of night to be bringing over Brooklyn copy. You have been lounging somewhere."[25]

The messenger said nothing to the scolding and left so fast he seemed to be trying to catch the door before it swung closed. Meanwhile, the clerk had just received the all-in message—which read simply, "good night." He laid the new AP dispatch alongside the all-in slip in the box of received stories, ready to go into type, and whistled up the pipe. Upstairs, a young assistant in the editorial rooms began pulling the box up to begin processing the news for the papers.

Ever since Grant crossed the Rapidan, *The World*'s night editor had stayed on duty as late as six o'clock in the morning. But at that particular moment, he had stepped out. The copysetter found the text of the manifold pages in the box exceedingly messy, to the point that he and his coworkers had to rewrite two sentences while the story was on the press. Nevertheless, the proclamation had run.

Fear now gripped Prime as he listened to these various accounts. Had he and Marble been tricked into running a fake news story? It would not be the first time that lies slipped into newsprint. To offset the scurrilous reports often circulating from the front, many newspapers published a slug above major battle news: "This is important if true."

Readers often doubted even official government reports. "Dubious documents considered reliable are given almost daily to the public by the Secretary of the War Department," lamented the editor of the *Metropolitan Record*.[26] Those official reports of battles were so positive toward the Union side that the public came to believe that the real (and darker) updates from journalists were the hoaxes.

Back in February 1864, three and a half months earlier, Secretary of State Seward had been taken in by a fake report circulating in Northern papers, allegedly written by Confederate Secretary of the Navy Stephen Mallory, in which he described detailed movements of his fleet and, as an aside, noted the help the Confederates had been receiving from England and France.[27] Seward sent the clipping to the U.S. minister in France, who then forwarded it to the French diplomat. The implication from Seward: why were the Europeans supplying the Confederacy with ships? When the Mallory report proved to be fake, Seward was forced to apologize to the European governments.[28] "The truthfulness of our newspapers has been greatly impeached in Europe, and a serious fabrication of this kind, even though innocently used by the government, places us in an unpleasant and awkward position," the U.S. minister to France wrote to Seward.

If this new proclamation were false, the *Journal of Commerce* could not simply brush the matter aside with a correction. Lincoln, whose administration already loathed the paper for its Democrat politics, would likely unleash his full, presidential fury.

Lincoln's postmaster had previously blocked the *Journal of Commerce*, as well as eight other New York and Brooklyn papers, from using the mail to distribute its editions due to their outspoken criticism of engaging in war.[29] Although the case went to court, the postmaster general leapt ahead of the grand jury's legal decision and halted distribution. Struggling with the subsequent loss of business, the *Journal* made a bitter deal with the administration. It broke ties with a thirty-two-year veteran of the paper, cofounder and editor Gerard Hallock.

Hallock's whole life had been the *Journal of Commerce*. His family lived in New Haven, but he saw them only on weekends; he otherwise stayed overnight at the office and took lonely meals at restaurants. As a fellow newspaperman of the era said, "Hallock slept on his arms."[30]

He personally ensured that no major event went unreported. Once, on his way to cover a fire, sprinting through the narrow, pitch-dark streets, he tumbled into a newly dug cellar but kept going. "I sat down on the curbstone to rub myself, and, seeing the light of the fire brighten up, I started for it," he reported to a friend.[31]

On August 31, 1861, a devastated Hallock wrote his farewell note to the paper he had so loved, signing the operation over to William Prime, David Stone, and the early investors, cofounder David Hale and his own son, William H. Hallock.[32] "Although we have denounced secession again and again as a dangerous heresy, unauthorized by the Constitution, and never justifiable," he wrote, the "heavy oppression the government had inflicted" on the *Journal of Commerce* gave him no choice but to resign. He had been so slandered by the government as a secessionist he "received anonymous letters by the dozen, threatening personal violence and the destruction of [his] office. Volunteer committees have waited upon numbers of our subscribers, urging and sometimes significantly advising them to stop taking the *Journal of Commerce*. Anonymous letters and circulars have been served upon advertisers, warning them that if they continue to advertise in the *Journal of Commerce*, their own business will suffer in consequence."[33]

Congress worried over the administration's love of censorship and began hearings in the House Judiciary Committee focusing particularly on whether the telegraphs in D.C. were censored and if the restraints had violated the Constitution. The Washington correspondent for the *New-York Tribune*, Samuel Wilkeson, testified on January 24, 1862: "I am not allowed to send anything over the wires which, in the estimation of the censor, the Secretary of State, or the Assistant Secretary of State, shall be damaging to the character of the administration, or any individual member of the Cabinet," or that is harmful to "the reputation of the officers charged with the prosecution of the war."[34]

Journalist Benjamin Perley Poore wrote of his efforts to cover the administration:

> The surveillance of the press—first by Secretary Seward and then by Secretary Stanton—was as annoying as it was inefficient. A censorship of all matter filed at the Washington office of the telegraph, for transmission to different Northern cities, was exercised by a succession of ignorant individuals, some of whom had to be hunted up at whiskey shops when their signature of approval was desired. A Congressional investigation showed how stupidly the censors performed their duty. Innocent sentences which were supposed to have a hidden meaning were stricken from paragraphs which were thus rendered nonsensical, and information was rejected that was clipped in print from the Washington papers.[35]

When two journalists angrily confronted Lincoln about censorship, he "listened in his dreamy way," according to a fellow reporter of the time, and he told them, "I don't know much about this censorship, but come downstairs and I will show you the origin of one of the pet phrases of you newspaper fellows." They dutifully followed the president to the basement where he threw open a door to show a large sheep carcass hanging in storage. "There," he said, somberly, "now you know what *revenons à nos moutons* means." The French phrase meant "let's return to the matter at hand." The reporters were too confused to respond. The journalists to whom Lincoln retold the story were also too perplexed by the strange tale. Did he mean that the matter at hand was the war, not censorship? Or was it a grotesque threat? Or mere trickery? Diversions tended to be a favorite tactic of Lincoln's for getting through a difficult conversation.[36]

In June 1863, just after the controversial arrest of Ohio congressman Vallandigham for his fiery speech, New York governor Seymour and a group of Democrats crafted a set of resolutions protecting constitutional rights and sent them to Lincoln. The president responded with a letter that he knew would be leaked to the press. He revealed his view of secession as a long-building conspiracy. "The insurgents had been preparing for it more than thirty years, while the government had taken no steps to resist them," he wrote.

The former had carefully considered all the means which could be turned to their account. It undoubtedly was a well pondered reliance with them that in their own unrestricted effort to destroy Union, constitution, and law, all together, the government would, in great degree, be restrained by the same constitution and law from arresting their progress. Their sympathizers pervaded all departments of the government, and nearly all communities of the people. From this material, under cover of "Liberty of speech," "Liberty of the press," and "*Habeas corpus*" they hoped to keep on foot amongst us a most efficient corps of spies, informers, supplyers, and aiders and abettors of their cause in a thousand ways.[37]

In his view, constitutional rights would need to be sacrificed to save the nation.

A year after Hallock's resignation, in 1862, the War Department targeted the *Journal of Commerce* for running information about a boat requisitioned by the army. One of Stanton's underlings telegraphed the New York chief of police: "Please send me the names of the editors and the publishers of the *Journal of Commerce*. Ascertain who is the writer of the paragraph that appeared in that sheet two days ago regarding the Vanderbilt steamer."[38]

If one paragraph about a boat could rile the government, if the government could force the career end of their deeply dedicated editor, what would Lincoln unleash after seeing nine paragraphs in the *Journal of Commerce*, allegedly written by the president's own hand and signed by the secretary of state?

Ruefully, Prime posted a warning on the public bulletin board that his paper possibly had been duped. But as he still hadn't received a disclaimer from Washington or the Associated Press, he also did not declare the proclamation an outright lie. There was a chance that his staff might just have been a jump ahead on the news, as all the other newspapers were likely too far along in their printing due to the late hour.

Outside his offices, the crowd grew fiercer, demanding the retraction. Prime had not yet heard from the Associated Press, and the telegram to the Board of Brokers that some in the crowd had shown him might itself be a lie.

Word of the president's dire announcement raced through the city as the citizens confronted the impending new draft. The "working population" gathered at street corners to discuss the terrifying, astonishing news. As they talked, their surprise turned to anger. More of their loved ones would be fed to the grisly war machine. And not only that, the president, with his laments, confirmed their worst fears: that their sons, brothers, and husbands, already serving and dying, would likely see not victory but brutal defeat. Daily they had been told that Union generals found success after success, and now, in a signal of desperation, the administration demanded an enormous number of men ripped from their families within weeks.[39]

The deadline to send news—or news corrections—through the mail to the *Scotia* before it sailed had already passed at 10:30 a.m. M. S. Roberts of the American Telegraph still hoped for a denial or confirmation from Washington. A boat could still speed to the transatlantic vessel if they could reach it before it officially pulled up anchor at noon. He messaged again to Major Eckert.[40] He waited for a reply. Fifteen minutes later, he tried yet again. In forty-five minutes, an official response would be too late:

The proclamation is published in world & Journal of commerce no other Papers—European steamer sails at 12. If proclamation is bogus it should be made known officially immediately Gold opened at [1]84 now [1]81. Great excitement here in Boston.[41]

Speculators, having begun to suspect a fake, had started selling their gold at peak, and now gold's value had dropped. A three-dollar difference in a few hours signaled an upset market; three dollars was half a week's teacher's salary. Normally, values moved in increments of cents.

Over at Forty-Nine Bleecker Street at the Department of the East, the headquarters of the U.S. military administration for New York and New England, sixty-five-year-old Major General John Adams Dix wrestled with how to respond to news of the massive draft. Given the horrific response to the draft last July—when gangs killed and looted—an uprising in New York could be imminent. It would be Dix's job to maintain order. He'd been assigned his post just days after the last draft riot. At that time, Dix wrote Stanton that he would not hesitate to declare martial law if the situation should arise again.

Yet, this proclamation was also another headache in his three years of serving Abraham Lincoln, only the last of them in this office. The gentlemanly, dignified Dix was a born New Yorker, with an impeccable record, a graduate of Phillips Academy at Exeter, and an army man from the age of fifteen. He had worked as a respected attorney and financier, forging powerful friendships from the pulpits to the courts to the banks.[42] Twenty-three years earlier, he had joined the Democratic Party. A year later, he won election to the New York State Assembly, and the U.S. Senate three years after that.

Lincoln deemed him "a very wise man" after their first long conversation.[43] Now the Democrat Dix found himself facing the daunting demand of Republican Lincoln to rally a new four hundred thousand recruits or, if the locals resisted, enforce the dreaded draft.

If Dix had his druthers, he would be living far away, serving in an idyllic post promised to him by Franklin Pierce two administrations ago but never realized: minister to France. He would spend his days translating poetry and penning more memoirs of his European travels, like his *A Winter in Madeira and a Summer in Florence and Spain*. "It is ... in the freshness of the evening," he wrote dreamily, "that the Alameda is most thronged. It is then that it presents a scene richer in female beauty than any to be found elsewhere ... The man who passes often through this ordeal of fiery eyes and comes out of it unharmed, must be exceedingly cold or exceedingly fortunate."[44]

But Dix found himself still in New York. He possessed such long experience in public service—from New York secretary of state, to member of the state assembly, to New York City postmaster general, to President Buchanan's treasury secretary, ending his term as the Republican Lincoln took office. He had also displayed acumen in business operations, including serving as president of the Union Pacific during the historic completion of the transcontinental railway just a year earlier. He had been an obvious choice for Lincoln when filling his military posts.

Above all else, Dix was a patriot. When the rumbles of the Civil War began, he famously fired off a telegram that was leaked to the press: "If anyone attempts to haul down the American flag, shoot him on the spot."[45]

All day, every day, messages flew between his office and Stanton's in the War Department. Recently, Stanton had initiated a war diary pretending to be his leaked telegrams to Major General Dix but, in fact, were messages he prepared to deliver directly to the newspapers through the Associated Press. He intended those official-looking reports, with precise time codes and headed "To Major-Gen Dix," to preempt news correspondents' interpretations of battles.[46] He would shape the news one way or another.

But today Dix had so far received no notice from Stanton about the proclamation either over the wire or in print.

Dix sent off a message to Secretary of State Seward in the Capitol Building at 11:35 a.m. He knew he'd already missed the mail delivery to the *Scotia*. The next deadline was a hard stop, no later than twenty-five minutes away, when a military schooner could still catch the *Scotia* with last-minute messages. Dix's tone was a bit leisurely for the situation:

> A proclamation by the President countersigned by you, and believed to be spurious, has appeared in some of our morning papers, calling for 400,000 men and appointing the 26th instant as a day of fasting, humiliation, and prayer. Please answer immediately for steamer.

In Washington, Stanton read Dix's message with the text of the proclamation Lincoln had allegedly put out under the banners of *The World* and the *Journal of Commerce*. He could barely contain his fury. The *Scotia* was scheduled to sail in five minutes, and the man Lincoln nicknamed "Old Mars," due to Stanton's single-minded focus on the war, was not one to be trifled with. Ulysses S. Grant would describe Stanton in his memoirs as "caring nothing for the feelings of others. In fact, it seemed to be pleasanter to him to disappoint than to gratify."[47] A British journalist described Stanton as the "most repulsive character in America," with a "brutal, arrogant manner."[48] McClellan had once considered him a friend, but after working with him in the Lincoln administration, McClellan would write to his wife, "Stanton is without exception the vilest man I ever knew or heard of."[49]

Reverend Henry Ward Beecher disagreed with those assessments. To his family and dearest friends, Stanton revealed a softer side. "Stanton was tender as a woman," Beecher would recall. "He was as tender as a lover."[50]

Visually, Stanton cut a somewhat remarkable figure, with small, dark, piercing eyes and a long, black, fuzzy cape of beard. His round spectacles and thin lips made him look like a prim parson. But when at work, he presented none of a parson's tranquility.

Working late into the night from a standing desk in a general workspace off his private office, the tightly wound Stanton forced every meeting to be public, to ensure few digressions and to eliminate pleasantries and backstabbing comments. He ran a rigid operation, even bringing President Lincoln to talk openly in the scrum of clerks and secretaries.

Stanton maintained tight control over the press. "No newspaper reporter ever came to Mr. Stanton or to any officer of the War Department for news," remembered Stanton's private secretary, Major A. E. H. Johnson. "He held all officials to a rule of strict non-intercourse with reporters and correspondents. Of all the branches of Government, the War Department was the last resort of reporters. For this the newspapers reveled in denunciation and abuse of Mr. Stanton. But if ever a tyrant was right, it was the great War Secretary, and his persistent and unrelenting tyranny was the colossal factor that made this nation what it now is."[51]

Stanton fired off a telegram to Dix:

I have just seen a copy of the spurious proclamation referred to in your dispatch. It is a base and treasonable forgery.

Someone, somewhere would be facing court martial with potential military execution.

6

STOP THE PRESSES

[Washington, D.C. - May 18, 1864]

S ecretary of State William Seward not only received Dix's query at 11:35 a.m., he'd received a telegram from D. H. Craig, the general agent of the Associated Press, at 11:00 a.m., alerting him that the association suspected the proclamation was inauthentic.[1]

Seward had cosigned a call for humiliation and prayer a year ago, but he and Lincoln had sent nothing out in the last days. And given their deep personal relationship—involving long evenings as teetotaling Lincoln listened and talked and Seward quaffed copious amounts of claret—Lincoln would not have cut him out of the chain of information. But Mary Todd never trusted Seward. He had been a favorite for the 1860 Republican nomination and took his time recovering from his pique when denied the presidency. She commented plainly to her husband, I hate to see you "let that hypocrite, Seward, twine you around his little finger as if you were a skein of thread."[2]

Now, a half hour past the scheduled departure for the *Scotia*,[3] Seward issued a statement to the New York press and foreign ministers abroad, stating emphatically: "This paper is an absolute forgery."[4] He added more: "No proclamation of this kind has been made, or proposed to be made, by the President, or issued, or proposed to be issued by the State Department, or any other Department of Government."[5]

No denial could be more complete.

When Lincoln received word that the so-called proclamation signed by his hand had been published in the New York papers, he blasted into one of the worst tempers witnesses had seen him—or would ever see him—in the entire course of his presidency.[6] Despite his reputation for sagacity and calm, Lincoln could get riled to a terrifying degree. An eyewitness to a speech Lincoln once delivered, inspired by an injustice, remarked on his temper: Lincoln reportedly "stepped cleanly out of character, and became . . . a different person—fiery, emotional, reckless, violent, hot-blooded—everything what at other times he was not."[7] In the past, he had physically tossed people he considered schemers from his office. Now someone had dared to write a nine-paragraph lamentation over his name.

Lincoln summoned Seward, who went out into the pouring rain to find Stanton and demand to know if the document had gone over the War Department line. Seward and Stanton assured Lincoln that it had not, since they could easily search every message. That left one likely culprit, the Independent Telegraph Company, at Twelfth Street, near Pennsylvania Avenue, which operated free of government surveillance.

Stanton ordered Lincoln's trusted telegrapher, Major Eckert, to hurry there in the downpour, to gather all of the messages he could find at their offices, and to shut down their operation. Stanton would follow up with a file of soldiers to arrest staff members on the charge of circulating contraband, but without submitting evidence to a judge.[8]

Up in New York, Dix and the Associated Press agents now had Seward's denials but had missed both of the *Scotia*'s regular deadlines. Someone in Washington had telegraphed Postmaster Abram Wakeman, a close friend of Mary Todd Lincoln, to keep the mails open to allow the *Herald*'s report of the fraud onboard, but that time too had passed.

The *Herald*, the *Chicago Tribune* suspected, would likely not keep such a transaction clean. "It would be very like the Scotch shrewdness of the satanic *Herald* to ship its whole 'suppressed' edition of 20,000 by the Scotia, to meet with ready sale on the other side of the water. True, it may be overhauled by a Government contradiction at Halifax," meaning a disclaimer could be telegraphed when near land in Nova Scotia, "but a robust, strong winded lie, with a good start, is not easily run down by truth, especially when running among its friends. That bogus proclamation is designed as a news *coup d'etat* in Europe. The foreign rebels will give it circulation in all the Government purlieus friendly to their cause. They will have it translated into French, German and Russian. Grave Lords and brisk parliamentarians will introduce it in their debates. It will not be so easy to throttle it with a denial."[9]

Now, at 12:30 p.m., Dix got M. S. Roberts at the AP to hire a carriage to race to the dock and dispatch a military steamer to stop the *Scotia*'s progress.[10] Seward had begged the *Scotia* to hold in quarantine, but the vessel couldn't delay indefinitely. A man on the masthead must have seen the steamer coming.

The steamer pulled alongside and officers climbed aboard. They tramped across the vast deck to search from stem to stern for copies of *The World* and *Journal of Commerce*. What they found were passengers clutching little paper slips printed by the offending newspapers and warning that the story of the president's proclamation might very well be a hoax.[11]

The officers left Seward's vehement denial on board to be telegraphed from Queenstown, Ireland, plus a message to the U.S. ministers in London and Paris, assuring them that the fabricators would be arrested and punished.[12]

That is, if the fabricators could be found.

The Associated Press announced a reward of $1,000 for evidence leading to the conviction of the proclamation's author.[13] That sum represented enough to purchase ten work horses, or for those more disposed to luxury, sufficient funds to purchase the camel hair and cashmere shawl that Mary Todd Lincoln acquired at A. T. Stewart's in the first months of her husband's presidency.

James N. Worl, a superintendent of the Independent Telegraph, found Lincoln's favorite War Department telegraph officer, Major Thomas Eckert, standing before him that rainy day demanding every message and news report on the Telegraph's premises.

Worl had been in the business for sixteen years, starting in quieter times and in a quieter place, Philadelphia, and he did not stand for the mayhem of government interference.[14] Any message passing through his office, he protested, was confidential and privileged, and he refused to sacrifice the people's confidence. Among the full record of telegraph papers that Eckert was now demanding were thousands of private transmissions from across the country: the word of births, deaths, and love affairs, business dealings, and political plans.

But as Worl fended off Eckert, Lincoln's military reinforcements arrived. General Moses Wisewell, the military governor of Washington, barged in with his soldiers. They began arresting everyone on the premises, including two unfortunate ladies who happened to have chosen the wrong morning to send their telegrams. While Eckert rummaged through the office's contents, another War Department telegrapher and decoder, Charles A. Tinker, arrived to confiscate all of the documents. Wisewell's soldiers lined up the operators, putting Worl at the head. They freed the women, but they marched the unfortunate telegraph operators up busy Pennsylvania Avenue under double guard in the pouring rain.[15] To Worl's embarrassment, senators, congressmen, and other friends of his witnessed the shameful procession.

After being interrogated at the provost marshal's office, the telegraph operators were sent down to Old Capitol Prison, the jail for spies and prostitutes.[16]

There, Captain Woods led Worl into a large, filthy third-floor cell with the bad weather blowing in through broken windows. Worl's new rough cellmates looked up. They were six of Confederate Colonel John Mosby's band of weather-worn guerrillas, famous for striking on horseback from out of nowhere in the hills of Virginia and vanishing without a trace. Their arrests had filled the newspapers in the last weeks.

As Worl took in one then the other of his new and dangerous mates, he became keenly aware of the money bulking his pockets, his gold pocket watch, and his gold studs. He stopped Woods before his departure from the cell, and while the guerillas watched, he handed over all his valuables for safe keeping, holding on to just fifty dollars.

Then the captain clapped the door shut, leaving Worl alone with the enemy.

By noon, up in Hartford, Mary Prime had gotten word that *The World* and the *Journal of Commerce* had published the hoax. She wrote:

Good morning, dear Love,

   . . . Pa has gone downtown. He is very much excited over the "Proclamation" which as yet we do not understand, only knowing that it was published and has been pronounced a forgery. Still, he is excited and anxious.[17]

When her father, an esteemed elected official of the Connecticut Republican Party, returned home, he reported that the newspapers that published the proclamation—including the *Journal of Commerce*—had been suppressed. In fact, no newspaper had been ordered shut down, only the Washington telegraph wires, and even that order had only passed along the military wires. Misinformation seemed rampant, even from her father's insider Republican sources. Mary wrote to her husband, Will:

Of course I believe nothing that is not officially announced but I am worried and anxious. I wish I could be with you to know how the world goes on with you.[18]

She suspected that the false proclamation's intent was to snare *The World* and the *Journal of Commerce*, both Democratic papers, and shut them down in advance of the Republican Party convention three weeks hence.

It is a Republican trick and is aimed to stop you all off during this season of excitement of which they take advantage.

With Eckert off securing the D.C. office of the Independent Telegraph, Stanton conveyed a new order from the president to Dix: arrest the telegraph operators in New York. It was 2:00 p.m.

The President directs that immediately upon receipt of this order you take military possession of the Independent Telegraph Company at New York.[19]

The president wanted military occupation of not only the offices at Twenty-Six Nassau Street, at the corner of Cedar, but its outposts at William Street, the Gold Room, and the Brokers' Exchange. Lincoln ordered Dix to seize "all the instruments, dispatches, and papers" both "in the office or upon the person of the manager, superintendent, and operators."

The president ordered Dix to personally oversee the task. "Strict diligence, attention, and confidence is desired in the execution of this order, and you are requested to give it your personal attention and employ your best officers."[20]

At the same time, Stanton sent ferocious commands to Philadelphia, Harrisburg, and Pittsburgh, as well as to Baltimore. Every office of the Independent Telegraph and the Inland Telegraph should be seized, its transmissions confiscated, and its operators arrested.

By 2:15 p.m., Eckert reported his work in D.C. complete. "I have the honor to report that the arrests have been made and offices closed."[21] But when the telegraph operator Tinker returned to the War Department, he had disappointing news: he had searched every document in the Independent Telegraph office and found no signs of the proclamation.

As evening came on, the military officers directed by Stanton throughout Pennsylvania reported on their successful arrests. Those Harrisburg and Pittsburgh telegraph men—until moments before, diligently typing out the messages of the people—had been marched like criminals through their city streets. The soldiers now controlled all communications and the Telegraph's employees.

Stanton was delighted by the thoroughness. He thanked the officers and ordered their entire haul of prisoners and papers sent some two hundred miles to him and to the Old Capitol Prison in D.C.[22] Stanton seemed not to care whether these men deserved constitutional rights, or if their private property merited constitutional protections. He knew he controlled the communication network of the United States. No skullduggery would escape his investigation.

In New York, Prime imagined that a nefarious culprit had sent that boy running through the darkened streets. Someone had concocted that whole long proclamation. Someone knew the particulars of the Associated Press reports, and more sinister yet, he knew the hour when the newspapers would be most vulnerable. Dark motives must have compelled him, perhaps bloodshed in the New York streets.

Prime sent Mary a telegram: "I am investigating and hope to catch the forger." Later, he would write, "I would give a thousand dollars myself to find him—The man that hoaxes a newspaper commits a personal crime against the editor & a public crime against the people."[23]

By early afternoon, he and Marble agreed they should head uptown to see General Dix at the Department of the East and share the details of their sleuthing, as well as the news that they were offering a reward of $500 to catch the culprit.

They found the general inundated with communications, including from AP headquarters and Washington. Throughout New York, the population had been buzzing with fear about the impending draft. Dix had spent most of the day trying to calm the populace by sending out word that the proclamation was a hoax.

At 2:00 p.m., Dix had received Stanton's order from the president to arrest the telegraph operators and seize their possessions. But he resisted. He had not yet gathered all the facts. More information was needed to know where to even send the culprit. For example, if the act was criminal in nature, the culprit would head to "the Tombs," the city's gloomy limestone prison for men, women, and boys, where high slit windows allowed only the barest punctuation of sunlight.[24]

Or the traitor might be sent to Fort Lafayette, dubbed by those who had suffered within its walls the "American Bastille." The austere quadrangle sat five hundred yards out into the brown-green sea, down near where the New York Harbor narrows. The prison occupied most of its island, and the American flag stuck up from the compound's center like the candle on a birthday cake. A ring of more than forty massive cannons pointed outward, threatening arrivals, and the officer in charge told the prisoners that one cannon was fully loaded and pointed at the New York sheriff's headquarters should he try to enforce habeas corpus. People who were arrested and sent there essentially vanished. Men trembled at the mention of its name. Some prisoners suffered in solitary confinement for weeks, refused even a Bible, and were fed their bread and water by a taciturn guard.[25] The main prison population waited in vain to hear the charges against them. "Who can form an idea of the dull monotony of Bastille life at Fort Lafayette?" wrote one former prisoner. "Language is inadequate to describe, the anxiety and ennui of the prisoners, as hour after hour, and day after day, they longed for their release."[26]

To gather more information about the case, Dix was happy to meet with the well-known editors Prime and Marble. He listened to their entire saga with interest. According to them, the newspapers had been mere pawns in a larger plot, leading Dix to suspect that the trick had been crafted for Wall Street speculation, possibly with the hope of the false rumor going to England by steamer to affect investment in the Cotton Loan. This investment fund loomed large in the minds of the Union citizenry. After Union forces created a blockade of Confederate shipments of cotton overseas, the Confederacy, in 1863, created a futures offering—dubbed the "Cotton Loan"—for the whole stock of cotton when the war ended. European investors, in particular, bought into the offering on the British exchange. They could pay a low rate now for an enormous cache of valuable cotton as soon as the war ended. The dire news laid out in Lincoln's proclamation would make Europeans believe the Confederates would soon win a clean secession, making the loan ever more valuable.

Satisfied with the meeting, at 4:35 p.m., Dix sat down and began writing a telegram to Stanton:

I am investigating the gross fraud of this morning.[27]

He then went on to report the delivery's timing, the type of paper used, the newspapers targeted, including the *Herald*, which had printed it but not disseminated it. He itemized the steps taken by the editors who arrived at their offices to discover the hoax, including their generous offer of a $500 reward.[28]

I have sent to all the newspapers for their manuscripts and have received three. They are alike in respect to paper and handwriting. I think the authors will be detected, and I need not add that I shall in that case arrest and imprison them for trifling in so infamous a manner with the authority of the Government and the feelings of the community at this important juncture in our public affairs.

In the middle of Dix's writing, a staff member delivered a long message signed by President Lincoln. It came direct from the executive mansion, and the president's fury pulsed off the page.

Lincoln named both *The World* and the *Journal of Commerce* specifically as lone culprits, which meant that even by that afternoon, even from Washington, the administration believed it had conducted a rapid and thorough search to determine the full extent of the dissemination.

He described the two newspapers as having acted "wickedly and traitorously."[29]

He damned the proclamation as "false and spurious."

He declared the action "treasonable ... designed to give aid and comfort to the enemies of the United States and to the rebels now at war against the Government and their aiders and abettors."

Dix knew whom Lincoln meant by the rebels, but which people did the president consider the enemies of the United States?

Then came the most shocking demand:

> You are, therefore, hereby commanded forthwith to arrest and imprison in any fort or military prison in your command the editors, proprietors, and publishers of the aforesaid newspapers.

He also authorized imprisonment of anyone who would reprint the story:

> You will hold the persons so arrested in close custody until they can be brought to trial before a military commission for their offense.

A military commission held the power to order the death sentence. Since the beginning of the American Civil War, military commissions tried thousands of prisoners, doling out the most severe punishments. In February, twenty-two soldiers had been hung for desertion in Northern Virginia. Just three weeks earlier, two deserters had been shot to death by muskets in Boston. President Lincoln intended to arrest newspaper editors—famous ones at that, pillars of the community—and subject them to a potentially fatal punishment.

And then Abraham Lincoln demanded an even more comprehensive seizure.

> You will also take possession by military force of the printing establishments of the *New York World* and *Journal of Commerce*, and hold the same until further orders and prevent any further publication therefrom.

Dix could not believe the order. Lincoln, not content to order the shutdown of the telegraphs, to halt the *Scotia*, to disavow the proclamation far and wide, would, at this late hour, order the arrest of the newspaper editors and essentially demand the death of their presses? Such a decision was not only personally humiliating for Dix, as he had spent the afternoon with Prime and Marble, but also blatantly unconstitutional. No charge had yet been filed against them. No judge had signed a warrant. Dix wrote a postscript to his earlier, as-yet-unfinished letter to Stanton:

> Since writing the above, the President's order for the arrest of the editors, proprietors, and publishers of the World and Journal of Commerce has come to hand. I shall execute it unless the foregoing information shall be deemed sufficient by the President to suspend it until my investigation is concluded.[30]

He sent the telegram off.

The response from Washington, from Stanton in the War Department, came back quick and ferocious. Stanton clearly indicated that Dix should not misinterpret the order as coming from him as secretary of war. It had come from President Lincoln himself:

> The President's telegram was an order to you, which I think it was your duty to execute immediately upon its receipt. I have no further orders to give you.[31]

Dix loitered an hour more with that scolding, still taking no action, and then he wrote to Stanton:

> There will be no delay in the execution of either order. The telegraph offices will be seized immediately, and the newspapers, editors, &c. . . .[32]

But he added a plea:

> . . . unless I hear from you before the guards are ready.

He signed off again.

Stanton, down in Washington, hit a higher boil. Not only was Dix attempting to weasel out of seizing the newspaper offices, he had blatantly delayed in shutting down the New York telegraph offices, an order that had been issued nearly four hours earlier. It was 6:30 p.m. By now, Stanton expected that the order would have been completed. All the other military officers across Pennsylvania had marched their cuffed culprits to train stations to send them to D.C., and Dix had not even begun to make arrests?

> Your telegram of 5.40 is just received. A great national crime has been committed by the publication. The editors, proprietors, and publishers, responsible and irresponsible, are in law guilty of that crime.

He released his fury.

> You were not directed to make any investigation, but to execute the President's order; the investigation was to be made by a military commission. How you can excuse or justify delay in executing the President's order until you make an investigation is not for me to determine.

Dix struggled. He decided he would resign rather than execute such an extreme order and wrote a letter declaring the same.[33] But then he was convinced to back down and left the resignation letter in his drawer. With no other recourse, he sent out soldiers across the city to begin making the arrests.

That evening, a squad of soldiers marched down Nassau Street in New York City. It was not uncommon to spot such military movements through Manhattan and Brooklyn, day or night. The army often sent armed force to arrest deserters. But this platoon was larger and more ominous than usual. The soldiers halted just past the office of the Independent Telegraph Company. The officer in charge and his men fell into position, blocking the front and side entrances from arrival or escape.

After the soldiers established their perimeter, three carriages rolled to a halt at the Telegraph's door. Colonel Ludlow and an assistant stepped down from one of the carriages and marched into the office.

Wallace Leaming, the well-known manager of the New York office, had stepped out for a moment, but Ludlow found there Leaming's chief operator, A. N. Aplin, along with the night team of J. W. Fish and Edward Johnson. The third operator, Robert C. Edwards, was in the midst of sending a telegram to Boston. As the soldiers took possession of the office, Edwards keyed to his fellow operator in Massachusetts, "We are all under—"[34]

Just as he was about to type "arrest," a sword blade slid below his arms, lifting his hands off the keys. Colonel Ludlow was staring down at Edwards, his weapon now controlling the telegraph operator's ability to work. The ever-clicking telegraphs in the office fell silent as each operator stopped communications. Ludlow ordered Edwards up and into the line of other operators.

Soldiers searched the telegraph employees' pockets. Then Colonel Ludlow directed the prisoners to the carriages, the telegraph key left open; the machines could still receive messages, but they would be neither transcribed nor answered. They would be codes rattling in an empty office.[35]

Leaming had returned and identified himself at the door. He managed to get inside. But the officers immediately arrested him as well and put him into the line.

As the officers rifled through the office files, the arrested operators still believed that, surely, the authorities would understand this all to be a silly mistake. They would be back at their machines within moments. Ludlow had mentioned that he intended to take them to the Park Barracks, but the operators assumed that the incident would end there, and they would head back to work.

They were mistaken. From the Park Barracks, they were driven to officers' headquarters and placed under guard. The charge against them was "aiding and abetting in the transmission over the wires a forged document purporting to be a proclamation by the President."[36] But they appeared before no judge, and no evidence was presented against them.

Leaming pled to be taken to Dix's office on Bleecker Street to petition for his men's release.[37] Two hours later, he returned, despondent at having failed. The operators now understood the danger before them. They were under Dix's control, Dix of the famous order to shoot "on the spot" a person who would take down the flag. That line had seemed so patriotic in the early days of the war—if reckless. Now his words sounded like destiny.

Around 8:30 p.m., the day clerk heard what sounded like marching outside *The World* offices. Then he heard a barked, "Halt!"[38] An officer entered the office and positioned two soldiers, with their revolvers drawn, at each door. The commanding officer spoke only to his men, ordering them to let no one in and to shoot anyone who tried.

"Who is in charge?" he asked the day clerk.

"The editors are?" the day clerk replied, confused.

"Where are the editors?"

Up in the warren of dingy rooms, *The World*'s writers and editors heard the noise on the stairs. When a few officers filed in, the staff barely looked up.[39] They assumed the uniformed men came on benign business. In the office of managing editor David Goodman Croly, the officers showed him an order from Dix requiring them to seize the premises.

Why? Croly demanded but received no answer. So he insisted on continuing his editing work. He saw nothing in the order telling him he couldn't keep producing the newspaper, even with the soldiers there. This parsing of the spirit of the demand flummoxed the commanding officer. He sent a messenger back to Dix's office for clarification.

Not long after, Lieutenant Gabriel Tuthill from Dix's office appeared, along with a command of twenty men. Tuthill ordered everyone to immediately stop what they were doing, asserting that the orders to Dix had come directly from Washington, D.C. Tuthill then went downstairs and told the day clerk to stop working, too.

Advertisers arrived to place ads. News carriers came in with telegrams. All were driven away. The day clerk then noticed the night clerk arriving at the Park Row door. Somehow his colleague had maneuvered through the phalanx, unaware that *The World* was under military occupation. A soldier leveled the barrel of a gun against the night clerk's temple.

"That is the night clerk, you must not disturb him!" the day clerk shouted. The soldier lowered his gun, but grumpily ordered the day clerk to lock up the newspaper's cash box and get out.[40]

Upstairs, the reporters and editors struggled to reckon with the enforced requirement: stop work. One writer had been typesetting an event announcement for a festivity their readers would want to attend but now never would know about. A reporter condensing the transcript of a tedious session of Congress stilled his pen, but then wondered how the readers would monitor their elected officials. *The World*'s special correspondent, just back from the Virginia battlefield that day, held nine days of notes in his coat pockets, news that anguished families waited with great anxiety to hear and now wouldn't.[41]

The staff left the offices but found a place to gather nearby. Thinking surely that the insane order would be reversed and they could go back to their desks, they waited until two o'clock in the morning when they finally realized the terrible truth that *The World* had been silenced.

Down in the press vaults, the soldiers ordered the press engineer out. But the boiler, which supplied steam for the presses, could not simply be left idle. The engineer asked permission to stay long enough to extinguish the power.

"I want no 'tender scenes,'" the soldier snapped. "Move on!"[42]

Some moments later, the engineer returned to the sentries at the door. "I guess that I've left steam enough on down below to blow the neighborhood up come the next twenty minutes," he observed.

That got the soldiers' attention. They ordered the engineer to go fix the problem, but he was so angry, he wanted them to suffer. He vanished into the streets.

Now the soldiers eyed each other nervously. The guards in the publication room watched each tick of the clock, one minute, two minutes . . . The officer in charge seemed ready to offer a reward for one of his men to go scour the streets to bring the informer back.

A rumble sounded. The soldiers shuddered. But it was a distant carriage wheel on the cobblestones.

At 8:30 p.m., Prime, knowing nothing of the events at the *World* office, left the *Journal* and went uptown toward home, stopping to get dinner along the way. It was after 10:00 p.m. when he arrived at his house to change his collar, readying to go to Barlow's to see if Marble had been there and if he had any new information about their investigation. At that moment, he believed them to be heroes for spending so much time—and even offering money—to catch the author of the fraudulent document.

Prime knew the military had swarmed the offices of the Independent Telegraph Company earlier that evening. Though he didn't know for sure, he had assumed the soldiers were there to search for information about the bogus proclamation.[43] Aside from that, he had no further sign of the government's reaction, nor had he received any thanks for all that he and Marble had done to catch the perpetrator.

When he arrived at Barlow's, he failed to find his friend in his usual spot in the library and "all looked cold and dismal."[44] A few moments later, Barlow came down from upstairs. General Dix, Barlow informed Prime, had put out an order for Prime's arrest. Not only that, but the *Journal of Commerce* was in the hands of the military.

Less than an hour earlier, Captain Winston Barstow from Dix's staff had led twelve Reserve Corps soldiers, fully armed, to the *Journal* newsroom and presented arrest papers to the editor still at work: William Hallock, the son of the retired founder, Gerald Hallock.

Hallock asked that he be allowed to keep putting together the paper, but the soldiers assured him that there was no need, as the paper would not be going out the next day. Deeply disturbed, Hallock reluctantly told his newspaper foreman he might as well go home. Then he sat down to write a letter to his wife, as she would wonder why he had disappeared.

The officers took Hallock on their search for Prime and the co-editor, David M. Stone, although they found neither. At their stop at Stone's house in Brooklyn, they tormented his wife with news of his imminent arrest.[45] From there, they took Hallock to Castle Garden, the port at the southern tip of New York City, which served as the boarding for the water voyage to Fort Lafayette.[46]

Prime had no time to process Barlow's news of all that had occurred at his newspaper offices. Barlow informed him that Assistant Adjutant General Charles G. Halpine of the general's staff was at that very moment in the house to arrest Prime. *The World* had also been seized and Marble too would be arrested.

Marble suddenly arrived, having been to dinner with a friend nearby, making Halpine's task of arrest extremely easy.

Back at Bleecker Street, now at 10:40 p.m., late in that very long day, Dix wrote to the rageful Stanton that he had done—despite his private misgivings—exactly as he had been ordered.

> The investigation was made by me as commanding officer of the department before the President's order was received, as my dispatch showed. There has been none since. I understood the President's orders as commands to be executed, and there has been no unnecessary delay in the execution. The telegraphic offices were seized as soon as my officers could reach them. The *World* and *Journal of Commerce* printing offices are in possession of my men. Two of my officers, Major Halpine and Captain Barstow, are engaged in the arrest of the editors, proprietors, and publishers, and a steamer is waiting at Castle Garden to take them to Fort Lafayette. The only delay has been in making proper arrangements to secure, as nearly as possible, simultaneous and effective action.[47]

That message, Dix could assume, would assure Stanton that he had done exactly what duty, not conscience, urged him to do.

7

THE HUNT

[New York, N.Y. – May 18, 1864, 10:40 p.m.]

---

s Dix waited for the arrival of his prisoners—strangely, two very famous New Yorkers—he found a telegram from Stanton that had been
sent at 8:30 p.m. Dix had missed it in the flurry of activity around
the arrests.

> The officer in charge of the investigation, respecting the forged procla-
> mation, reports that he is led to believe it originated in this city [Wash-
> ington], and that the New York publishers were not privy to it. If your
> conclusions are the same you may suspend action against them until
> developments are made.[1]

That telegram offered enormous relief to Dix, if poorly timed since he had
already sent out the armed soldiers to cuff these men. In the afternoon,
Dix's relations with Marble and Prime had been so cordial. It was impossi-

ble to believe they had conspired to humiliate the president or dispirit the citizenry, or worse yet, capitalize on the stock market. Dix's view of their innocence now had been authenticated.

But though the newspaper editors would face no prosecution, Stanton's telegram did not free the telegraph officers. If Stanton believed the fraud was initiated in D.C., then the wire service operators would have played a part in getting the message to the New York papers. Dix responded to Stanton at 10:40 p.m.:

> Your dispatch in regard to the probable origin of the forged procla-
> mation is just received. I am satisfied the publishers of the *World* and
> *Journal of Commerce* had no knowledge of it. I shall, therefore, suspend
> the order as to them, but shall keep possession of their printing offices
> until you otherwise direct.[2]

He assured Stanton that he had arrested the manager, superintendent, and operators of the telegraph line at five o'clock in the evening and would be sending them to Fort Lafayette in an hour.

It was a deep dark night with thunder in the distance when the telegraph operators were marched to the Battery and loaded onto the police boat, the *Berdan*. The other Independent Telegraph offices in the city also had been seized. Since it was past regular business hours, the soldiers found no one working in the Gold Room or in the telegraph offices just off the trading floor. The soldiers confiscated the Independent's messages and machines, and they occupied the place from then onward.[3]

The Independent operators still had no idea what their future held. One of the officers guarding them at Castle Garden thought they would simply stay on the *Berdan* for the night. But then the crew began to cast off the *Berdan*'s lines to take the boat out to sea. The old Trinity Church bell chimed eleven o'clock. As the boat steamed down the harbor, the lights of Governors Island and Castle Williams vanished behind them. They were headed far beyond the city's embrace.

Over the course of the hour-and-a-half journey, the thunder intensified. A stiff wind curled white-crested waves over the deck, leaving trails of foam. A vivid flash of lightning lit up the sky and revealed the grim walls of Fort Lafayette, the last stop before the New York Harbor opened to the vast Atlantic. The *Berdan* bumped up against the fort's dock. Rain came in torrents as the crew fastened the boat to the wharf of the massive prison. The telegraph operators, shaking themselves awake from their fitful dozing, grabbed hastily for their hats and were ordered to line up.

The soldiers marched the operators toward the gloomy portals. In that deep night, the men were separated from their families and friends, their jobs and their city, and were jailed along with "secessionists, pirates, blockade runners and bounty jumpers."[4] Whether guilty or innocent, as they well knew, people sent to Fort Lafayette remained there a very long time.

The prisoners met Colonel Burke, a thick, balding sixty-year-old man, with "altogether a war-worn and stern face." He favored an old coat and Buffalo robe, smoked a pipe, and had at heel his dog Carlo, who reminded people of Cerberus, due to his ferocious appearance and his job at the gates of hell.[5] Burke had come to this post after serving under General Scott during the Mexican War and earned his promotion due to his lack of hesitation in his assigned task for Scott: executing deserters.

He asked the operators to sit, and his assistant wrote their names in a ledger. Why had they been sent to Fort Lafayette? Burke asked.

They replied they had no idea.

"Ah! Yes," he said, "No one ever knows what they come here for. This is a Temple of Innocence."

He then escorted one of the operators into an adjacent room that housed a glorious downy white bed. The operator thrilled at the prospect of getting such a nice place to sleep so late in the night. Burke told him it was a mere formality. The operator assumed "it" meant the arrest, and he would soon be freed from Fort Lafayette after a luxurious slumber. By "it," however, Burke meant a thorough body search. All the operators endured the same. The jailors then escorted the prisoners to various barracks where they found thirty-two men to a room, their baggage stacked about their cells. Two of the operators slept in chairs with their heads on the transoms of cannons, and one found a dining table in the mess to use as a bed.

At Forty-Nine Bleecker Street, at Dix's Department of the East, it was nearly 11:00 p.m. when Prime and Marble walked through the doors to be interrogated. Ten hours had made a dramatic difference in their fates. That afternoon, Dix had received them warmly. Now they stood before him under armed guard, at strict orders issued by the president. What revelation now could have made Dix drag them to the docks? Were they about to be shipped off to Fort Lafayette, where traitors, draft dodgers, and spies festered?

Thankfully, given the terror they'd been put through, Dix again adopted his favored graceful tone. "Gentlemen, I regret the necessity of having brought you," he began, as if he had not roused them from their homes, snatching them from their families and friends in the late hours of the night.[6]

He tried to offer a courtesy in lieu of an apology: "and have only to request you to take the carriage at the door and go to your homes again."

Of course, Prime and Marble were relieved not to be headed to the infamous prison. But these sudden shifts in treatment also spoke to a strange chaos within the administration. How could they be headed to the infamous Fort Lafayette one moment and the next enjoying the comforts of the general's carriage on their way back home? Who exactly was in charge?

Dix boasted that he, along with Thurlow Weed, boss of the Republican Party, had intervened to get them released. Still he had alarming news. He said their newspaper offices would be held indefinitely. It was eleven o'clock at night and Dix hoped he would receive orders to reopen the presses, but that word had not yet arrived.

The newspapermen would be barred from their own businesses, but Dix would tell them the instant he heard otherwise.

Prime and Marble traveled back to Barlow's to find Barlow's friends gathered in vigil. Stone, the editor and proprietor of the *Journal*, soon joined them. With this convention of key editors, they discussed the brutal treatment they had received.

That the government, without evidence or charge, had struck so severely was humiliating, even horrifying. The *Journal of Commerce* had been published daily for thirty-seven years. In the four years that *The World* had been in operation, it had been a crucial champion of the Constitution, protecting it against administration excesses. As Prime would later note, the *Journal of Commerce* had supported Lincoln's administration even at a cost to the newspaper:

> Mark this. We have within three years done more than fifty thousand dollars' worth of gratuitous advertising for this same Administration . . . every order coming to us in almost *facsimile* of this forged dispatch, and with no verification whatever. There is scarcely a night in the year that the War Department does not send us, on manifold paper, now in this and now in that handwriting, at one, two, three or four o'clock, some such proclamation . . . If we should refuse to publish one of these we should be denounced as Copperheads. If we demanded verification or pay we should be hooted at as traitors . . . we were ourselves arrested, and our paper was suppressed, on a supposed order from Washington, written out by a telegraphic operator, which Gen. Dix took on trust, because he had seen others that resembled it which were true.[7]

The editors were furious. Though their presses had been stopped, they understood they still had access to the Associated Press to vent their rage.

Their *cri de coeur* to be put out over the wire, which they titled "A CARD FROM THE JOURNAL OF COMMERCE," started with a condemnation of the evil forgery.[8]

The editors reassured readers that they always took "utmost care and vigilance" in putting out their newspaper. They were powerless, however, against a perpetrator with such intricate and vast understanding of the practice of newsrooms.

> The fraud was so perfect that we venture to affirm that ninety-nine men out of a hundred, placed in the situation of the foreman would have been deceived . . . The moment when editors have left and the foreman is the responsible man is well known to newspaper men as one of the most critical moments in the day's history of a newspaper. If any one suggests that it is better to reject everything at such a time, let him reflect that we frequently receive as late as 3 1/2 o'clock A.M. all urgent dispatches from the War Department and other departments, the value of which to Government and people depends on their immediate publication.

They posited that had they blocked the president's message, they would have been lambasted. They then went on to set out their theory. "There must have been more than one man concerned."

Other newspaper members of the Associated Press, they pointed out, had benefited from their locations along Park Row. "Our own remoteness from the offices of other papers forbade any such comparison of notes among the men employed."

They then expanded the notion of threat. "It is important that our readers and the public at large should know what ingenious scoundrels are at work devising every possible method of deceiving the people, either for purposes of stock speculation or with intent to aid the enemies of the country."

They ended by insisting that they believed the forger would be caught—with their help as well as with the aid of the other victims in the press.

The declaration completed, the editors headed down to the Associated Press in the carriage lent by Dix. It was now very late and the streets of Manhattan seemed all but abandoned.

As they traveled in the night, a police officer stopped them. Were they about to be arrested once again?

But after a few sharp words from the officer about the darkness, the driver stepped down from the carriage and lit the headlamps. The officer had merely warned them about the hazards of driving without sufficient light.[9]

By then, it was three o'clock in the morning.[10] *Journal of Commerce* editor Hallock arrived at the AP office, anxious to tell of his arrest six hours earlier and the search for Stone and Prime. He had stood in the storm at the docks of Castle Garden. He had readied for his voyage to the imposing Fort Lafayette, only to learn he would be released. He then went looking for Stone and Prime at Prime's home, but discovering them gone, had come back down to the AP office.

After the AP clerk keyed the *Journal* editors' statement and put it out on the wire, they all headed back to their homes, Marble and Prime still traveling in the carriage Dix had lent them.

That night, Prime felt too restless to sleep. On the way from the Associated Press headquarters, they had passed *The World* and saw the soldiers standing with bayonets crossed at the door.[11] Prime wrote Mary, it was "a sad sight in New York in May 1864." All was darkness except on the ground floor where the soldiers patrolled.[12]

"I will keep you fully informed," he assured her. "Stay where you are—Don't think of coming down here—It is atrocious that such a hoax on us should be so serious in its results."

Distrustful of the mail, Will Prime sent his letter by private hand. At four o'clock in the morning, he finally closed his eyes.

By morning, the severity of Lincoln's retaliation dawned on New York citizens as they hurried past the armed soldiers occupying not only a private business but also a bastion of the free press. The *Brooklyn Eagle* said the site made anyone passing by feel ashamed of himself and his country.[13] When the Gold Room trading floor opened, soldiers watched over the action, inspiring unusually demure bidding by the swaggering brokers. The sight of gleaming bayonets tamped down their customary vigor.[14]

With the dawn of morning, it was also clear that *The World*'s office building would not blow up, as the machine's engineer had threatened the soldiers the night before. He had taken pity on the building's neighbors and snuck the previous night through a side door to shut down the machinery the proper way. He left the soldiers in the dark about his fix, but also left the city block unharmed.[15]

When the first sleepy news courier arrived at *The World*, one of the soldiers occupying the premises roughly demanded to know what he wanted.

His ticket, the courier replied, to receive his copies for selling.

The soldier brandished his revolver. "I'll give you your ticket out of this," he said, and the courier hurried away.

That courier was only the first of many to be repelled from the paper's offices.[16]

Angry crowds gathered outside *The World*, among them the employees who were now blocked from their desks. They clustered in little groups discussing the outrage and what action they should take next. One employee started delivering a bold speech.

A well-dressed man came up to the outer ring of the crowd and asked what was going on, to which he received the reply, "Only this damned traitor's office shut up."

"What for?"

"For getting up a bogus proclamation to injure the Government."

"Oh, but I understand that all the papers had been deceived by that proclamation and came near publishing it, as well as *The World*."

"Oh, that's all very well, old man, but Gen. Dix isn't to be gammoned in that way. The loyal papers knew better than to publish it. Gen. Dix ought to have sent every God damned man in the office to Fort Lafayette."

Policemen sensing a fight brewing came up and scattered the throng.[17]

Soldiers also guarded the entrance of the *Journal of Commerce*. When a *New York Herald* reporter managed to make his way through the weaponized perimeter, he found the commanding officer in the accounting room, reclining in the bookkeeper's chair, carefully smoking a Havana cigar.

Passersby asked the reason for the soldiers' presence. When they were told the military had taken possession of the newspaper, some looked pleased, others nonplussed. Others muttered "damned tyranny" under their breaths.[18]

And indeed, Manton Marble reflected, the U.S. citizens did seem to be living under tyranny. Almost fifty people had been taken into custody that previous night. Journalists trembled at guns leveled at their heads as they went about their jobs.

In broad daylight, without trial or warrant, the U.S. government had thrown civilians in jail and seized private businesses. No evidence of conspiracy had been produced and no official charges filed.

The media at first was conciliatory toward the administration. On May 19, Sidney H. Gay of the *Tribune*, Erastus Brooks of the *Express*, Frederick Hudson of the *Herald*, and M. S. Beach of the *Sun* telegraphed Lincoln "respectfully" explaining to him in detail the workings of the Associated Press.

They begged a second chance for the newspapers. "The suspension by your excellency's orders of the two Papers last evening has had the effect to awaken editors & publishers and news agents, telegraph companies &c., to the propriety of increased vigilance in their several duties."[19] They then begged his "excellency" to rescind the order of suppression.

On the day the hoax unfolded, the *Chicago Tribune* had called the newspapers' action "a fraud which should consign its perpetrators to all eternity of infamy, if not the nearest lamp post."[20]

But on the second day, even the government censor, Sanford, the head of the American Telegraph, noticed a shift in mood in Washington, D.C. He wrote Eckert:

> The feeling here yesterday was very strong against the Paper which published the proclamation. Today it is pretty evident that an imposition was practiced on them.[21]

The newspapers that had been lucky enough to avoid getting duped and remained functioning amplified this upset on behalf of the victims in the free press. Normally, the editors enjoyed pointing out each other's stupidity, laziness, and partisanship. The *Tribune* might refer to Bennett as "the little villain of the *Times*," or the *Herald* would disparage Greeley as "the white-coated philosopher" of the *Tribune*, but that hostility ended in the printed columns. If one were to visit the tables of Delmonico's at the lunch hour on any given day, one would find a collegial crew. "Conservatives and Radicals, Democrats and Republicans, Catholics and Protestants, conductors of the press, strike hands over a plate of soup; and, after unbending for an hour, go back to their several dens to renew the paper warfare."[22]

And in this week in May, despite a few minor shots across the bow, the editors joined forces to battle Lincoln's overreach. "It is very likely [Lincoln's actions] will injure the political aspirations of the Administration seriously, and may lead to a rejection of Lincoln by the Baltimore

Convention [to choose a Republican presidential nominee]," the *Sunday Mercury* predicted. Alternately, "The Cleveland Convention [for the Democrats] will take very high grounds in favor of personal rights and the rights of the press."[23]

The *Brooklyn Daily Eagle*, where Joseph Howard Jr. served as city editor, blasted its support for the occupied newspapers: "SHALL WE HAVE A FREE PRESS?" the headline demanded. The editorial writer emphasized that the *Journal of Commerce* and *The World* had been "unlucky enough to be imposed upon by unknown rascals."[24]

The *Tribune* called the forgery "bold and wicked," seeing it as both a stock manipulation and a way "to nullify the influence of the news of Grant's successes, to be taken out by steamer yesterday." But they urged the government to release the newspapers. The *New York Daily News* could barely believe the seizure true: "It was too palpable, too gross, too wanton an outrage upon the liberty of the press."[25]

Press indignation spanned out to the hinterlands. The *Daily Register* in Wheeling, West Virginia, remarked:

The government has acted like a rash and angry man who, when incensed, strikes in blind fury those within his reach, without waiting to consider whether they be the guilty ones or not . . . It is true that a great crime was committed by the man who issued the forged proclamation. The highest prerogative of the chief officer of a great nation, has been usurped; public confidence in the stability of the government, was, for a time, almost overthrown; and the reliability of all the dispatches, which are so eagerly sought for, and which exert such an important influence in affairs of business, or of information, is almost destroyed. No punishment can be too severe for the man who has perpetrated the fraud, but, in the name of justice, we protest against the punishment of innocent men.[26]

The Wheeling Daily Register urged that, if guilty, the newspapers would suffer. But the editorial writer also invited readers to speculate as to why these particular newspapers had been targeted—perhaps because they opposed the policy of the Lincoln administration. The paper asked readers to imagine what would have happened had the *Tribune* been duped. It was impossible to imagine Lincoln suppressing it.

Who had, in fact, perpetrated the hoax? Who might have gone through this considerable effort to craft the long declaration, to painstakingly counterfeit the AP's distribution, and time the action to the workings of the papers? And for what purpose? Did the agent of the hoax intend to upset feelings about Lincoln before the election, hoping to influence the nominating convention only weeks away? Painting a dire picture of the war effort would certainly make Lincoln look weak in this campaign season. Lincoln could be predicted to overreact to the hoax, demonstrating the president's fragile commitment to constitutional rights.

Perhaps the hoax had been placed by a Confederate to break the Union spirit and inspire wider military desertions. Or perhaps a scheming Lincoln administration official had planted the story to stir up violence in New York and thus justify martial law. During the last draft riot, the federal authorities had crept awfully close to seizing control. With New York's able men at the front, the city lacked muscle to stop the carnage. The final resolution had involved the New York State National Guard, but they had accepted the help of Michigan Volunteers and the Army of the Potomac.[27]

Mary Prime believed in such conspiracies. Her favorite theory was that the entire fabrication was likely a Republican plot to silence the Democrat papers going into the election. The authorities, she believed, wanted an excuse to shut them down. She wondered what revenge the government would next exert on her husband. Certainly, he had been released, but perhaps only because the government planned to execute a true search warrant.

On the other hand, Republicans suspected Prime and Marble of pretending to be hoaxed. McClellan, Lincoln's likely Democratic opponent, certainly was Prime's close friend. And wouldn't it be helpful for McClellan's ambitions to damage the president? Was it not odd that McClellan had shown up at the *Journal of Commerce* office first thing on the morning of the fraud?

In the nearly eighty-eight-year history of the United States, hoaxes had been used for multiple public and personal purposes. People placed bogus advertisements and marriage notices simply to stir up trouble in domestic relationships.[28]

Several decades earlier, a six-installment Moon Hoax had gripped readers of the *Sun* with meticulous descriptions pulled from an alleged Scottish scientific journal about animals scampering across the lunar landscape. "We beheld continuous herds of brown quadrupeds, having all the external characteristics of the bison, but more diminutive," the scientist explained about the terrific visions through his telescope. "It had, however, one distinctive feature . . . namely a remarkable fleshy appendage over the eyes."[29]

In 1838, an annual message from President Van Buren to Congress turned out to be fake. More recently, in May 1862, a memorandum marked "private and confidential," supposedly issued by Jefferson Davis, predicted the Confederacy would be defeated in three months if his people did not demonstrate more zeal.[30] An accompanying proclamation, allegedly authored by Davis, called for "Fasting and Prayer."[31] The *Chicago Times* admitted the next day that their reporters had played the hoax.[32]

As mentioned earlier, only six months before, Seward had been taken in by what became known as the "Mallory report," in which the secretary of the Confederate Navy wrote to an aide that France and England had supplied them with boats. *The New York Herald* complained the fraud "placed us in a false and ridiculous position before Europe."[33] The *Journal of Commerce* had made fun of Seward for falling victim to it, and now Will Prime wondered why they had been punished for falling victim to a dupe but Seward had escaped similar censure.[34]

Moreover, on May 8, just ten days before the bogus proclamation ran, *The New York Times* had published a detailed correspondence between Lord Lyons, the British minister to the United States, and Jefferson Davis about whether or not England could honor a shipment of vessels for war use. The *Times* indicated that they had picked up the supposed leaked letter from the *Mobile Tribune,* and that even that paper had noticed the letter date as April 1, April Fools' Day.[35] A week later, just three days before the bogus proclamation went into the newspapers, the *Times* announced that Lord Lyons was denying he ever wrote the letter.[36] *The New York Herald* would later say of the fraud's effect, "it slandered and vilified an ambassador."[37]

And those were just the hoaxes known to the public. Who knew how many stories circulated that would one day be proved false? The *Daily News* raged over the illness of the era: "The present is emphatically the age of lies. We have lying news, lying journals, lying histories and lying prophecies. The spirit of mendacity rules everywhere and little wonder when the Spirit of Mendacity is the Great Spirit of our rulers."[38]

Observed the *Weekly National Intelligencer* about the bogus Lincoln proclamation: "The criminal fraud does not rise to the dignity of the famous 'moon hoax' of Mr. Locke, but is about as ingenious as the pretended annual message of President van Buren to Congress in 1838, though not as innocent as was that amusing invention."[39]

This fraud smelled of more sinister purposes. The key would be to find out why someone now wanted to trick the public. Or did they hope to trick President Lincoln?

U.S. federal marshal Robert Murray, the cherub-faced forty-three-year-old who ran a one-stop shop for investigations, arrests, and interrogations out of his office at Forty-Eight Chamber Street in New York, was put in charge of the investigation. Murray had a reputation for being everywhere in the city at once. He fearlessly boarded vessels in New York Harbor to free illegal slaves. He pushed his way into New York's American Express office to halt a package of twenty-four first-class revolvers and five hundred percussion cartridges on their way down South to the rebels. He led a necklace of iron-bound pirates through the streets of New York City to court and uncovered a cache of government-issued bacon sides and barrels of beef headed to the black market via the wharfs. In just one year, the goods he seized from ships alone totaled millions of dollars.

He appeared to be the perfect detective, with the requisite personal virtues that a great sleuth needed: "an unblemished character . . . for the temptations are many" and a "good memory." He needed to be "cool, unmoved, able to suppress all emotion . . . [able to] put on all characters, and assume all disguises; pursue a trail for weeks, or months, or years; go anywhere at a moment's notice, on the land or sea; go without food or sleep; follow the slightest clew till he reaches the criminal."[40]

Illegal operators loathed Murray, and he received his share of death threats. But he also earned the respect of the condemned. When Lincoln ordered an execution of a citizen he deemed a traitor, it was Murray who visited the Tombs to deliver the brutal news. In those somber moments, Murray revealed his compassion. He would offer to personally buy the doomed man his last meal or promise to support his wife and children in perpetuity.[41]

Sometimes, in Murray's fervor to create moral stability in a scheming city, he would cross the line by becoming one-man judge and jury, arresting individuals without warrants. He was at that very moment fending off charges of taking Don Jose Arguelles, the lieutenant-governor of a town in Cuba, into U.S. custody without legal authorization and sending him back to his home country for punishment. Originally, Arguelles had arrived in the United States as a hero for having blocked a shipment of African slaves into Cuba. As it turned out, he had sold 150 of them on the side for profit.

While Arguelles was no hero, the U.S. had no extradition treaty, and without an official legal policy, Arguelles's arrest and return to Cuba equaled kidnapping.

Now Murray joined General Dix and John A. Kennedy, the head of the Metropolitans, the city's official police squad, in working up the bogus proclamation case. Democrats considered Kennedy's police force Lincoln toadies. During the draft riots, a mob had beaten Kennedy nearly unconscious and thrown him over an embankment into muddy water. When word spread that he was dead, a group of citizens performed a war dance in celebration.[42]

This formidable team of police authority had little to go on at first in solving the case. Who might be at the end of this proclamation hoax trail? A rebel? A foreigner? One could certainly imagine someone wanting to damage the Union cause, but how would that schemer know so much about newspapers?

It was, in Murray's estimation, the work of the messenger boy, if only they could find him. Public pleas went out to sway the messenger's conscience. "Besides the rewards already offered, some $2,000, a subscription paper has also been put in circulation for the raising of a fund as a reward for the discovery," *The New York Times* reported. "This will undoubtedly swell the amount (already $3,500) to a very large sum."[43] That kind of money was enough to buy thirty-one wagons with their oxen teams, twenty-three work horses, or three Philadelphia rowhouses with money to spare. "Citizens should enlist themselves in the matter and let this fact be generally known."

The newspapers, such as *The New York Times*, tried to work on the psychology of the messenger, sympathizing that he was "but a tool, doubtless ignorant of any wrong." He should have great motivation to turn himself in, they noted. Not only would he receive thousands of dollars to give up the person who tricked him into the scheme but also "the thanks and approval of the public." The newspaper also offered a strict alternative: "If he does not [turn himself in] he will be considered equally guilty, and on detection will doubtless be as severely punished."[44]

Down in Washington, the Independent Telegraph supervisor, Worl, had found himself in a bizarre new world. After the captain slammed shut his cell door on May 18, leaving him at the mercy of the six rough-looking Mosby guerillas, the apparent leader of the group confessed to Worl that, although they looked like barbarians, they were, beneath the filth and tatters, gentlemen. Only war had made them appear so feral.

Stanton had designated Worl as a prisoner allowed to use his own money to buy food. By the time the cell door shut, it was 4:00 p.m., and Worl had had nothing to eat all day. He exercised his privilege and ordered dinner with his remaining fifty dollars—enough for seven people to dine. Amazingly, the guards made good on the delivery, bringing not just the bounty but a fine tablecloth and napkins for each place.

The guerillas marveled. They hadn't had a square meal in two years.

After they ate their fill, they asked Worl if he would allow them to stash the leftovers for a day when they would not have access to his hospitality.

That first meal cost Worl a full $19.75, but he was so pleased with his new friends, he sent a servant with two dollars to fetch them cigars and the evening newspapers.

Worl slept poorly that first night. The filth, the broken windows, and the mean beds conspired against slumber, but in the morning, he cheered his new friends by ordering breakfast for them all again.

Later in the day, the guards escorted him out of his cell, away from the guerillas, for a privileged walk in the prison yard. Here stood both Confederate and Union men who had been thrown into jail, for horse swindles or draft scams, or for reasons unknown to them. It was said that Union soldiers picked up people for even private conversation critical of the government. From a high window, a woman looked down at Worl and waved, and he believed her to be the famous Confederate spy Belle Boyd, mistaking him for someone else.[45]

Days after the release of the proclamation, Stanton reasoned that if it were not the American telegraph line that had sent the bogus proclamation, nor the Independent line, there was only one other possible conduit from Washington, D.C.: the Western Press Association, a new competitor to the Associated Press, started by Henry Villard, the German-born journalist who had covered Lincoln from his election through the first days of the inaugural train trip. Villard had been remarkably scrappy breaking stories, which included a string of scoops that he'd landed while embedded with Grant at his headquarters during the Battle of the Wilderness. Villard had been the first reporter to return to D.C. with eyewitness accounts of the brutal firefights in the thickets.

Villard's fledgling news service had already won subscribers in Springfield and Boston, Massachusetts; Rochester, New York; Cincinnati, Ohio; Chicago, Illinois; St. Louis, Missouri; and farther west. His partners in the enterprise were Adam Hill and Horace White, the latter being one of Stanton's pets who recently had resigned from the War Department.

Now suspecting Villard and his team of circulating the "bogus proclamation," Stanton brought in White for a long interrogation. He jailed Villard for two days at the provost marshal headquarters and put Hill under constant surveillance.[46] To reporters and government critics, Stanton's new arrests seemed sinister. He was extending the reach of his press harassment. By doing so, he also happened to be silencing reporters who had delivered a clear view of the gory war to their civilian readers.

Relative to the bogus proclamation, a reporter uncovered Stanton's supposed justification. These three reporters sent information on the draft over the wire the night before it appeared in New York:

> We learn from the well informed correspondent of the *Commercial Advertiser*, that on Tuesday night a dispatch was sent by members of this Western Press Association, or purported to have been sent by them, announcing that there would be a proclamation, calling for a new draft, about the 1st of July . . .
>
> Whether the bogus Proclamation was concocted by one of the Association, or whether another person based it upon their news, is not yet officially known. It is fair to infer, however, that either some member of the above Association was the author of the bogus Proclamation, or that some person connected with them, knowing the fact that a call was about to be made, wrote the Proclamation upon the predictions furnished by their dispatches.[47]

No matter the alleged reasons, the public read these new arrests as Stanton expanding his ruthless reach to repress organs of war information. A former telegraph operator in the War Department later called it an example of Stanton stretching "his Briarean arms to the newspaper men of Washington."[48]

Thomas Eckert received a cryptic telegram from Pittsburgh at one o'clock in the afternoon on May 20:

> The following has been handed to me by a Gentleman whose initials will be recognized by the party addressed – To C A Dana Asst Secy of War – Allow me to direct your attention to D A La – vine Junior & Senior as the possible perpetrators of the Proclamation fraud The

father has a position in the Soldiers home the son I think is with
Surrogate Tucker – C. D. B.[49]

"Surrogate Tucker" likely referred to Gideon Tucker, a Democrat politician
and newspaper editor. He served as a kind of judge who heard last will
and testament cases in New York. The Soldiers' Home was the summer
residence of the Lincolns, which was being readied for their return in the
month ahead.

The same day Eckert received the tip about the La-vines, Marshal Murray received a new lead, to his great excitement. It was a letter lacking punctuation in places:

Sir, I see by the newspapers this morning you offer a reward for the
person who delivered the copies of the bogus proclamation in the press
the person who delivered is your obedient servant. I am in the employ of the Independent telegraph line. I delivered the copies to all
the offices getting 25 cents each for so doing. I have been informed
by my brother who is a compositor in the herald office that they destroyed 25,000 copies when they found it out. I am willing to furnish
any evidence you may need without the reward.

The author of the letter added a tease:

. . . if you can find me.
Yours,
A Telegraph Messenger[50]

Murray seemed unfazed by the taunt at the end and held on to this notion:
if they could find the telegraph messenger, they would get their man.

Meanwhile, he sent detectives fanning out from dingy newspaper office to dingy newspaper office, confiscating the manifold copies and talking

with reporters, editors, foremen, and clerks about their routines in putting out the news. They, as well as Dix's aide, cross-examined witnesses as to a description of the messenger and his behavior. For newspaper reporters, it must have been a strange reversal, accustomed as they were to doing the questioning.

The detectives discovered that around April 1 a complex hoax had been gotten over on the Brooklyn newspapers. Joseph Howard's *Brooklyn Eagle*, in particular, had fallen for the bait, announcing, "Gen. Grant Coming North." Supposedly Grant would be arriving at the Brooklyn Navy Yard to meet with General McClellan and other "dignitaries" about a scheme to land the Army of the Potomac by ship in an unknown location. They would discuss the "tonnage which can be concentrated at given points on the Potomac," reported the *Eagle*. The article named the members of Grant's staff and congressmen who were arranging the public receptions for the illustrious visitors.[51]

Under a separate dateline of Trenton, New Jersey, the paper reported McClellan had been ordered to the meeting by the War Department in preparation for a new strategy for "the advance on Richmond."

On April 1, readers received an extreme reversal: the *Eagle* had filled almost a full column on how happy a "bright-eyed telegrapher" must have been to have tricked "our community" about the meeting at the Brooklyn Navy Yard. Commented the *Eagle*, "Of all the jokes we have met recently that was the most successful. In all the places of public resort last night the greatest excitement existed on the subject. Politicians rubbed up their wits for able and 'impromptu' speeches which they hoped to get off at the 'Reception,' which was to be given in front of the Academy; the Long Island Historical Society made arrangements to give the distinguished gentlemen a huge parchment entitling them each and every one to enjoy to the full the many rare and valuable curiosities of their collection . . . Mayor Wood and the civic dignitaries generally put themselves to bed, that they might wake up bright and early to-day to do honor to the Head of the Nation's armies, and the people at the Navy Yard were in a state of frenzied excitement bordering on lunacy."

The paper had tracked each player down, trying to check the facts, and found the featured people in the story otherwise occupied. They then realized that the entire story had been a trick.

The new presidential draft hoax had been written on similar paper. The detectives even discovered who the authors had been.

Back at headquarters, comparing notes, the detectives became confident. A key clue emerged when they showed one of the newspaper foremen a copy of the manifold: "Well," he said, "it looks very much like our Williamsburgh copy. If I did not know it was not from there, I would almost swear it was written by the same hand."[52] Even the taunting note from the "messenger" appeared to be handwritten by the same person.

The investigators headed back to Brooklyn. As it turned out, a stylus—the particular pen used to make multiple copies of a report on manifold paper—was missing from the Williamsburg newspaper office of the *Tribune*. Such a finding might have led the detectives to suspect that the "wrath-y" Greeley, the editor who thought Lincoln too tepid in his opposition to slavery and too languorous in his prosecution of the war, had played a role in the hoax to make Lincoln lose the Republican nomination.

But Murray had an opposing theory. To prove it, he needed to visit the most powerful man in newspapers, who just happened to be one of Lincoln's favored editors. He took the original copy to a meeting to pose key questions of none other than the kingpin behind *The New York Times*, Henry Raymond.

As the investigation unfolded, Will Prime insisted on sitting in his dead newspaper's office, even if he could not produce the *Journal*. Each morning, he managed to talk himself in the door, even if he had to remain idle.[53] By the following day, he feared the paper might not ever be allowed to resume. He wrote to Mary: "Nothing new this morning . . . The delay is not explained & it is by no means certain that we shall be permitted to resume publication at all."[54]

In the *Journal of Commerce* statement on the first day of publication after the military occupation, Prime had poured out his sorrow. "It was a sad and somewhat solemn view, for an American, that rush of the busy world along the street, by the guarded doorway of a suppressed newspaper," he wrote. "It was not for this, some thought, it was not for this our brave boys were dying on the field.[55] Men recently arrived from foreign lands were unable to explain to themselves the strange sight. Some citizens went along chuckling complacently over the accomplished suppression of a free press; but those were very few, very few in New York; and the vast throng, in the main, passed by with saddened countenances. The dim sight of old men was dimmer with the mist of tears when this sorrowful exhibition of bayonets was made in our great commercial street. The exceeding beauty of our national character was marred; the splendor of our historic freedom was tarnished; the glory of our American boast was gone. A man of more than eighty years, born in New York, whose long and peaceful life had blessed himself and benefited his country, as he passed along the street, uttered his sorrowful wish that God had let him die before his old eyes looked on such a scene. Young men, strong and earnest, were not moved to tears, but resolved that henceforth they would recall the old traditions, restore if they might the old laws and be content, when the land was again as of old united and free, to say their *nunc dimittis*. Not till then! Oh not till then! God grant that we may live and work till this story is remembered as a hideous dream, and from ocean to ocean the breeze that sweeps down from our mountains shall again be the breath of freedom."

Prime's sentiments were warranted. But the precious and self-satisfied tone had been one that Mark Twain noticed and marked in his private copy of Prime's best-selling travelogue, *Boat Life in Egypt and Nubia*. In those pages, Prime described scolding one of his Muslim riverboat pilots: "nothing short of Mohammed himself could save him." Twain had written below: "How terrible is this man."[56]

8

CLUES AND MISSTEPS

[New York, N.Y. – May 20, 1864]

The detectives watched Henry Raymond examining the copy of the Brooklyn Navy Yard hoax that they presented to him. Raymond said he believed it to be the handwriting of one person he knew all too well: Joseph Howard.

Detectives also discovered that a man in Brooklyn had been seen buying unusual tissue-like paper similar to that used by the Associated Press. Howard lived and worked in Brooklyn.

Out in Brooklyn, the detectives shrewdly tracked down a young man who matched the description of the Associated Press messenger. They questioned him and finally learned that he was "on intimate terms with Mr. Joseph Howard."[1]

The detectives then staked out all of Howard's favorite spots, asking his friends and associates if they knew of his whereabouts on the night of May 17, as well as the next day's early morning hours. At least one witness said that several days earlier, Howard had intimated that there would be a sudden change in the money market, and that fortunes could be amassed. The detectives pressed further and found that Howard was in the city late in the evening when the bogus proclamation was delivered to the printing presses. He had allegedly been seen buying the tissue paper.

By one o'clock in the morning on May 20, the evidence was said to be conclusive.[2] Detectives Radford and McDougal went to make their report to Mr. Kennedy, who in turn went and conferred with Dix.

William Kent of the brokerage firm Kent & Clapp had reached out to Dix after the proclamation had appeared in *The World* and *Journal of Commerce* and told him that the proclamation was the one shown to him by Howard. He had dealt with Howard on previous matters. He said that Howard had come to him a week earlier—around May 11—to "ask what would be the effect if a proclamation from the president calling for 300,000 men were to appear." Howard showed Kent a draft of a proclamation he said was soon to be issued and which had been procured from what *The New York Times* described as "secret channels of intelligence at Washington."

The surfacing of Howard's name must have shocked the detectives. Why would the reporter so beloved to readers, a Republican at that, want to concoct a story to rattle the nation? The public and even the detectives might have suspected a Confederate, a foreigner, but a bon vivant? The city's tenacious journalist and most loved humorist? A strong supporter of Lincoln?

Within a few hours, Dix issued an order to Murray, who sent Deputy U.S. Marshal Tooker with detectives Radford and McDougal to Howard's house at No. 16 Willow Street, at the corner of Middagh in Brooklyn Heights.[3] It was three thirty in the afternoon.

Ushered into his rooms, they found Howard, with his distinctive jet-black mustache and eyeglass. He seemed startled at their arrival and their announcement that they were there to arrest him. They related all they had found of what they understood to be his part in the hoax and charged him with writing and uttering the bogus proclamation.

Howard's reaction took them utterly by surprise. He appeared thunderstruck, as if they had come to him with the most outlandish story imaginable. "Blank astonishment and injured insouciance appeared upon the countenance of Howard as these revelations were made," reported the *Sunday Mercury*. "A great emphatic and general denial was made and his well-known and established loyalty alluded to as a guarantee of his innocence."[4]

But when taken across the river to Marshal Murray and presented with the full evidence again, Howard reportedly confessed all. "He admitted that he had originated the idea of publishing the bogus proclamation, and had dictated but not written it."[5] He claimed he was as astonished as anyone that the proclamation had made a big sensation.

What was the cause of Howard's original surprise? That the detectives had uncovered his actions? That Kent had done him in by revealing their conversation so swiftly to the authorities? That the entirety of guilt now lay on his shoulders alone?

Howard, like all New Yorkers, had spent two and a half days tracking the storm of activity. He might have been horrified when he learned that troops had marched into the newspaper offices, including *The World*, where he had pleaded for employment so recently. He likely had read the outrage in the editorials of Prime and Marble as they tried to fight for the freedom of the press.

"He said he had no other motive except to make a little money on the Stock Exchange, and that it never occurred to him that his performance could produce any more important or serious effect," reported *The New York Times*.[6]

Apparently, Howard had lost at the market before and was on the verge of ruin. "The idea entered his mind that a well devised story, that would send a chill over the entire nation, already getting exuberant over the victories of General Grant, would be sure to send up gold and stocks, and if he could manage to buy for the rise he would pocket a snug profit. To do this he was obliged to lend himself to the designs of other gamblers as desperate as himself, and even more unscrupulous; those who had a two fold object in view—first, to make money, and second, to damage the Union cause abroad. Hence the selection of Wednesday morning (steamer day)."[7] Howard declared that his inspiration had been a bogus proclamation allegedly written by the president of the Confederate States of America, Jefferson Davis, that had run in the *Metropolitan Record*, a Catholic weekly, on May 14 and called for the people of the Union territories to simply give up the fight and grant peace. This hoax had been adjacent to a reporter's allegation that Grant's forces had been soundly beaten in the battles around Spotsylvania. That hoax had been somewhat obscure. Howard had asked financial experts how the markets would react if Lincoln "were to acknowledge his own recent defeats."

Next the guards brought Howard to Dix's headquarters, where he continued to add details. "He at once made a full acknowledgment of his agency in the matter, and exculpated all the newspapers, which he succeeded in victimizing, from any connection with it, directly or indirectly. He employed another person, whose name we believe is Morrissey, to make the copies which were sent to the press," wrote *The New York Times*.[8]

The man Howard mentioned was not Morrissey but Frank Mallison, whose full byline was Francis A. Mallison. He also wrote humorous pieces under the alias Francis O'Pake. He worked at several newspapers, including with Howard at the *Brooklyn Eagle*. One of his other employers was the *New-York Tribune*, the sole member of the Associated Press that apparently had not received the proclamation and the office that had been missing its stylus.[9]

Mallison was known to his friends as "Ave." He was keen and bright and renowned for his practical jokes going back to his first job upstate in Rome, New York, where he operated the town's telegraph in the window of a clothing store, typing out the messages for up to seventy-five dollars a year. His friends and colleagues regularly teased him about his voracious eating.

Howard had convinced Mallison to join the scheme. The planning was formidable: how could they get the story in the newspapers without leaving their fingerprints? It would have to look as if the false proclamation were telegraphed and at a time when no editor could check the usual channels. They needed the AP's distinctive paper, the particular type of AP stylus. They needed a boy, similar to the usual AP boy, to counterfeit the delivery.

Howard had arrived to meet Mallison on the evening of May 17. Mallison had brought the stylus and paper. Howard dictated each word. What would Lincoln say exactly? Which phrases were particularly his? In addition, the proclamation had to sound absolutely dire.

After delivery, the news would flow out, first streaming through New York City, then over the broader tributaries—the trains bearing their bundles to cities in the North and South, as well as the locomotives headed out to the West. The wires would pick up the dispatch, the information clickety-clacking across the country, operators all across the country hearing the semaphore and taking down the message.

It was possible that Howard had intended for the proclamation merely to make news in New York and then be crushed before it went farther. Lincoln would be exasperated, but it would have been of a piece with the fake "Rebecca" stories even Lincoln himself had put out in Sangamon County, albeit Howard's would have national import.

Unfortunately, it had all unfurled so much faster than Howard could have expected. His little fiction had ignited the worst of Lincoln's fury. Soldiers occupied the offices of the victims. The partisan vitriol boiled over into accusations and condemnations.

And Howard sat at his home, realizing that before too long his wife and daughters would see him led away in cuffs, taken to the docks to journey to Fort Lafayette for years. Even, as people said, court martialed.

In an agitated scrawl, Dix crafted a message to be sent to Stanton, marked confidential:[10]

I have arrested and am sending to Fort Lafayette Joseph Howard, the author of the fraudulent . . .

He crossed out "fraudulent" and wrote "forged."

> ... forged Proclamation. He is well known as a newspaper reporter
> and intimately connected with Henry Ward Beecher and says he has
> accompanied the ...

He scratched out the connection to Beecher and the part about accompanying someone somewhere.

> ... known as a newspaper reporter "Howard of the Times." He has
> been very frank in his confessions, says it was a stock-jobbing oper-
> ation, and that no person connected with the press had any agency
> in the transaction except another reporter, who manifolded and dis-
> tributed the Proclamation to the newspapers, and whose arrest I have
> ordered. He exonerates the Independent Telegraphic line, and says that
> the publication on a Steamer day was accidental.

Dix wrote, "Not considering your despatches of May 18, a prohibition of,"
then crossed it out, concluding with:

> His statement, in all essential particulars, is corroborated by other
> testimony.

Stanton conveyed the news to Lincoln. At 9:10 p.m., Stanton let Dix in on
his private conversation with the president:

> Your telegram respecting the arrest of Howard has been received and
> submitted to the President. He directs me to say that while in his
> opinion the editors, proprietors, and publishers of the "The World"
> and the "Journal of Commerce" are responsible for whatever appears
> in their papers injurious to the public service and have no right to

shield themselves behind a plea of ignorance or want of criminal intent, yet he is not disposed to visit them with vindictive punishment; and hoping they will exercise more caution and regard for the public welfare in future, he authorizes you to restore to them their respective establishments.[11]

Escorted by Assistant Adjutant General Halpine, a former writer for the *Herald* and *Times* and author of burlesque poetry, and his intimidating phalanx of soldiers, Howard marched to New York's waterfront. Journalists were soon to report that on the way there, Howard reiterated his confession and listed off a half dozen other people involved in the fraud, including well-known stockbrokers.

Howard had, of course, heard about conditions at Fort Lafayette. In early September 1861, Republican Party boss Thurlow Weed ventured out to investigate complaints from prisoners and their families. After his review, he assured the public that the fort was like a hotel, its only drawback being a strict proprietor. But plenty of other dire reports had made their way ashore. One prisoner described sleeping on fourteen pounds of straw, eating half-rotten food, drinking water from a dirty tin cup full of tadpoles, and being locked from six o'clock at night to six o'clock in the morning "without any natural conveniences."[12]

Howard had to realize that Lincoln did not take press impudence lightly. How would he treat a prisoner who had dared to pen nine paragraphs as if from the president's own mind? A reporter noted: "As days, weeks, and even months elapse without any event to break the monotonous round of confinement, [Howard] may find, as many a man has who has been confined for a far lesser crime, that the opportunities for reflection upon the mischief he has caused may afford him some adequate idea of the enormity of the offence for which he is beginning to suffer the just punishment."[13]

Even as Howard steamed across his city's harbor, newspaper editors prepared their vitriolic condemnations: "It is as bad as it would be to cut General Grant's communications," a *Boston Herald* editorial declared. Howard's own newspaper called the hoax "cruel"—"One of the most flagrant and heartless impositions ever practiced upon the public."[14]

On the steamer to Fort Lafayette, Howard assessed his guard, Halpine. General Dix's aide had contributed popular satirical columns to *The New York Herald* under the pen name Miles O'Reilly, allegedly a fictitious, hapless soldier. Lincoln's press aide, John Hay, was just one of O'Reilly's many fans, deeming the lampoons classics, and wrote to Halpine in 1863 that a military officer had figured out the authorship of the letters and that O'Reilly should be careful not to come to D.C. lest Stanton figure it out, too, and crack down. "The Tycoon of the War Department is on the war path: his hands are red and smoking."[15]

Hay even tried at one point to honor Halpine's request for real White House details to give his satire more punch. Wrote Hay in reply to Halpine: "Ever since I got your letter I have been skulking the shadows of the Tycoon [Lincoln], setting all sorts of dexterous traps for a joke, telling good stories myself to draw him out and suborning [Lincoln's other assistant] Nicolay to aid in the foul conspiracy. But not a joke has flashed from the Tycoonial thundercloud. He is as dumb as an oyster. Once or twice a gleam of hope has lit up my soul when he would begin 'That puts me in mind of Tom Skeeters out in Bourbon County' but the story of Skeeters would come out unfit for family reading."[16] With this background likely in mind, Howard shared an entirely new motive with Halpine as they headed to Fort Lafayette: the proclamation was a joke on the New York newspapers. In fact, Halpine's former employer, the *Herald*, later reported that Howard thought the "newspaper novelty" would "eventually do him great credit."[17]

Howard kept talking. He allegedly predicted, "As for Fort Lafayette, I shall be detained there only long enough for my father and Henry Ward Beecher to proceed to Washington, make a trifling explanation and procure the order for my release."[18]

Howard's boat passed the last lights of civilization and entered the Brooklyn narrows. Gloomy at night, enfolded in the briny air, Fort Lafayette was no kindly hotel. Howard was led up the stairs from the dock to the fort where yet another cannon pointed through the entrance door. Up a great, twisting stone staircase lay the office of the towering Lieutenant Wood, disliked by the prisoners for his severity, with his piercing black eyes and frowning brow.

Upon arrival, an officer greeted Howard with the words: "Young man, did you write that proclamation?"

"Yes, sir," Howard admitted. "I did."

Shocked, Wood turned to his fellow officers. "Look at him, boys; look at him! He's the only guilty man that ever came into the fort. All the others say they didn't do it."

As with all prisoners, Howard emptied his pockets and received a receipt to present to get the items back should there ever come a day when he would be released. Like all prisoners, he was placed in a first-floor room, although some witnesses said he was put in solitary confinement for a while.[19]

In the cells, narrow beds lined the walls, as did all the prisoners' baggage and pots and pans. Some prisoners played dominoes in the center by candlelight. Some played the card game whist, although gambling was forbidden. Howard found the telegraph operators there, at that point on their second full day of confinement. He said little to his fellow inmates but did tell the telegraph operators they would be released the following day.

One of his fellow inmates asked why he was being held, and Howard made a vague reference to having put the false proclamation in the *Brooklyn Eagle*, playing down his actual role. Aside from that brief exchange, Howard found himself shunned. Long before his arrival, the prisoners had discussed what they would do should the perpetrator of the hoax be placed among them. They condemned the fact that the hoaxer had injured *The World* and the *Journal of Commerce*, two newspapers bold enough to resist the Lincoln administration's spin. They decided they would not admit Howard to their "mess."[20]

At Fort Lafayette, other prisoners sometimes got visits from their spouses, but not Howard. On shore, his distraught wife broke the hearts of those who saw her. "It was pitiable to witness the grief of this estimable lady, and the friends of the prisoner, when they became convinced that Mr. Howard was actually on his way to Fort LaFayette."[21]

Here he was, one of the most famous journalists in all of New York City, a man who could call upon the benevolence and influence of his highly placed friends. But the authorities told him he could not contact anyone, not even his powerful mentor, Reverend Henry Ward Beecher.

Even with Howard's arrest, *The World* and *Journal of Commerce* newspaper offices and the Independent Telegraph wire remained under military guard, the employees barred from the premises. No newspapers could be prepared or published. No wire transmissions could be sent or translated by the Independent. The soldiers controlled all of the property of these establishments and were able to comb through every private document at will.

On top of that, the authorities seemed to grow ever more interested in the communications between civilians. Mary Prime wrote to her husband: "My dear love—I did not sleep much last night. I was in too excited a state & my heart in constant palpitation. I awoke with congestion of the lungs & a high fever, which alarmed me with the fear that I was breaking down. I felt as if I could not live another day away from you—that this suspense was more than I could bear without some sympathizing words from you . . . Darling—your penciled note has just reached me (by private hand). Your letter did not come at all—but was taken from the mail, as this to you may be . . . Father is very much troubled. He told me that my letters had been taken from the mail—which is a good deal for him to say."[22]

On Friday night, May 20, Will Prime wrote to Mary, having no idea yet of Howard's arrest: "There is no change yet, darling wife. I have been sitting all day in the office waiting for the order permitting us to go on . . . I still wait & while I wait, I talk with you . . . They cannot intend to hold military possession with bayonets and soldiers forever. They may simply order us to discontinue & that ends it. We can sell our presses & types & probably pay all that we owe in the world. The firm owes nothing.

"We can start in the world free of debt, with light hearts and trust in God."

Will Prime had prepared for the end.

Meanwhile, Dix's detectives continued to prowl through the city making arrests. That Saturday night, two detectives visited the *Sunday Mercury*, which boasted the highest circulation for a weekly, and asked after a "prominent attaché" of that paper. A man stepped forward to identify himself, and he was taken to Dix's office for interrogation and locked up overnight. The next morning, while being examined, he was told he was suspected of a connection with the crime. He denied the charge and was paroled.[23]

The police also sought Mallison, whom the *Sunday Mercury* would describe as a "harum-scarum, thoughtless fellow." Their stakeouts of his home and office yielded nothing.[24] But on the morning of May 21, an officer from the Forty-Fifth Precinct came across him on the street, a block from the police precinct where Mallison was going to report on the draft.

"He seemed much frightened and made a desperate effort for some time to regard the affair as a joke."[25] He kept up that story even when brought before Marshal Murray, who had been awaiting his arrival. Mallison went on to talk to detectives Radford and MacDougal, who took him to Dix.

He confessed that he wrote the proclamation from Howard's dictation and had gone to the city at eleven thirty at night, lingered around the streets until he knew the newspapers would be vulnerable, and directed the runner. This admission of guilt also earned Mallison a trip to Fort Lafayette.

On Saturday, May 21, one of Mallison's employers, the *New-York Tribune*, expressed doubts about the correctness of the arrests, arguing that Howard could not have been part of the scheme.[26] Howard was too loyal to Lincoln to cause so many problems for the president.

At 9:00 p.m. on May 20, Will Prime added a note to his unfinished letter to Mary: "We have just rec'd great news if true." Prime revealed that the authorities had caught the forger and it was Howard. "If this is true—it is great—great—For a hundred reasons!"[27]

The next day Mary gloated to him that she had been correct in her suspicions: a Republican had manufactured the hoax to cause trouble for the Democrat papers. Even now that they had arrested Howard, she didn't believe Lincoln would lift his military occupation. She told Will Prime that her mother had entered her room and asked, "What will they do to the Forger? Hang him? Make him leave the country?"

And Mary had replied, "Neither . . . They will pamper him and feed him. No Democrat will dirty his fingers by touching him and the Republicans will find a thousand 'extenuating' circumstances.

"He will pocket the reward money & his pardon. If form, & the state of feeling, requires it, he'll have a feather bed in Fort Lafayette for a night, & then—be a good fellow suffering under temporary aberration."[28]

A day later, Mary wrote to Will a new suspicion: "Do you suppose any of the Tribune people are implicated in this? It is strange they were left out of the list in sending out the Bogus Proclamation. I hear too that they give Howard the benefit of their affectionate interest.

"Are you sure the man did it simply for purposes of speculation?

"I still feel anxious for you to ferret out the motives & search into the thing. Who were his accomplices? Let their names be known. I think it looks strongly like some political management & I shouldn't be surprised at learning some of the *Tribune* men were in on it."[29]

The World's editor, Manton Marble, whose wedding day of May 19 had been postponed because of the crackdown, still fumed over his shuttered press. His editors sat idle as news of battles in Spotsylvania unfolded, day after day. Grant had been unable to oust Lee. Now he planned a retreat and a march toward Richmond to pull Lee into an attack.

Marble noticed an envelope among his other mail. The sign-off was from Ohio representative Samuel Sullivan "Sunset" Cox. The letter, dated the same afternoon as Howard's arrest, sharply reordered his reality.

After all Marble and his colleagues had endured, after all of the arrests and the armed seizures, the revelation Marble found penned on official congressional stationery, under an engraving of the U.S. Capitol Building, was mind-blowing: "The forged proclamation is based on a fact . . . A proclamation was written and similar in impact to the base and damnable forgery for which you are under ban," Cox wrote. He had a theory as to its source: "It may come from Mrs. Mary Lincoln."[30]

9

SHADOW MANEUVERS

[New York, N.Y. – May 21, 1864]

At Fort Lafayette, jailors swung open the cell doors and the telegraph operators walked out, leaving Howard and Mallison behind. For the hoax, no telegraph wires had been required. At Dix's office, the operators signed an affidavit that they had not aided or abetted in the conception or construction of the proclamation and that the first they saw of the hoax was in public print.

Down at the Old Capitol, the imprisoned telegraph agents who had been arrested in Baltimore and throughout the cities of Pennsylvania stepped into the day, hundreds of miles from home, and tried to reckon with what damage the soldiers might have wreaked on their machines and files in their absence.

It would be another week before the government would hand back the telegraph offices to the operators. For a total of eight days, their telegraph in New York, Pennsylvania, and Maryland remained silent, as if the "earth had swallowed it."[1]

The government had gleaned all they wanted from every message sent through the Independent Telegraph wire, and now they offered a small recompense. Lincoln tended to hand out plum positions to people whose favor he hoped to curry. Stanton now gave the Independent Telegraph a cut of government business, which he said would improve their reputation with the public.

At 10:00 a.m. on Saturday, editor Hallock walked into the *Journal of Commerce* office accompanied by Captain Barstow. Hallock had heard the premises would be released to the editors that morning.

The rooms where Hallock worked daily producing the breaking news lay as if under a spell, silent, soldiers sprawled about the floor in various positions, sleeping. Barstow barked for them to wake up and ordered for them to leave, so they rose and lumbered out.[2]

About an hour later, Will Prime burst into Dix's office on Bleecker Street to claim whatever paperwork was needed to restart his *Journal of Commerce*.[3] Dix was so jovial about the reversal of the suppression, he even gave Prime his arrest order as a souvenir.

Prime, too, felt elated. Upon arriving at his office, he asked the officer who had commanded the occupying force to share a glass of wine with him across the street at Brown's. The celebratory gesture took all of ten minutes, but such a throng had gathered outside Ninety-One Wall Street in his absence that Prime had to push his way through the crowd to reach the door. This time, the tenor was entirely different from the rage he had witnessed on May 18. Inside, he found his friend McClellan, the former Civil War general and the front-runner for the Democratic presidential nomination, writing him a note. They hugged as Prime shouted with joy at the reunion. McClellan stayed two hours, watching the rooms fill to the walls with well-wishers—Democrats and Republicans alike—offering donations and denouncing the evil of Lincoln's order.

The closure of the newspapers had pushed even political enemies to side with the Democrat newspapers. "Men shouted, 'I am an abolitionist, but I go *The Journal of Commerce* hereafter for its bravery and its wrongs.' Many—very many—said this," Will Prime reported to Mary. "The outburst through the city was noble—and so all day long it was impossible to do anything."⁴

Even Republicans seemed troubled at Lincoln's actions. Mary wrote to Will on May 22 that *The Hartford Times* had picked up the hoax, and when it was discovered to be false, the "indignation was great & having no one else to direct it against, the citizens directed it all against the *Times*— & everyone was shouting for its suppression—but the moment it was announced that you were taken possession of, the clamor ceased, men seemed frightened at what had been done & the injustice & wickedness of it."⁵

Prime postponed his own thoughts of protest until later. He had so much work piled up, so many stories to get covered by his staff. It was only in the evening that he could turn his attention to his first editorial. He labored over it for three hours. Once satisfied, he read the completed work repeatedly to Stone and Hallock.

In the first editorial published in his newly freed newspaper, Prime raged at Lincoln over multiple paragraphs, but he ended up on a pitying tone. "It is not we that have been harmed so much as he [the President] who so fiercely struck at us," Prime wrote. "We are grieved for him." He then offered an olive branch: "He has withdrawn his grasp, and we are again free. And now for the private wrong done us, we find it in our hearts to forgive him."⁶

Despite his docility, Prime worried that Stanton might be riled enough to arrest him again. "I must wait to see how they will take my article tomorrow," he wrote Mary. "Stanton may retort with another 'Lettre de Cachet' [a letter of imprisonment]. But I don't think he dares."[7]

Meanwhile, the *World* staff was not quite so easy to appease. They'd been blocked from their own possessions and paychecks for days. Soldiers had stolen two overcoats, including one belonging to the special correspondent who had just returned from the Virginia battlefield the day of the crackdown. Inside his pockets had been all of his notes from nine days covering the campaign, a valuable pistol he had carried to fend off guerillas, private letters, and cards from the staff of a Union general serving at the front. His flask, drained during the torrential rainstorm before the battles in Spotsylvania, had been swiped, and his quinine pills left littered on the floor.[8]

With respect to these affronts, as well as his own mistreatment, their boss, Manton Marble, harnessed all of his rage in writing his editorial response to the events. "Sir, That the king can do no wrong is the theory of a monarchy," he opened in his three-column public letter to Lincoln.[9] "It is the theory of a constitutional republic that its chief magistrate may do wrong... [Our Constitution] ... in providing for [the president's] impeachment ... admits that he may be guilty of crimes." After posing the threat of impeachment, Marble went on to emphasize his right as a citizen to question the president's actions. He pointed out the irony that the proclamation had been produced by the president's friend, "who ever since your departure from Springfield to Washington in 1861 has enjoyed private as well as public opportunities for learning to counterfeit the peculiarities of your speech and style," he wrote. Later, Marble added that Howard "represents himself a favored visitor at the White House since your residence there." He had enjoyed special access to the president at such press opportunities as Lincoln's visit to West Point to confer with General Scott in June 1862.

Lincoln's own "party principles" had "been the daily meat and drink of this forger," Marble said. "He has denounced [Democrats] as faithfully as you . . . He has been the noisy champion of an exclusive loyalty he has preached in clubhouses and at street corners, those politics which stigmatize constitutional opposition to the administration as disloyalty to the government."

He slammed the stockbrokers who had conspired with Howard—Republicans, too—who favored paper money and its inflation "heedless of the misery to poor men which such inflations breed."

Marble pointed out his efforts to aid Dix and the detectives, all of which Lincoln was well aware of before ordering his imprisonment. "Not until today has the *World* been free to speak. But to those who have ears to hear, its absence has been more eloquent than its columns could ever be."

He then hinted at vengeance. "Do not imagine, sir, that the governor of this state has forgotten to do his duty, do not imagine that the people of this city or state or country have ceased to love their liberties or do not know how to protect their rights. It would be fatal to a tyrant to commit that error here and now. A free people can at need devise means to teach their chief magistrate the same lesson."

Marble listed the sacred rights he insisted on protecting. "That the people shall be secure in their persons, houses, papers, and effects against unreasonable seizures and that no warrant even shall issue except upon probable cause supported by oath." A search warrant needed to be specific, "that no person shall be deprived of life, liberty, or property without due process of law."

He then issued a passionate complaint. "These are the most priceless possessions of freemen and these you took away from me . . . the proceedings taken against the *World* were of the nature of a summary execution of judgment."

He accused Lincoln of targeting political opponents. If the *Tribune* and *Times* had fallen for the hoax, he guessed Lincoln would not have suppressed them. "You know you would not," he wrote. "If not, why not?

"Can it be possible, sir, that for a moment you supposed that journals like ours could afford to be guilty of this forgery? Let the unanimous voice of your own Press answer. Such a trick would hardly have succeeded in San-gamon County, Illinois," he said, referring to the place where Lincoln had practiced law and, in fact, perpetrated his own editorial hoaxes.

Marble argued that since the beginning of the war, his paper had been a cheerleader for the Union cause and the country. But it had also not been si-lent when witnessing what Marble considered wrongs. It had opposed paper money because the government had broken the tie between paper money and gold, making it unstable in value. It vindicated General McClellan for his military decisions, contradicting the Lincoln administration's critiques. Marble accused Lincoln of targeting the paper before "the underling, your partisan" had even concocted the plot. "When you answer these interroga-tories, I will produce the proof of threats made against us by those nearest you, and assuming to exert your prerogative, before this trick of forgery fur-nished you with the specious pretense of an accusation." That last sentence got cut by some newspapers reprinting the editorial. Perhaps the editors considered it too bold an accusation against the president.

Marble insisted he was not guilty. Lincoln was the criminal. "It is you that in transaction stand accused before the people. It is you who are con-spicuously guilty. It is upon you that history, when recording these events, will affix the crime of a disregard of your duty, oblivious of your oath and a pitiable subserviency to party prejudice and to personal ambition." He pointed out that elections were imminent. "And the right of impeachment yet remains to their representatives."

"The law may break down. It will then disclose to a watchful people the point of greatest danger. Courts may fail; judges may be intimidated by threats or bribed by the allurements of power, and those who have sworn to execute the laws may shrink from the fulfillment of their oaths. A craven Congress may sit silent and idly watch the perishing liberties of the people whom they represent, but this can not deter him who, in defending his rights, is determined to do his whole duty."

Marble's three-column screed went out in the first *World* to be published after the silence. Letters from supportive readers poured in.

The New York Times, on the other hand, while admitting the wrong of suspending the newspapers, called the commentary of the two victimized papers "laughable."

In particular, they hammered Marble's letter: "The *World* . . . over the signature of its editor, which in itself is contrary to all good taste—and looks like coxcombry—tries to rail and threaten . . . Through three columns it tears passion to tatters."[10]

The two tricked newspapers, the *Times* suggested, suffered from incompetence. The *Times*, on the other hand, had "suspected the spuriousness of the production before five lines of it were read, was entirely convinced by the time the reading was completed." The night editor had sent a runner to the telegraph office to check if such a story had come over their wire.

"What was done by the TIMES might have been done by any of our contemporaries, with competent men in their editorial rooms," the *Times* editorial said. It questioned the *Journal*'s excuses of having only a foreman on the premises. "The plea is an insult to the business habits of this City. No business house could keep public confidence for a day if it should intrust its most important acts to a subordinate who should 'go it blind' in that fashion for one minute of the day. The pretence, too, that it was a specious counterfeit that might deceive any one, is absurd. No man in this country, writes a more unique and unmistakable style than ABRAHAM LINCOLN. Never was there a coarser and more palpable counterfeit of a bank bill than this counterfeit of one of the President's official documents. The editor, who is supposed to know the marks which make style, stultifies himself by affirming that the style of that document had any resemblance to Mr. LINCOLN's. A bank teller would be instantly dismissed who should accredit a forgery so clumsy . . . Had we been guilty of it, we should have deemed the Government perfectly right in calling us to personal account for it."

The *Times* not only insulted the standards and intelligence of the rival papers, it suggested the editors should face severe punishment. "An editor is personally responsible for whatever appears in his paper, whether through design or negligence. If he thus accredits and gives currency to a forgery, he ought to answer for it in court. If the forgery was one of a military order, as was here the case, he must expect to be tried by a military court, in accordance with the army regulations."[11]

In other words, the *Times* hoped Marble, Prime, and their associates, charged in Lincoln's order with treason, would face a potential death penalty, the punishment for that crime.

All sides trusted that the truth would be known when Howard himself stood trial. A few months prior to the incident, Dix had sent a military commission out to Fort Lafayette to review cases so trials could proceed more swiftly.[12] The semiweekly *Albany Evening Journal*, edited by Thurlow Weed, likened Howard's publishing of the bogus missive to a case in 1814 in England that earned harsh punishment. Operators of a large investment fund faked a letter by a high government official stating that Napoleon had been slain by Cossacks, Paris had been saved, and peace was imminent. The perpetrators were discovered and found guilty of conspiracy against the public welfare. They paid a hefty fine, were imprisoned for a year, and were clamped in a stockade opposite London's Royal Exchange in a backbreaking position while subject to public violence and harassment for an hour at midday.[13] Howard, the paper implied, should receive the same punishment.

The *Memphis Daily Appeal* was more definitive: "It is thought [Howard] will be executed," the paper reported.[14]

Meanwhile, the editors of the *Brooklyn Eagle* faced the horror of having employed both forgers—one their city editor and the other a humorist and reporter. In their own defense, they attested that, of all the "millions of people" now aware of the "clumsily worded" proclamation, no one had been more surprised than they to learn it had emanated from someone at the *Brooklyn Daily Eagle*.[15]

On the morning of May 18, Howard had reported to work at the paper at his usual time, complaining of fatigue. He had credited that to a heavy bout of champagne drinking the previous night with *New York Times* editor Henry Raymond.

That the culprit should be a person from Lincoln's party shocked the *Brooklyn Daily Eagle* editors: "We mention these facts, not to implicate his party in his transgressions or to attempt to trace any connection between Republicanism and heartless cheating."[16]

They itemized the many bogus reports that had been issued during the war—particularly by Republicans—just to boost stocks. Oddly, in another column on the same page, under the headline "The Draft—The Government and the Local Authorities," the paper also reported what Sunset Cox had alluded to—that a draft of three hundred thousand was imminent. "It is now understood that the government will soon issue a call for three hundred thousand men, to fill the vacancies caused by the expiration of the terms of service of the three years' regiments, and to keep the army up to an efficient standard. A draft will take place about the 1st of July."[17]

In noticing the veracity of the core fact from Howard's proclamation—that hundreds of thousands of more bodies were now needed at the front—one wondered, What exactly was false other than Lincoln's voice in the matter? That he mourned the state of the Union cause? Why was he so enraged if the core issue were true?

The *Brooklyn Eagle*'s mention of stock manipulations drew attention to a practice that had been plaguing the Lincoln administration. In fact, at that very moment, the administration was in a critical fight to corral the market, a battle secretary of the treasury Salmon Chase had led since his first moments in office. In one of the first telegrams on the morning the hoax appeared, Chase had queried Lincoln about its veracity. Lincoln responded:

> I have issued no proclamation lately.

He then admitted:

> I signed a very modest paper last night for the Sec. of War, about draft-ing 300.000 in July, as I remember, but the document now rampant at New York is a forgery. A. LINCOLN.[18]

That phrase "as I remember" seemed strange. Lincoln was saying he had been engaged in the matter only the night before—in other words, no more than fourteen hours before he telegraphed Chase and no more than four-teen hours before the news broke in New York. That "paper" was signifi-cantly close to the detail of the proclamation now circulating, now causing such turmoil, now causing civilians to be arrested around the country. How could he have such vague recollections of a document of such importance, a document he not only signed but also handwrote? Three hundred thousand men was no small call for reinforcements. What had happened to that "very modest paper"? And what was its relationship to the so-called forgery?

10

FUN AHEAD

[Washington, D.C. – May 18, 1864]

Back in D.C., on the day the proclamation was published, Treasury Secretary Chase was determined to find out if Lincoln had sent out such a document. The nation's survival hung in the balance. To understand the seeds of that concern, one had only to revisit Chase's travels just over a month earlier.

On Wednesday, April 13, 1864, the elegant Salmon P. Chase snapped shut his travel bags in D.C. Journalists immediately began to whisper gossip. A sentence or two slipped into the evening papers: the secretary of the treasury had headed out in a late-in-the-day exodus from the capital to New York City on unnamed business.

Arriving in Manhattan, tall, stately Chase moved through the bustle of the city's streets to the five-story Fifth Avenue Hotel, a lodging of plush carpets and gilt wood that took up the block between Twenty-Third and Twenty-Fourth Streets and had been favorably compared to Buckingham

Palace. Few on the street would fail to recognize the treasury secretary. He had put his own face on the one-dollar greenback.

At the hotel, the doors to Chase's room firmly shut. People tried to call on him, but, as *The New York Herald* reported, "Mum's the word."[1]

All of Wall Street began to buzz. Before his arrival, gold had threatened to go up to 200, but by the next morning it plummeted, to open at 180. Around the columned subtreasury on Wall Street, which resembled the Parthenon, brokers jammed the streets. The hallowed location where George Washington took the oath of office as the first president of the United States now was home to one of the prime storehouses of the nation's gold and silver. To those outside financial circles, the meaning of the morning's commotion was hazy. Brokers and traders flooded in from all directions, packing Pine Street and all the avenues to the point that no carriages could pass. Chase's presence in the city had put brokers into a panic.

Later, Chase came downtown to do business, as *The New York Times* reported, teasingly describing him as "the Golden Bear":

> Gold, early [in the day], was at a premium . . . but in the course of the day Mr. CHASE, having come to town, took a walk down through Wall-street, and it at once tumbled . . . If such was the effect of Mr. CHASE's perambulating . . . we think he had better stay in town permanently, and take a walk among the bulls and bears every morning. Gold would possibly soon be at par—who knows?[2]

Before examining why Chase's presence caused gold to tumble, one first should understand why so much interest rode on gold's value standing at par—or, more to the point, on the end result of gold's value tumbling. At par, as *The New York Times* referenced, would mean that one ounce of gold would be worth $20.67 in silver dollars, as it had as far back as 1834 when the government first set a fixed value. The Lincoln administration ended that direct, exchangeable relationship. For more than two years, gold had floated in value relative to the silver dollar and ultimately to the greenback, to disastrous effect on the U.S. economy. In fact, that very spring, the entire economy teetered on the brink of collapse.

The decline began with the war's financing. When Lincoln took office in 1861, the government already carried a deficit of over $65 million with an estimated $27 million more anticipated July 1.[3] That deficit had to be addressed. But Lincoln also understood that to crush the rebellion, he required a great infusion of money, and quickly. Foreign and New York banks demanded outrageous interest on their loans. Lincoln rejected the option of the foreign loans. To swiftly gather capital, Congress passed a package of $250 million in domestic bank loans, federal twenty-year bonds, and interest-bearing notes that would pay out in three years.

The collateral on those loans was said to be the true property of all the people in the Union. That meant should the government fail to pay its debts on time, the true property of the citizenry allegedly could be sold off to make those loans real—for example, every house, every horse, every business owned privately was said to be owed to the banks as collateral. It was an outlandish notion but frequently referenced. A Union citizen's ability to keep his or her private property hinged on the Union surviving.

As the war dragged on, and inflation climbed, anxiety rose. "People have up to the present managed to quiet their apprehensions on this score by a sort of blind reliance on the borrowing powers of the Government, and by the insane notion that the entire property of the country could be and was 'pledged' for payment of all debts it might contract," *The New York Times* explained. "A good many writers, who ought to have known better, helped to propagate this delusion, until it at last became quite common to see the difference between the total amount of the public debt, and the estimated value of the real and personal property of the people of the North, gravely set down as a fund on which we could draw for the prosecution of the war to the last cent, as if any people ever consented to the confiscation of all their possessions for the payment of any collective liability, or as if any such measure was physically possible."[4] It was a delusion because it was impossible to imagine government authorities wresting away private property to pay off war debt.

To supplement the loans and create more war financing, the government needed to literally manufacture money. Three months after the start of the war, the federal treasury had issued its first "demand" notes, meaning that, beginning three years from their printing, these paper notes could be redeemed at an interest rate of seven and three-tenths per year. In New York, St. Louis, and Cincinnati, they could be redeemed for gold.[5] Congress authorized fifty million silver dollars' worth to enter circulation. This money could be used for all transactions—salaries and purchases of goods.

But greenbacks could not be used for everything. Imports required gold payment to the merchants in these other countries. Foreign economies did not recognize greenbacks. Therefore, any U.S. merchant selling foreign goods in a shop, say, in New York or Philadelphia, needed to purchase gold to pay those overseas bills. With the wealthy citizenry of America on a binge of extravagance—foreign fabrics, jewels, art, cigars, suit broadcloth, champagne, and delicacies—gold poured out of the country.

But that wasn't the only cause of gold's scarcity. The U.S. government required its customs and tariffs to be paid in gold, which meant gold accumulated in the U.S. subtreasuries. The government could use the gold to pay off interest on its loans, but, otherwise, that gold was not released back into the economy.

The U.S. Treasury's holdings created scarcity, and the merchants' requirements to pay import fees in gold produced need.[6] That made gold ever more valuable.

Meanwhile, greenbacks dropped in value. Those paper monies originally represented the U.S. government's promise that they could be redeemed at value, so their worth served as a barometer of how much the people trusted the Union to honor its promise, including its likelihood to survive long enough to honor it. If the Union government entirely failed, the paper would be worthless.

At the very end of 1861, in crisis as the cost of war continued to grow, Chase let the country know that the U.S. Treasury would not be able to reimburse its paper money for gold for the foreseeable future. Gold became detached from use as legal tender and became a commodity, like beef or cotton.

Stockbrokers started trading gold two weeks after Chase's announcement. More significantly, a separate tribe of brokers set up a dungeon-like space at Twenty-Three William Street, between Wall Street and Newspaper Row, nicknamed the "Coal Hole," intended for the separate and exclusive dealing in gold. From that point on, newspapers reported the value of gold as the number of dollars necessary to buy what had originally been $100 worth of gold.[7]

The brokers bought and sold large amounts. For example, the bidders so often sold hundreds of thousands of dollars' worth of gold at one time, they simply dropped those extra words and would say "one hundred" to mean "one hundred thousand dollars in gold." They would offer a "half" or "five-eighths" to mean they would pay that much over the previous bid. If they made no mention of time, the gold purchased was to be delivered the next day. If they shouted "buyer three" or "seller three," it meant the gold would be delivered three days later. That space of three days allowed for speculation. A broker could sell at one price on Monday and hope by Thursday to have bought cheaper gold to fulfill the purchase, thus pocketing the profit.[8]

Meanwhile, the government required more currency to pay its war bills. Only seven months after the first distribution of greenbacks, the Legal Tender Act augmented the first $50 million greenbacks with $150 million worth of U.S. notes, still with no direct backing in gold. Five months later, the treasury issued another $150 million, and seven months later, yet another $150 million. In the Lincoln administration's ideal scenario, faith in the government and trust in the success of the Union would make the green-back as valued one day as the precious metal. But speculators saw the scenario differently.

The whole history of the Civil War could be read in its most simple form in a little publication of unusual format that came out several times from 1862 to 1864. Howard's Gold Chart, put out by a small Wall Street publisher, tracked on a long accordion of paper the value of gold from the moment the government divorced gold's direct correlation to the greenback. The years 1862, 1863, and 1864 ran concurrently on the folded paper—for example, the page for January showed the month's progress for all three years—so the dramatic leap in gold's value over the earlier years could be easily absorbed by the stacked lines visible at once.

In 1862, the line started at the bottom of the chart, at a value of about 103, meaning $103 would buy what, prior to the severing of gold's relation to the greenback, had been $100 worth of gold. It simmered along in that region until July, when it began to climb. But starting with 1863, it rocketed to 145 then made vertiginous leaps and dizzying drops. The creator of the chart, Joseph P. Howard—by all evidence, a different individual than Joseph Howard Jr., most likely a Tiffany jeweler—had written notes next to the most dramatic changes explaining the causes, for example, "General Sherman repulsed before Vicksburg" for a rise. A Confederate victory meant that gold became more valuable because it would outlast the Union. The successes of the Union dropped gold's value, as shown, for example, by Howard's note—"Favorable news from Mississippi"—in March 1863.

These rises and drops meant that any person who needed gold, such as importers, hoped for a price drop, in other words hoped for a Union success; anyone who held gold, such as foreign investors and speculators, hoped for a Union defeat.

People from all walks of life—educated and illiterate, doctors and priests, young and old—suddenly became fascinated with gold trading. The number of brokers willing to pay twenty-five dollars a year for the privilege to trade in the Coal Hole became so numerous, the operation moved out of its space in October 1863 to Gilpin's News Room, at Twenty-Six Exchange Place, a larger space that at least had the benefit of letting in some sunlight.[9] With a $12.50 commission on every $10,000 in gold, brokers racked up thousands of dollars a day. Orders poured in over the telegraph wire from all over the country. The majority of orders came from D.C. and Baltimore, followed by Louisville, since people closest to the front had the best war updates.

Gold speculation responded wildly to any breaking news. A journalist of the day compared the din in the Gold Room as headlines rolled in to a "den of wild beasts . . . The chaos of voices and the stamping of feet shook the building as in an earthquake, and boomed out of the open windows into the street below like the discharge of artillery."

Brokers sometimes wrestled with their conflicting emotions over a bad turn of the war. Their country suffered, perhaps their loved ones at the front as well, but their greed was satisfied.

At other times, the trading floor became a war zone of its own. "Men leaped upon chairs, waved their hands, or clenched their fists; shrieked, shouted; the bulls whistled 'Dixie' [the ostensible Confederate anthem], and the bears sung 'John Brown' [the Union marching song]; the crowd swayed feverishly from door to door, and as the fury mounted to white heat, and the tide of gold fluctuated up and down in rapid sequence, brokers seemed animated with the impulses of demons, hand-to-hand combats took place, and bystanders, peering through the smoke and dust, could liken the wild turmoil only to the revels of maniacs."[10]

On the street outside, where the gold clock showed the changing prices, men and boys bet each other, not on gold's value, but simply on how much the price would go up or down in a certain number of minutes.

The chaos of the Gold Room wreaked havoc on salaries and common goods. A teacher's salary of $5.80 a week in greenbacks could be worth 10 percent less in buying power before week's end. Something needed to be done to suppress the value of gold so that greenbacks could hold a steadier value.

In December 1863, Chase gave a speech before Congress that he intended to make it his goal to bring down the price of gold and commodities. The country could not withstand the market fluctuations, given the terrible effect they had on the value of greenbacks and the inflation they caused. He believed that if he released the government's holdings of gold into the market—flooding the market—he would reduce the value of gold, thus restoring greater value to the greenback. He also thought that if he could be granted his own discretion as to the timing for the sale, speculators would fear his choice. Not knowing when Chase would suddenly reduce the value of gold, speculators would view it as a less valued commodity for trade. It was a strange plan, a true gamble. He was attempting to make a precious metal valued through the age less valuable instantly by a dump of holdings into the market. He would make gold less sought after by making it suddenly less rare.

In the early spring of 1864 (two months before Chase's secretive trip to New York City), he pushed through legislation that allowed him to sell the government's gold holdings at his discretion. He would retain just enough gold to make the next payment of interest on the public debt—which would occur at the end of May. Another payment of interest would be due six months later, but Chase bet that U.S. tariff payments would refill the gold coffers enough by then to pay the next round of interest.[11]

Legislators, including Samuel Sunset Cox, who opposed the bill, feared that no one man should be able to sell off the people's property.[12] It was risky, even if Chase proved trustworthy. If he proved corrupt, it was outright reckless.

The *Detroit Free Press* argued that the government had no more right to cheapen gold than it did flour, cotton, or tobacco. Lowering its value would wreck the whole economy—because unlike flour, gold marked value around the world and had for ages—and therefore, the value of all other commodities.[13]

By April 1864, one month before the bogus proclamation would appear, the country had borrowed and spent approximately $2 billion, yet a million men were out of the labor force at the war.[14]

The New York Times highlighted the financial stresses of the time, a fear that gripped the general public. "[The people] know full well that the only danger in this struggle of the Government is the financial danger, and that this danger must be fatal, unless there be timely and wise action. . . . They do not intend that their business and industry shall be smothered with worthless paper; that their children shall be bowed down by a mountain of debt; that their brothers in the field shall shed their blood for nought; that the flag of the country shall go down in ruin and disgrace."[15]

The *Times* argued that Congress needed to show courage to deal with the financial woes. The first income tax in U.S. history had been imposed in the summer of 1861 at 3 percent, but more taxes were needed.

On March 21, Lincoln signed into law the bill to allow the selling of the U.S. Treasury's gold. On April 13, Chase reportedly paid the May interest on the public debt a month and a half early. Then he headed to New York that night.

On the day of Chase's walk down Wall Street, gold experienced "rather startling fluctuations" on the New York Stock Exchange.[16] Ten minutes before the opening, the price stood at 1.80¼ in paper—meaning what had originally been $100 in gold now would require $180.25 in greenbacks to purchase. Another way to look at it was that one dollar in greenbacks was at that point worth only fifty-five cents. Since April 13, gold prices had climbed, likely because Congress had decided to adjourn session without passing a tax or otherwise trying to raise revenue in the face of the nation's catastrophic financial situation. Additionally, General Grant contended with torrential floods down South that had wiped out whole sections of the railroad, potentially jeopardizing future troop supplies. When the Union cause looked dire, gold absorbed hope. It could be considered a reliable investment.

Chase's presence in New York set off a very different reaction on the gold market. "Within an hour our paper money suffered a depreciation of nearly nine per cent and recovered six of it; and at the close of the day the price ran down," a reporter observed. "This is, indeed, gold gambling run mad. There is no cause for these violent fluctuations."[17] The reporter still didn't understand that Chase had instigated the wild swings by sending private brokers to sell off $9 million worth of bullion owned by the U.S. government suddenly in the market, creating "a day that has been one in financial and business circles of almost unparalleled excitement and anxiety."

The next day, with Chase still in town, the market boiled again. "The excitement on the gold market to-day beggars all descriptions," wrote the *Chicago Tribune*.[18] Chase had now announced that the U.S. government would sell gold at $160, far less than the going rate. That meant every seller would be forced to drop their selling price. Brokers and traders, some of them holding stacks of greenbacks a foot high, paid people who had queued up earlier at the treasury as much as $100 for their place in line so they could purchase the cheap gold. The price of gold at one point "advanced by four and a half percent in three minutes and then reversed track to fall the same amount in five minutes."[19]

Chase was unloading even more gold. To counter Chase's efforts to drive down gold's value, the biggest gamblers sent their own brokers onto the street corners to buy as much gold as possible to create sudden scarcity and artificially inflate the price. When gold raised to mad heights, the gamblers sold their new holdings, pocketing a large profit.

"Gold was . . . staggering like a drunken man," the *Chicago Tribune* reported about the events of Friday, April 15.[20]

On Saturday, Chase left town.

When the markets opened on Monday, the commotion on Wall Street was beyond anything witnessed since the start of the war. The stodgiest bankers ran about as if insane. Curses and fistfights filled the air. The most solid banking concerns desperately tried to sell any stock they owned to remain solvent. That panic resulted in $15 million in stocks being dumped on the market on that one day. The value of railroad and bank stocks dropped as much as 50 percent.[21]

Prior to Chase's visit to New York, one of the largest stock and commodities traders of the time, Anthony Morse, had offered Chase that he would buy all of the government's gold outright. Chase ignored the outrageous insider bid; anything less than selling gold on the open market was clearly corrupt. That Monday, with panicked investors calling due their payments on their loans, and the value of usually stable stocks in their holdings, such as railroad stocks, plummeting, the big trading firms teetered. Suddenly, they owned less of value and owed more in payments to banks that had extended them loans in the past.[22] Morse's mammoth firm collapsed, and it had to request a sixty-day suspension of payment to investors and clients.

Governor Curtin of Pennsylvania, visiting Lincoln in Washington, D.C., in the days of Wall Street's terror, took note of the newspaper reports. "I see by the quotations that Chase's movement has already knocked gold down several per cent," Curtin said.

An observer claimed Lincoln twisted with fury. "Knotting his face in the intensity of his feeling, he said, 'Curtin, what do you think of those fellows in Wall Street, who are gambling in gold at such a time as this?'

"'They are a set of sharks,' Curtin replied.

"'For my part,' the President said, pounding his fist on the table, 'I wish every one of them had his devilish head shot off!'"[23]

Within a few days, it became clear: Chase's seven-day experiment selling about $11 million in gold had failed. He only temporarily depressed the price of gold, or seen alternately, he had only temporarily raised the value of greenbacks. The government gold was gone, into the pockets of foreign investors or even rebel speculators. Gold stood four days later higher than it was when Chase arrived in New York.[24] The debt was increasing by $2.86 million a day, and the Union side was spending $2.25 million a day on the war. Congress had adjourned without passing a tax.

The only savior for Union finances would be good news. "We look, therefore, to General Grant and his gallant armies for a rescue," read a *New York Herald* editorial. "With his success we shall have better times; but should the Washington Directory of the accidents of war entangle him so as to bring upon him misfortune instead of success, why then we may look for the deluge."[25]

Chase did not want to leave the Union's financial stability to the ups and downs of news reports. He devised yet another attempt to block his nemeses, the gold traders. He would drop the value of gold internationally by selling U.S. Treasury gold on the London exchange below the market value. He hoped that dropping gold's price in what was essentially the world market would drop the value in New York markets as well. The planned date for this international mission of financial scheming: May 19.[26] The only thing standing between him and his imagined success was bad news about the Union that would raise the value of gold at the same time or directly after his sale. Bad news, whether real or fraudulent, would staunch his scheme. And these gold speculators were both smart and devious enough to show him that they were in charge. The bogus proclamation painting the Union cause in dire terms landed on May 18 and made its way into newspapers headed overseas.

When considering the particulars of the hoax the day after it published, the *Daily National Republican* in D.C. said that it was clear that the fast day was for London and the military draft for New York. The latter would affect gold; the former would drive investors into the Confederate loan in London.[27] On May 18, Chase found himself wiring off a worried telegram to the president asking if he had sent a proclamation.

Out at Fort Lafayette, each of Howard's mornings began with the piercing screams of a fife and the belligerent rhythm of a drum. The barrack's window casements cracked open to let in the barest glimmer of light. The sprawling forms of more than thirty men, clinging to whatever combination of surfaces might be considered a bed, were revealed. All the prisoners received breakfast at six o'clock in the morning, soldiers' rations, which another inmate reported to be "one-sixth of a loaf of soft bread, a pint of coffee, and a passable quantity of meat, cold."[28] The food was doled out punitively, depending on the level of rage the prisoner inspired in his guard. Interrogations followed.

The morning newspapers arrived, with the exception, starting in June, of *The World*, and one other banned New York newspaper. *The World* had resumed publication on May 23, but the government authorities felt the "Copperhead" contents of the newspapers would inflame the prison population with a stronger dislike of their government. The prisoners could talk over the news.[29] They joked about the strange quirks of the often-inebriated Colonel Burke. They invented hobbies. A prisoner, who explained he had found himself at Fort Lafayette "for borrowing a piece of rope with a schooner at one end of it," worked at training a rat to fight another rat.[30] Like all prisoners, Howard likely received his hour of exercise in the morning and his other in the evening. Later in the day, the men were served barely cooked pork or beef, potatoes, rice, and tarry coffee. They drank rainwater, which was sometimes acceptable and sometimes so disgusting they needed to boil and skim it. At six o'clock in the evening, the jailors closed the men into their rooms. The guards snuffed out all the lights at 9:00 p.m.[31]

What had seemed such a brilliant idea to Howard, a hoax similar to his previous pranks, now put him in this company, miles from his wife and daughters, who were said to be in the "greatest distress over his disgrace and incarceration."[32] Only a month earlier, Howard had written to Marble about his desire to get deeper into the election season's political fray, and now he was as far from the political conventions as could be, surrounded by ocean on all sides.

The *Brooklyn Eagle*, Howard's employer, wrote an assessment of the situation that almost sounded like an extended epitaph: "We have little or nothing to add except to say that Mr. Howard is by relationship connected with the warmest supporters of the administration in this city. No doubt they regret, as every generous man will, that a young man with ability for the performance of better things, should, at the outset of his career, bring shame upon his friends, trouble upon those very dear to him, and disgrace upon himself."[33]

The New York Herald slammed his character: "a superabundance of egotism, a superficial education, and a brain completely turned by infatuation with Wall Street gambling and manipulation by the most desperate gamblers of them all."[34]

In the society of Fort Lafayette, Howard's scheme would make him a member of the minority "white-washed," the most loathed type of prisoner. These were Northerners who had tried to play the war both ways, Unionists who profited from the misery. Within the fort's walls, they complained the loudest and vented the most hatred for Dix and his ilk. The other prisoners—the "secechs"—were pure Confederate rebels, who loved their new nation and loathed Lincoln. They did, however, hold a grudging respect for Northern abolitionists who were true to their cause. And they still cared what the Unionists, their former fellow citizens, thought of them. Many urged Northerner prisoners, should they ever be released, to assure the public that their Confederate cell mates were not thieves or cutthroats.

And then there were those Northerners stuck at Fort Lafayette with no idea why they had been imprisoned. Federal or Republican state officers across the country had seized them from the streets, their workplaces, or their beds, often on a trumped-up charge, and shipped them off without trial. A writer for the *Knickerbocker* magazine wrote about the arbitrary arrests: "In Philadelphia, in the State of Ohio, and even in New-England . . . some have been dragged out of their beds at dead of night and immured in dungeons for mere private conversation . . . while others, who neither by word nor deed had offended the tyrants at Washington, were consigned to the same quarters because somebody had merely suspected them ... [or] they might possibly say or do something offensive or dangerous to despotism."[35]

The writer went on to describe the experience of Dr. Edson B. Olds, a former Democratic Ohio congressman. An unnamed accuser tagged Olds for delivering a speech at a schoolhouse encouraging draft dodging and praising secession. Olds found fourteen witnesses to vouch that his speech had been patriotic. He claimed the language for which he had been denounced had been quotations pulled from Lincoln's inaugural speech. In the middle of the night, armed men kicked down his door and hauled him out of his sickbed at gunpoint. He was sent to Fort Lafayette; stripped of his glasses, medicines, and money; and denied a Bible in solitary confinement. He drank from a filthy cistern in a room so damp that mold grew on everything that touched the floors. Rats roamed. After twenty-two days, he won a place in a fifteen-by-twenty-five-foot cell shared with eleven other men. None of them held much hope of getting out. During the brutal confinement, Olds suddenly decided that the reason Lincoln didn't want him to have a Bible was because the president had violated the biblical injunction not to "forswear" himself: Lincoln had sworn to uphold the Constitution, with its protection of free speech, right to trial, and protection against cruel and unusual punishment.

Olds recalled a prisoner at Fort Lafayette, "partially deranged," who had already been in solitary confinement for ten months when Olds got out because "on one dark, stormy night, with a life preserver made out of oyster cans, he jumped into the sea to escape." Another had been pulled from his work in his potato patch in Chester County, Pennsylvania, for not informing on his Democrat neighbors. "The idea that this poor laboring man would be dangerous to a nation with nearly a million of soldiers in the field, seemed more Lincoln's jokes than a reality," said Olds in a speech to his town upon his return from prison. His wife tried to smuggle a letter to him: "I can not tell you how much trouble I have been in about you since you have been stole away. I sat up all that night waiting for you." At the "first peep of day," she had gone to town and asked if anyone had seen her husband. One neighbor thought he had been taken to a Philadelphia prison. She then received a letter from the War Department that her husband would be sent to Washington. "I was told that they were very well paid for stealing you," she wrote in the smuggled letter. Olds got elected to the Ohio legislature in absentia while behind bars.[36]

One Maryland inmate noted bitterly in his diary when a new prisoner arrived: "[I] suppose as he is a 'British subject' he will be released as soon as the British Consul hears of his imprisonment; lucky thing now-a-days to have been born in England, or any where outside the 'Land of the Free and Home of the Brave!'"[37]

Howard's fate hung in legal limbo. An editorial in a Boston political and cultural journal discussed how difficult it would be to try him. "It is a somewhat singular fact that forging a proclamation of the President of the United States should be an offense without a name," Boston's *The Independent* explained.[38] "We are told by some that no existing statute covers the case; by others, that the prosecution will be made under the law of libel; by others, reference is made to an old English law against conspiracies to defraud the public, as a precedent; by others, to the law of Congress of July 17, 1862, reaching those who give aid and comfort to the enemy; while still others hold that the offense, being against the military head of the Government, the trial should be by a military tribunal, and the punishment a military penalty." That could include execution or banishment to the Dry Tortugas, the feared military fort in the remote islands off Florida.

If Howard could not be tried under any of those legal structures, the writer threw up his hands. "[Otherwise] this strange case will be parallel to that of the ancient code that provided no punishment for parricide, on the theory of the law that no man would ever commit it."

In Manhattan and Brooklyn, everyone talked of Howard and the motive behind his action. A journalist's thirst to land a scoop could be useful, argued *The Independent*, but such contests between reporters tempted some to win "by inventing fictions instead of reporting facts." They then turned the mirror on the readers. "The public, too, is an accomplice with the forgers. The eagerness with which the multitude devour extraordinary bulletins, the popular greed for a large story instead of a true one, the unsatisfied air with which even temperate men throw aside a newspaper which has no striking capitals or startling announcements . . . A community that cries out for the punishment of such offenders ought to be told how far it is itself a like offender."

The newspaper wanted a solution but did not trust the Lincoln administration to devise it. "Of course, we do not mean to be understood that the cure for these evils is to come from any action of the Government. In fact, the Government itself has been a many-headed author of hallucinations, a spinner of false prophecies, a rainbow-painter of delusive hopes and ninety-day wonders."[39]

A correspondence that year between Assistant Secretary of War Charles Dana and a major general in the army indicated that these government lies were even tactical: "If indiscreet newspaper men publish information too near the truth, counteract its effect by publishing other paragraphs calculated to mislead the enemy." The order went on to indicate the leakers within the army should be arrested and sent to do "hard labor."[40]

Mary Prime wrote to Will on May 22 that she thought *The World* and *Journal of Commerce* had been specifically targeted with false news. "It seems as if whoever had managed it had special designs against you and meant you should publish it . . . Can it be that the Bogus Proclamation was put out as a feeler? Or could it have been sent out to create an excitement, to direct the public mind from the depression that was coming over it? To act as a counter-irritant? Or could it have been done in a bold attempt to throw odium upon the Democratic party, or to paralyze its efforts by destroying its organs before the upcoming election campaign—making this the pretext? If so they have done a bold thing and it looks to me like it."[41]

Her exile in Hartford had given her plenty of time to think. She urged her husband to use his newspaper to investigate the subterranean motivations: "Be sharp & look into the affair thoroughly. It is truly your affair now & for your interest to know how deeply the plot lies."

"Give the devil his due," she said, urging more mistrust and an investigation of the future legal case. "Is it right that Howard be put in Lafayette? Is it a state offense? By what process can he be treated?"

She warned her husband not to be caught up in retaliation against Howard without due process. "Be cautious not to approve wrong & illegal action however much you may feel personally against the scoundrel. Remember that it is the feeling & error of the day. Let Howard receive the scorn & contempt of the world. Pitch into him & abuse him & his crime. But see if there is any legal way of bringing him to punishment; demand it for him & see that he gets it by process of law."[42]

She wanted the explanation that would come from a trial. Simply sending Howard to Fort Lafayette did not answer the question of why he had engaged in the act. "Fort Lafayette is not only made use of to the injury of the innocent, but it also protects the guilty from his proper punishment," she wrote. "The friends of the administration rarely suffer there & I believe Howard will be kept there until he is lost sight of & the thing blows over, & then will be quietly released."[43]

Despite Mary's hopes, Howard was not the first figure in these events to stand trial in the courtroom. The wheels of justice turned onward, revealing an unexpected defendant.

Up in his mansion in Albany, on Hawk Street in Dudley Row, New York Governor Horatio Seymour, a man with meditative eyes and a taut bearing that became electrified during impassioned speech, fumed. Seymour had been in office only a year and a half, but he found himself repeatedly jousting with President Lincoln over constitutional issues. During Seymour's first days in office, the president admitted how much he needed Seymour's support, writing him that though they were strangers, they needed to work together due to the importance of New York in the Union. At the time, Seymour withheld his agreement of partnership, preferring to judge Lincoln on his future acts, not his words.

Already a well-known political figure from having served as New York governor for one year some ten years earlier, Seymour had been considered an early Democratic presidential favorite on the 1864 ticket. But the need, as he saw it, to publicly combat Lincoln put him in the role of tireless scold, making him an unpleasant choice to some voters.

Even in Seymour's inaugural address he had highlighted his criticism and suspicions. Lincoln had conducted arbitrary arrests, disregarded Congress, and appointed "the least intelligent class of officials" to serve as "spies and informers" to seize people without due process of law and take them over state lines. He considered his own election a rebuke of Lincoln by New Yorkers committed to expressing their outrage in a lawful, constitutional way: at the ballot box.[44]

On the date of that speech, Seymour pointed out that Lincoln had cracked down on publications that opposed his politics. "Unconstitutional acts cannot be shielded by unconstitutional laws," Seymour declared. And now Lincoln had exercised his might against *The World* and the *Journal of Commerce*. "It is a high crime to abduct a citizen of this State. It is made my duty by the Constitution to see that the laws are enforced."[45]

With the Republican nomination looming only two weeks away, Governor Seymour knew he would seem like a spoiler if he outwardly opposed the president's conduct in the seizure of the two New York papers, as well as give the president yet another worry at a difficult, politically charged time. Yet, really what were his options? Horatio Seymour faced a crisis ably described by one newspaper: "Governor Seymour swore solemnly to execute the laws of the State. He has no choice but to do so, or violate his oath and degrade himself personally and officially."

Manton Marble was badgering him too, filling his aide's mailboxes with letters complaining about the governor's silence in the matter. "Why . . . when I was being driven down to Gen. Dix's office," wrote Marble, "it did not so much as occur to me to look to Albany for help. Help for other men unlawfully dealt with had not been in the habit of coming from that quarter. I took pains then and later to get Republican influences, personal purely, at work here and in Washington but it did not enter my mind to appeal to the State authorities for protection . . . My telegram of Saturday was an inquiry not whether the Governor would meet the trespassers on the threshold of the World office and by force of arms return to us the property seized by illegal violence—the opportunity for that had long passed—but it was a late inquiry of you whether—the Governor having failed to choose that better part, could be relied upon to enforce judicial mandates—to unlimber the guns of the State behind the breastwork of the Supreme Court."[46]

Seymour answered by doing just that. He wrote to the district attorney of New York, thirty-eight-year-old Abraham Oakey Hall, asking him to pursue a grand jury indictment of General Dix and the other officers. Hall could handle the high stakes. A graduate of New York University and student at Harvard Law, he had risen quickly in the legal profession, having argued a case before the state supreme court by the age of twenty-seven.

In his letter, Seymour pointed out that during the 1863 draft riots, he had warned that the laws of the State needed to be enforced and the people's property protected. Not just working class men should be liable for seizing and destroying property. "Unless all are made to bow to the law it will be respected by none. Unless all are made secure in their rights of person and property none can be protected."[47] He pointed out that if the newspaper owners violated state or national laws then they needed to be held to account. But any action taken against them outside legal procedures was criminal. "At this time of civil war and disorder, the majesty of the law must be upheld or society will sink into anarchy." Seymour pointed out that soldiers were fighting in vain if those they left at home had their rights trampled.

He went on to explain why law and order particularly mattered in New

York. "If this great centre of wealth, business, and enterprise is thrown into disorder and bankruptcy, the National Government will be paralyzed. What makes New York the heart of our country? . . . The world-wide belief that property is safe within its limits from waste by mobs and from spoliation by Government. The laborers in the workshop, the mine, and in the field, on this continent, and in every other part of the globe, send to its merchants, for sale or exchange, the products of their toil . . . It is charged . . . in utter disregard of the sensitiveness of that faith at a moment when the national credit is undergoing a fearful trial, the organs of commerce are seized and held in violation of constitutional pledges . . . These things are more hurtful to the national honor and strength than the loss of battles."

He called for public support: "If the merchants of New York are not willing to have their harbor scaled up and their commerce paralyzed they must unite in this demand for the security of persons and property." He ordered District Attorney Hall to investigate the facts and prosecute the guilty, authorizing the county sheriff and police chiefs to help. If they failed to provide their armed muscle, he declared, he would fire them.

After sending the letter, Seymour hurried to the city the very next day.[48] Around him, the streets began to buzz. While *The New York Times* deemed Seymour's challenge "silly . . . puerile rhetoric" and "contemptible nonsense" that possibly could stir up riots, the citizenry did not dismiss the governor's actions so readily.[49] "In the cars, in eating houses, in the Park, at the street-corners, everywhere the threat of the Governor was discussed," the *Daily News* reported.[50] As soon as the order to District Attorney Hall was posted, people began gathering around all the newspaper office bulletin boards. At first, the crowds declared it a fake, penned by Howard. But, eventually, they accepted that the governor indeed had written it, and serious issues were at stake. Lawyers debated the technicalities. Tempers escalated as passersby further delved into the issues. "The eagerness with which everybody listened to his elbow neighbor in anticipation of hearing something fresh was remarkable. At intervals some waggish persons would essay a comical remark or retort which served to keep the crowds in very good humor."[51]

No one seemed to know how the governor would proceed. An old man walked up to the newspaper bulletin board and eyed the charges. An equally elderly elbowmate said that Lincoln should be locked up for infringing upon human rights, along with the "unfortunate and short-sighted Howard."

The first man asked how it was to be "did," how was Seymour to deliver up the body of "old Abe" and if he didn't "what would become of the Governor?"[52] That prompted his elbowmate into an endless soliloquy, but the question lingered. Even if the people supported Seymour, the technical issues of confronting the president directly could lead to problems. If the court issued an arrest warrant for Lincoln's officers, would the officers submit? "There seemed to be but one opinion in relation to it, and that was that [Seymour] had made another blunder." He had backed himself into a corner. He insisted on justice that he could not enforce.

On May 26, the *Detroit Free Press* assessed the case's likely path. The newspaper's editorial declared that Seymour and District Attorney Hall were right to see lawlessness in the president's action. Dix and his thirty or forty subordinates could easily be liable for damages to *The World* and *Journal of Commerce* in civil suits. They could also be convicted in criminal court for false imprisonment and trespass.

But what if Dix and his men were found guilty? The editorial writer described a possible scenario in which the sheriff and half a dozen deputies headed to the Department of the East offices on Bleecker Street to inform General Dix and his men that they were under arrest. The sheriff would show them the warrants and require Dix and his men go to court.

The editorial writer predicted tension would escalate. Dix's armed guard might refuse arrest, threatening the sheriff and his deputies with immediate imprisonment instead if they tried to execute the arrest. The sheriff, now left with no options, would call up a *posse comitatus*, that "being every man in the country," to assist in executing the process of law. In other words, every person thus ordered by the sheriff to assist him, was, by law, bound to obey the order. But the armed force at Dix's command, the U.S. army, held more weaponry than any strength the sheriff could muster from the U.S. civilians. The editorial writer believed the very army's purpose enabled offenders like Dix and his ilk "to defy the law of the land and the civil process of the courts of justice, and trample them under their feet."

Dix's military defiance would prompt the sheriff to plea for the governor to call up the state's national guard to execute the arrests. That meant "every man of the hundreds of thousands of the New York State militia" would have to appear in arms, resulting in a standoff between Dix's federal force and every other man in the country and state militia. The consequences were potentially gruesome. "All this presents a very plain question . . . It is a case which every lawyer understands, the vital point being the suprem- acy of the law of the land over lawless force and violence . . . Will Horatio Seymour, at present Governor of the State of New York . . . see that the proper legal process of the State is executed, and that the law of the land is maintained in all its supremacy? That is the simple question; and perhaps the question is also, incidentally, whether Horatio Seymour or John A. Dix is Governor of the State of New York . . . We shall watch the development of the proceedings with much interest."[53]

On the afternoon of May 30, Seymour traveled to New York City and spent hours in the mayor's office meeting with New York district attorney Hall. The newspapers reported that Hall had all the evidence he needed: "affidavits of proprietors, various editors, sub-editors, pressmen and print- ers." They speculated that even Lincoln and several members of his cabinet might have submitted affidavits. In their opinion, Seymour and Hall would find "plain sailing" in their case, clearly the party in the right, until a pivotal moment—the showdown when warrants to arrest Dix and his crew trig- gered a confrontation between the police and the military force.

"Guess the Governor and Oakey Hall . . . will find the navigation rather rough," the *Philadelphia Inquirer* wrote, "and that they have got into deeper water than they appreciated."

"Anyhow," they concluded, "there's fun ahead."[54]

11

A PRESIDENCY ON TRIAL

[Washington, D.C. – May 24, 1864]

The day after Howard's incarceration at Fort Lafayette, an edition of the *Brooklyn Daily Eagle* appeared and landed in the hands of Secretary of War Stanton in Washington, D.C. The day before its publication, Dix had reported to Stanton that he had shipped Howard off to the high-security, ocean-encircled prison. Now the newspaper where Howard had been employed as city editor ran an article on its second page with the headline "The 'Dead Beat' Redivivus: He Visits Fort Lafayette—and Stays There."[1] Dead Beat was Howard's frequent pen name.

Stanton read on.

The byline stated the writer's location:

Cell 5,311, Second Tier

Fort Lafayette

Dear Eagle—In the language of the 'magnificent' Vestvali, . . .

Dead Beat wrote, referring to the then-celebrated opera singer, an "enraged Amazonian beauty," who had recently punched a stagehand she suspected of touching her breast plate,

"I am here."

The letter continued:

> I think I shall stay here, at least till I get out.
>
> Perhaps you were surprised at my sudden departure. So was I.
>
> But I received a pressing invitation from General Dix to come down here, which I didn't feel at Liberty to decline—so I didn't.
>
> Bob Murray brought the invitation. Bob Murray is the United States Marshal, and he marshaled me in the way I should go, so I thought best to go it.
>
> Bob is a nice man; he has a very taking way with him, but I wouldn't recommend you to cultivate his acquaintance.
>
> You may have heard of Fort Lafayette; it is a great resort of friends of the Administration—over the left.

The joke played on Thurlow Weed's earlier reviews of Fort Lafayette, dismissing prisoner complaints by saying that the prison seemed like a hotel. Dead Beat went on to describe how he had arrived at the fort. He'd been loaded into a cannon at Fort Hamilton and fired off, to sail through the air and land in the middle of the military compound. He described the view in his arching trajectory—a scene so exhilarating with its perspective on Bath, Coney Island, and New Jersey, he had made a sketch. The sketch, he offered, could be compared to the war maps that appeared regularly in the *Herald*, which he facetiously praised for their accuracy of detail and guessed must have been composed on the fly as well. Of course, he was implying the War Department leaked the maps to the *Herald* since there would be no other way for a reporter to gain such an aerial view. Dead Beat described the menu:

TOO MUCH PORK

We have pork and crackers for breakfast.

Crackers and pork for dinner, and

Pork *with* crackers for tea . . . When you write me, enclose a bunch of radishes.

He claimed to have smuggled this particular message out by carrier pigeon, the best delivery system under "postmaster Lincoln"—which was a critique of Lincoln's allegedly putting spies in the post office. Dead Beat had received information since his arrival about goings on in Washington:

A meeting of the cabinet was called at the White House. Secretary Stanton introduced the subject.

The President said it reminded him of a story he once heard in Illinois. A man who lived in Sangamon County, in conversation with a medical student, said he didn't believe in vaccination. Says he, "It don't do a child a bit of good. I had a child vaccinated once, and in three days it fell out of the window and broke its neck."

The Cabinet saw the point at once, and laughed so loud that they woke up Secretary Welles.

Secretary Seward rang his little bell, and sent for Gen. Dix.

The bell referenced the widely circulated—and likely spurious—quote by Seward, boasting to the English ambassador that he had so much power, all he needed to do was ring a little bell and a citizen in another state could be arrested and held indefinitely. The Arguelles case, in which Marshal Murray had unlawfully extradited the Cuban citizen, had highlighted the view that Seward flexed his punitive capabilities without referencing law. Even Secretary of the Navy Welles had confessed in his diary about that case, "Mr. Seward sometimes does strange things, and I am inclined to believe he has committed one of those freaks which makes me constantly apprehensive of his acts. He knows that slavery is odious and all concerned in slave traffic are distrusted, and has improved the occasion to exercise arbitrary power, expecting to win popular applause by doing an illegal act. Constitutional limitations are to him unnecessary restraints."[2]

Wrote Dead Beat of the conversation between Seward and Dix:

"General," said William H., "how is Fort Lafayette?"

"Our flag is there," said the General, with military promptness.

As most everyone in the country knew, Dix was obsessed with the flag being kept aloft.

"Is there a reliable man to be found in the Department of the East," said Wm. H.

"If there isn't," thundered the General, "I'll shoot him on the spot."

"Who is he?" asked the Secretary.

"His name is Dead Beat," says the General.

The line about the Department of the East had to be mysterious to readers. Why would Dead Beat be part of the Department of the East? In other words, why would Howard be working for Dix? The column went on:

"Send him to Fort Lafayette."

So I came.

I am still here.

> Yours,
>> In retirement,
>>> Dead Beat
> P.S.—Give my regards to Chitty

Chitty was a reference to S. B. Chittenden, the owner of *The Union*, a Brooklyn paper and rival of the *Eagle*, who had urged on public placards that Howard be hung for circulating the proclamation. The newsboys had been so outraged about Chitty's remarks, hostile to the *Eagle*, they tore down *The Union*'s signs and ripped them to pieces.[3] Dead Beat continued:

> I understand that he was deeply affected on my account, and was anxious to see me elevated in society.
> Tell him to keep cool. There are some small men down here, but none quite so small as he is.

The letter concluded with a teasing, obtuse postscript:

> "And the little dog barked at the caged lion, and wagged his tail rejoicingly." D. B.

Dead Beat's column enraged Stanton. How had Howard, the scoundrel, managed to smuggle a message out of the infamous Fort Lafayette, five hundred yards out to sea? Not only had he gotten it out, he had it published in a newspaper with allegedly the largest evening circulation of any newspaper. On top of that, other newspapers, rejoicing at the flouting of government incarceration, picked it up as if the whole thing were a joke.

Inspector General Joseph Hardie wrote to Dix on Stanton's behalf on May 27: "The Secretary of War desires to know who is the officer commanding at Fort Lafayette and under what regulation prisoners confined there are allowed to write letters for newspapers." He drew attention to Howard's letter. "You are directed to allow no correspondence by nor with him or any personal communication."[4]

The next day, another missive from Dead Beat appeared in the *Eagle*:

There was a row about my last letter. General Dix blowed Burke up for allowing correspondence. Burke proved his innocence by the carrier pigeon which on that occasion became my letter carrier.

Whereupon Dix issued an order which will become historical, and I have already written it in chalk on a shingle, and sent it to the Historical Society.

"If any pigeon attempts to enter the Fort, shoot him on the spot."

"And serve him up in pot-pie," added the Colonel, who takes gastronomical views of things.

Hearing of this order I objected to staying a moment longer in a place where the fundamental principles of the Constitution and By-Laws were set at a defiance.

"Don't the Declaration of Independence say a man has an inalienable right to life, liberty and the pursuit of literature?" I immediately resigned my position as inspector of fortifications.

That level of inside knowledge was beyond belief. Not only had Howard smuggled out a first letter, he had learned of Stanton's furious reaction, which prompted Dix to lambast Burke. The following day, Burke wrote to Captain A. P. Fiske, the assistant adjutant general of U.S. troops in New York City, about the first column. "The letter referred to certainly did not leave the Fort through the usual channel, and I am confident that it was not written here *at all*. Shortly after its publication in the *Brooklyn Eagle* a copy of that paper was sent to Howard who, when questioned on the subject, denied its authorship, and stated that it was an imitation of his usual manner of writing."

The military authorities apparently now trusted the word of a prisoner they had incarcerated for lying. About Howard's alibi, the officer wrote: "This seems the more probable, as another letter in the same style, purporting to have been from the same source, appeared in yesterday's issue of the *Eagle*.

"Since I have commanded this Post nearly three years—I have never permitted any prisoner to forward an article, for publication, to any newspaper but have invariably sent such communications to Department Headquarters."[5]

The explanation failed to convince Stanton it seemed. Howard reportedly would never be eligible for visitors.

The court hearings, though, focused on the Lincoln administration. On June 28, District Attorney Hall hurried to the courtroom of city and state judge Abraham D. Russell in New York City, seeking an indictment of General Dix and his men. Russell and Lincoln shared warm relations, beginning three years earlier when Lincoln sent Russell to meet Secretary of State Seward with a recommendation from Bennett of the *Herald*.[6] A year later, Russell had secured from Lincoln the favor of a friend's appointment. But Russell stuck to the Constitution when passing along instructions to the grand jury on June 16.[7] The Constitution, he said, guaranteed every state a republican form of government protected from invasion and against domestic violence. He noted that New York had done nothing to jeopardize its standing in the Union. Instead, the state had loyally performed all of its duties. He wanted the grand jury to consider the following:

Had state laws been violated, and if so, by whom? No matter how lofty the criminal, he would need to be prosecuted. Of course, Russell meant Dix, and perhaps, even by suggestion, the President himself.

Secondly, if the president or other officer presumed a power the Constitution had not specifically granted them, then those who acted on his or their behalf were responsible for those illegal actions. Just following orders, Russell essentially said, was not adequate protection against guilt.

He reaffirmed that free speech and liberty of the press had always been the dearest and most sacred rights of the people.

He pointed out that Howard, clearly guilty, could be separately prosecuted by the district attorney. That direction implied that the jurors needn't feel that indicting Dix and his cohorts would mean exonerating Howard in any way.

Finally, he instructed the jury that if they found that three or more people took and maintained forcible possession of the newspaper establishments, those three or more people, by definition, could be considered liable for a riot.

Russell's instructions as a judge of the case, in their angling, suggested that he considered the government officers likely candidates for indictment. Then the grand jury went off to mull the charges. Dix's aide Barstow, corresponding with family members, confessed that his father feared he would be sent to prison.[8]

Nine days ticked by without a response.

On June 25, Oakey Hall arrived at court to prosecute the Arguelles case, which concerned Marshal Murray. As with Dix's case, the real argument pivoted on whether or not the Lincoln administration had acted outside the bounds of law.

That morning, as Hall entered the courtroom to continue arguments, someone handed him a note dated the day before. In a few lines, the foreman for the grand jury on the Dix case revealed the jury's decision.

The foreman did not say Dix was innocent.

Nor did he say Dix was likely guilty.

He stated that the grand jury had decided it would be "inexpedient" to look into the subject at that time. Right there in the courtroom, while arguing a completely different legal matter, an irked Hall declared he would not let the Dix case merely be shuffled aside. He intended to bring the case back before the grand jury next term.[9]

Inexpedient was also unacceptable to Horatio Seymour. From Albany, that very day that Hall learned the grand jury foreman would duck the case, the governor fired off an order to Hall.

> If the Grand Jury, in pursuance of the demands of the law and the obligations of their oaths, had inquired into the matter given ... their decision, whatever it might have been, would have been entitled to respect. As they have refused to do their duty, the subject of the seizure of these journals should at once be brought before some proper magistrate. If you wish any assistance in the prosecution of these investigations, it will be given to you.

Seymour hinted darkly at the intimidation that might be causing the grand jury to falter:

> It is a matter of public interest that violations of the laws of the State be punished ... If through fear, or other motives, [the parties immediately affected] are unwilling to aid you in getting at facts, it will be your duty to compel their attendance as witnesses in behalf of the people.[10]

Although Seymour sent the letter that very day, Hall failed to receive it. Instead Hall first read the letter—addressed to him—in the *New York Argus*, a conservative Democratic weekly. Seymour had previously complained about the delays, interruptions and surveillance of his mail by Republican appointees within the post office system. He'd announced that he would provide proof to any newspaper that wished to see it. Fremont, the former general now running on the Radical Democracy ticket, had also complained his mail had been tampered with, to the point where he began posting letters and telegrams under a fake identity. General McClellan, the Democratic front-runner, and Marble had also protested their mail's disruptions and tampering. Marble wrote: "General Butler violated the mails so openly where the *World* was concerned, that on two occasions he reinclosed our letters to us in his headquarters' envelopes."[11]

While prosecuting a previous case about the Lincoln administration's arbitrary arrests, Hall had gotten fed up with the harassment. He left the envelopes enclosing legal correspondence to his client unsealed, clearly scrawling his name on the outsides, along with a message to the government spies, in essence: this has been left open so you don't need to waste time trying to disguise the fact that you opened it; read it quickly and forward it on to my client so we can get back to business.[12] He'd given up on demanding they abide by the law; now he simply wanted to speed them along on their illegal interference so he could get his correspondence where it needed to go. General Dix wrote Stanton on June 27 requesting authorization to hire a defense lawyer due to the case's continuation. That meant somehow he had already learned the contents of Seymour's letter.[13]

Now, after reading the Governor's letter in the newspaper, Hall sent his clerk to his post box repeatedly to check for the letter's arrival, but the clerk came back empty-handed. Finally, on the twenty-eighth, the letter from Seymour appeared, along with a long-delayed letter Seymour had sent on the twenty-fourth.[14]

Hall sped back to A. D. Russell's courtroom with a request for witness subpoenas. On the stand, the victims in the arrest and closures of the newspapers testified that day and the following. Luckily, Hall happened to be deeply familiar with the workings of newspaper offices. A decade earlier, he had worked as a New York correspondent for the *New Orleans Commercial Bulletin*, where he wrote under the pen name Hans Yorkel.

Hall asked Hallock of the *Journal of Commerce* if he had been compelled to submit to his arrest. "I considered my compliance was yielding to a force that I had no power to resist," Hallock replied.[15]

How were the soldiers armed?

"They were armed with muskets or carbines, and the officers with their swords, sidearms and pistols."

And bayonets?

"Yes sir, fixed bayonets."

Washington Hills, night clerk at *The World*, described the government's intimidation tactics: "There was an armed man, with a pistol; he did not say anything; he had his pistol at my face."

Daniel Kirwan, day clerk at *The World*, testified about what Lieutenant Tuthill told him about the people clustered around the newspaper bulletin board heatedly talking politics: "He said to me that the first symptom of a fight he would shoot any man who made a row."

And with that, Russell called Sheriff James Lynch to give him the potentially perilous task: arrest Major General John A. Dix.

Lynch would be going off to take into custody a general in the U.S. army, and not just any general—the illustrious patriot John Dix, the man famous for threatening any rebel who so much as lowered the flag.

At noon on Friday, a sheriff appeared at Dix's office and took him and his men—Captain Barstow, Major Bowles, Captain Cundy, and Lieutenant Tuthill—into custody on charges that included inciting riots, forcible entry and detainer, and false imprisonment.[16] They went along without struggle. In Russell's courtroom, their lawyer, E. Delafield Smith, begged for more time to prepare his case. He was given four days.[17]

In the interim, the Lincoln administration showed signs of alarm as they began to assemble a powerhouse team to fight the charge. Dix brought in Wall Street lawyer Edwards Pierrepont, a Democrat, but a staunch supporter of Lincoln, who had served as New York superior court judge in the state supreme court. Known as one of the most eloquent speakers of the era, wise enough to see the Civil War coming a couple of years ahead, Pierrepont had advised Lincoln starting with his 1860 presidential campaign. He wrote an anxious letter to Stanton on July 3, angry that Dix's authority should be challenged.

> We are in civil war, and if a general commanding a department can be deprived of his liberty for obedience to the order of the President then all military men can be shut up while rioters revel—If the General submits to the arrest & is taken through the streets by a constable to the office of a criminal magistrate charged with no crime but that of obedience to the order of the President I think the effect will not be *very good.*

Pierrepont had personally advised Dix to resist arrest, saying he should not be deprived of his liberty for even an hour until the war was over. If Lincoln disagreed, Pierrepont would follow the president's direction.

> It is a matter of much moment and I wait a reply by Telegraph—Very serious consequences may follow unwise action—[18]

Lincoln now faced a choice. Either he acted as commander in chief and put military law over civil law, which could put his officers in legal jeopardy under civil statutes, or he submitted to civil law, also putting his officer in legal jeopardy. At his cabinet meeting on July 5, Lincoln brought up the matter, stating that he alone owned the paper's suppression, that it had been his act.[19] But he also believed the government needed to protect Dix. He asked for the cabinet members' opinions on what he should do. Stanton strongly agreed about the need to protect Dix. Postmaster General Montgomery Blair and Attorney General Edward Bates stayed silent.

Secretary of the Navy Gideon Welles also kept his own counsel but privately noted the "squeamishness" of the cabinet members over the issue. For ten years, Welles had been a part owner and editor of the *Hartford Times*. In his opinion, as he wrote in his diary, the government authorities had been wrong to harass and shut down newspapers, but he also believed Dix required protection.[20]

The *New-York Tribune* had reported at an earlier May 24 cabinet meeting that treasury secretary Salmon Chase "manfully denounced" the arbitrary arrests. The *Daily Post* of Pittsburgh picked up that news and commented: "The suppression of the New York papers ... were both condemned by him as devoid of policy and wanting law. The defence of those measures was more irritable than logical and assured—Mr. Chase has more brains than any member of the Administration, and he therefore opposes measures whose wickedness is only equaled by their silliness and folly."[21]

The article implied that the newspaper hoped to inspire Chase to revive his interest in securing the Republican nomination in June and end the Lincoln nightmare. But an anonymous reporter for the *New-York Tribune* insisted the subject of the proclamation hadn't been discussed in the cabinet meeting at all and Chase hadn't even attended. Later, it would turn out that the anonymous reporter was none other than John Hay, Lincoln's assistant secretary, the one who had written anonymously about the inaugural train ride and whom Lincoln apparently encouraged on an ongoing basis to write secretly for newspapers from the White House.

On the eve of the court date, Lincoln sent a message to Dix telling him to resist arrest the next day. The upshot: don't report to the court.

Now Dix faced a bitter conundrum.

Here he was, a man always loyal to his country and to his state, forced to decide if he were more a military officer obeying the orders of his commander in chief, or a citizen bound by legal oath to the sanctity of law. If he believed in the law enough to practice law, he ought to let the judicial system render its judgment. If he chose the former course, and the governor insisted on bringing him to court, he might find himself required to take military action.

Come morning, the lawyers and their charges assembled in Russell's courtroom. Hall, Attorney General John Cochrane, and General Miller, Seymour's chief of staff, represented the State of New York. E. Delafield Smith and Edwards Pierrepont appeared for the defense. Dix was not there. But at 4:00 p.m., when they assembled again, Dix appeared.[22] Hall recited the warrant and both sides agreed on the facts of the case. Judge Parker of Albany joined the prosecution team.[23]

No one disputed what Dix and his men had done. What was at stake was how their actions impacted the foundational rights of the country.

Ex-judge Pierrepont, with his peaked receding hairline and striking black mustache that blossomed into fat whiskbrooms of hair on either side of his face, stood to begin the defense. He explained that, since the warrant was issued, the president had given another order to Dix that he was not allowed to "relieve himself from his command or be deprived of his liberty for obeying an order of a military nature which the President of the United States directs him to execute."[24] Pierrepont said that Dix had come to him the night before to tell him of Lincoln's order.

Go ahead and submit the order to the court, Hall dared, so the prosecution could object, and it could be declared unconstitutional.

Judge Russell said he would need to see the order to decide and told them to bring it to the next session.

The magnitude of the trial seeped into the consciousness of all involved. Despite their differences, the lawyers on both sides agreed that the issues at stake were critical to the future of democracy. Pierrepont went even further, adding that the case was a "question of vast magnitude and more important than any matter that has ever been brought before any court in the history of any nation."

Hall considered it to be "one of the most momentous questions that had ever been brought before a court of justice." To that end, he said, he planned to spring no traps on the federal government nor argue technicalities. However, the State of New York, having acted with such nobility throughout the course of the war, deserved its dignity and the protection of its state's rights.

Smith, representing Dix and his men, argued that the federal government only wanted to follow the Constitution. New York was in the midst of a civil war that had torn the country to pieces. The issue was whether the federal government could be shorn of its power by the arrest of subordinates who were following the executive's commands.

Neither side wished to spend much time arguing the facts. They wanted only a date to set forth when they could win a decision about the larger matters of constitutional law.

As the session came to a close, Hall produced a document stating that if Pierrepont agreed that he would produce Dix when the court needed him, the court would waive bail for Dix as he awaited further proceedings.

Pierrepont, however, refused to sign it, saying to the judge, "Not if I know he may send me to Fort Lafayette." Pierrepont feared that if he did not produce Dix, Hall might push the punishment to its fullest.[25]

Hall replied that without Pierrepont's signed promise, he would have to insist on imprisoning Dix as he awaited trial. As district attorney, Hall had to consider Dix's status no more important than that of "a vagrant" and hold him accountable to similar rules.[26] Judge Russell, however, ended the dispute by accepting the promise that Dix would appear in court when necessary and did not insist on locking him up.

The official court date was set for July 9, 1864. *The New York Herald* reviewed even those preliminary proceedings: "This discussion, involving as it did, the question of federal and state authority, aside from the eminent legal talent engaged in it, will render the argument . . . in the hearing of a select audience, memorable in the judicial history of our time.[27]

As the parties retreated to prepare their arguments and evidence, a few disconcerting developments occurred. Despite Lincoln's protests that the proclamation was bogus and he did not plan to call up troops, on July 4, Congress voted to give the president power to call up troops of any number at any time for up to three years of service. Three days later, on July 7, Lincoln issued a call for a "Day of Humiliation and Prayer," endorsed by Congress:

> And to pray, that if consistent with His will, the existing rebellion may
> be speedily suppressed, and the supremacy of the Constitution and
> laws of the United States be established throughout the States.[28]

The phrasing was almost stranger than Howard's supposed "bogus" version, in that the president, as he had in 1863, asked each citizen "to repent of their manifold sins." In Howard's version, he had merely asked citizens to "aid this effort to maintain the honor, the integrity and the existence of the National Union, and the perpetuity of popular government." The new call also seemed to reference the struggle in the New York courts, as if to say Lincoln felt eager to abide by the Constitution, just not now.

On Saturday, July 9, the legal titans began to assemble at the Court of Sessions in preparation for the 2:00 p.m. trial.

Observers packed the room. The issues at stake would decide the future prosecution of the war, as well as the freedoms of the people and the press. Citizens were discussing the trial all over town, not just because it pitted a governor against a president, but because the proceeding engaged the debate of the greatest legal minds of the day, all ready to argue the core principles of U.S. democracy.

Before Hall's tenure as district attorney, back when he worked as a journalist, he had written a column about the sad fate of lawyers who exited school flush with excitement about their new profession only to watch as the elegant gold-lettered shingle outside their office faded and chipped as they scuffled for the crumbs of legal cases, copied "legal precedent for the sake of practice," or kept "hope alive upon the back benches of the court-rooms in listening to the eloquence of his seniors while *he* is waiting for clients."[29] Of the two thousand lawyers in New York, Hall assessed then in 1852, "out of these one hundred are 'notables,' fifty are 'distinguished,' and twenty-five are eminent." The trial in the *People of New York v. General Dix* was a battle of the famous, but also a battle of distinguished versus eminent.

Hall, John Cochrane, and Judge Parker—the men who constituted the distinguished—intended to hold Lincoln to account for three years of outrages. In Manton Marble's fierce editorial on the first day that *The World* regained its presses, Marble had expressed a mounting frustration. "To characterize these proceedings [of seizing the newspapers and arresting the editors] as unprecedented would be to forget the past history of your administration," he wrote to Lincoln.[30] The president had essentially ceased to shock the public because "men submitting once and again to lawless encroachments of power . . . lose something of the old free keen sense of their true nature and real danger." Lincoln, he said, could always find some men to applaud his "outrageous, oppressive, and unjust" acts because he had created their prosperity and could destroy the same.

The lawyers for the defense, the "eminents," included Pierrepont, E. Delafield Smith, and forty-six-year-old William Evarts, already famous for arguing the Lemmon Slave Case before the U.S. Supreme Court. They were there to protect Lincoln's ability to use whatever means necessary to prosecute the war. If Seymour's effort succeeded, Lincoln could be hampered and handcuffed by every Democrat in the Union. He'd be forced to let rebels and spies run free, causing untold damage to the nation.

But the task for Lincoln's lawyers was challenging. In a way, their job was to cover up the damage caused by the president and his aides' impetuous reactions to a multitude of crises.

Everyone wondered if General John Dix would come to the courtroom.[31] As the trial began, it became clear he would not. Instead, a few of the most revered figures of the era argued on his behalf.

Pierrepont began by reviewing the facts.[32] To begin, he read Lincoln's order to Dix telling him to avoid being relieved of his post. The stenographer took down every word.

Hall objected, explaining that he didn't consider the document legal. The case itself would decide if the president could issue unconstitutional orders. By reading the words aloud, Pierrepont had injected them into the transcript.

Pierrepont appeared surprised. His goal, he stated, was simply to establish the orders that resulted in General Dix's absence from court.

Judge Russell refused to decide this technical matter when so much lay ahead. The document's relevance would be determined, he said, after he had heard the case's details.

Pierrepont then began the substance of his defense by dividing the trial's key questions into three heads:

Did Dix and his subordinates kidnap Hallock, as alleged by the prosecutors?

Did he incite a riot?

And did the officers forcibly enter and detain the property of Hallock and Marble?

Right from the start, Pierrepont wanted the judge to consider the spotless character of the defendant. Dix was a patriot, Pierrepont stated, without equivocation. If Dix were found guilty, Dix "would bow to the supremacy of the law."

But Pierrepont was also subtly playing on the likelihood that the judge would prefer not to imprison a sixty-five-year-old public servant, who was also one of the nation's great patriots. "If, at his age, so loyal a man as Gen Dix had been guilty of kidnapping and inciting to a riot, then it was time he was punished." Those words forced the judge and audience to consider the tragedy of their beloved Dix behind bars. Contemplating the ultimate stakes would make the judge and audience search for evidence of his innocence.

On top of that, Pierrepont argued, justice had already been served in Dix's case. When the grand jury declined to indict Dix and his colleagues, Pierrepont argued, then "the majesty of the law ought to have been satisfied."

Pierrepont was implying that the grand jury had decided not to indict, when, in reality, they had merely expressed the belief that exploring the case would be "inexpedient." Pierrepont said Judge Russell now held the responsibility of "sitting there to act boldly and fearlessly," going on to flatter the judge by adding that "if ever he [Pierrepont] should be so unfortunate as to be arraigned for a crime of which he was not guilty, the greatest thing he would ask would be to be brought for trial before such an honest, bold and fearless judge."

The defense's position, argued by Pierrepont, was that the Habeas Corpus Suspension Act protected government officials from prosecution. He did not accept the prosecution's position, which they had introduced in the preliminary hearings: that New York was exempt from the suspension of habeas corpus because it was not a territory at war. Each state was not its own kingdom, Pierrepont declared, but part of a "great nation" involved in a "great and vast civil war."

He tried to shame the prosecution for its stance. "No state of war in the Northern States!" he exclaimed. "What meant then the trappings of woe on every third house in this great city? What meant then the sable weeds which clothed the forms of those who thronged Broadway? Did famine cause this woe? Did pestilence form this grief? No state of war! Let the learned attorney-general carry the glad tidings that New York was in a state of peace to one thousand of bereaved families."

With the country at war, he declared, someone had to hold the war power; the activities of the war had to be directed from somewhere. Was that from the federal government or the state government? Clearly, it was from the federal government.

He put forth a dramatic, even terrifying, alternative to questioning that ultimate government authority. If the people were aggrieved by Lincoln's actions, they should punish the man, not the office itself. The people should sacrifice Lincoln before upending the government structures that dictated an officer's obedience to the commander in chief. "If he usurped his power, impeach him, remove him, assassinate him," Pierrepont said, "but do not trammel this Government in their efforts to overcome this great, mighty, and stupendous rebellion."

He then circled back to the impeccable character of Dix. This case, Pierrepont insisted, was all about General Dix and his actions. The court's only job was to decide if Dix, by obeying the chief executive's order, "like a soldier and a patriot, had kidnapped his fellow man and incited a riot in this city."

Essentially, he rested on Dix's reputation, believing that no judge or jury would be able to believe Dix capable of criminal conduct. With that, Pierrepont took his seat.

As the handsome, graceful Hall stood to start his arguments for the prosecution, he too flattered Judge Russell, saying he was happy to agree with his "learned friend" that they stood before a "fearless Judge." Hall was known as one of the most charming men of New York City, witty and erudite, and it would help the prosecution's case to be seen as likeable while confronting the gentlemanly Dix.

To narrow the aim of the proceedings, Hall reminded the Judge—or more likely, the many viewers packing the large courtroom—that they were not assembled to establish Dix's guilt, but simply to establish the *possibility* of guilt and the grand jury could then take the matter from there.

Once again, he ran through the specific crimes of which Dix and his men stood accused.[33] When he got to "forcible entry and detainer," William Evarts, the eminent lawyer brought in to help the defense, stopped him. What facts constituted that crime?

"While these parties were in the exercise of their respective employments, men armed with muskets and fixed bayonets took possession of their offices, and retained the same for several days," Hall replied.

"And, I suppose, the further fact of incarceration," Russell chimed in. His remark suggested that the prosecution's view had begun to sway him.

Hall then took the court through the definitions of the various crimes:

First—Inciting to a riot . . . Any tumultuous disturbance of the public peace by three or more persons, having no avowed, ostensible, legal or constitutional object, assembled under such circumstances and deporting themselves in such a manner as to produce danger to the public peace and tranquillity, and which excites terror in the neighborhood, is an unlawful assemblage, which is a prelude to riot.[34]

Hall pointed out that the newspapermen had been stopped by not just three people, but up to a hundred. According to their subpoena testimony, the newspapermen were terrified. In respect to the alleged kidnapping, he cited legal precedent and definitions and said Hallock had been put in a carriage by people bearing weapons, thus a kidnapping. In respect to the "forcible entry and detainer," Hall again cited legal precedent, and noted that the awful act was so rare, he'd only seen the violation three times in his ten years in the district attorney's office.

After going over the charges and their merits, he then considered the defense's position by reading the relevant section of the suspension of habeas corpus. Hall declared that "this act might be entitled, 'An act to authorize the commission of wrongs.'" Not only was the first part, which gave the president authority to suspend habeas corpus, broadly unconstitutional, but the rest of the law included exempting any military officer for an action "derived" from the president's authority.

Before continuing on to discuss the criminal violation further, Hall segued to marvel that the "bogus" proclamation did not seem so "bogus" now. So what exactly was that document? "It was an interesting circumstance," he said, "that every single fact stated in the bogus proclamation had become so true as almost to give the unfortunate young man now in Fort Lafayette the mantle of the prophet."

He enumerated the ways Howard's proclamation matched reality: despite the victorious reports coming from the government during those days of mid-May—with the bloody battles around Spotsylvania which saw some 17,500 Union casualties—the military campaign had been judged by people with "considerable authority, a failure," just as the proclamation stated. Grant had been forced to retreat to coax Lee out of his unshakeable position.

Only a few days before this court date, Lincoln had issued a proclamation "for a day of humiliation and prayer," echoing Howard's very concept.

Six days earlier, on July 3, *The New York Herald* had reported that Lincoln would call for five hundred thousand men as soon as Congress adjourned that month.[35] Perhaps it was not precisely the same number of men as called for in the bogus proclamation—but a substantially large number of new soldiers, in fact, more.

Leaving mysterious similarities between the bogus proclamation and real events that had come to pass, Hall went on to argue the validity of his primary charges. In a speech richly woven through with legal citations, he insisted that:

One, without dispute, the officers had trespassed common law.

Two, if Congress held the power to trespass against common law, they had no authority according to the Constitution to delegate that power to the president in such vague, general terms as they did when they passed the law suspending habeas corpus.

Three, since each of the violations of common law were "odious" to the Constitution, the president's command for his officers to go commit them was still the act of a "superior wrong-doer." He had unlawfully seized authority not granted to him and sent out his henchmen.

Quoting from a speech at the first Republican convention in 1856, Hall continued that, in all free countries, any seizure of power must have a legal standing to support it. "The partition of Poland, the overthrow of the constitution of Hungary, the destruction of Irish independence . . . were consummated with a scrupulous observance of the forms of law.

"The effect of the section [of the law suspending habeas corpus] is to delegate to the Executive the right to practically legislate the exception to an act else unlawful," Hall said. "Congress generally authorized [the president] to perform unknown, illimitable, immeasured, boundless wrongs, and he is to select or create the specialties of them.

"Caligula wrote his laws but hung them up so high they could not be read, and the citizen was punished when he could not know the law," Hall said. "But Congress does not even specify the law. It allows the President to frame it within his own breast, and apply it after an offence has been committed."

He went on to lay out a hypothetical situation. "Suppose the President should, by telegraph, order Marshal Murray to arrest Governor Seymour, and if he resisted, shoot him. Suppose the Governor did resist, and the Marshal killed, and was tried in Albany for homicide. Would the President's order absolve him?" Congress could not grant a blanket ability to override the Constitution. It had to specify which constitutional law it was overriding. "A New York legislature might grant the corporation of this city power to legalize or permit an otherwise nuisance by specifying it. Could it grant such power by saying 'may permit any nuisance'?" he asked. He assured them, the state could not.

Hall then focused on the president's violation of civil law. "These seizures and destruction of May 1864, were clearly in the light of punishments in advance of investigation or trial. At this time New York was not a camp, and none of the parties who were injured were soldiers. New York was in full possession of all her civil immunities."[36]

"I understand our opponents to claim that the arrest and seizures were made by virtue of overruling military necessity, because New York was at war as an integral portion of the Union," Hall said, but he went on to explain that "overruling military necessity" in past precedent was always implemented under the same rules as martial law, and martial law could only be declared in the field of war operations. Therefore, "overruling military necessity" could not exist outside the battlefields.

Hall then considered if martial law and civil law could coexist in the same state or even the same city. On July 5, just four days before this court date, Lincoln had declared martial law in Kentucky, but claimed it would be confined to the battlefield territories. That meant Lincoln believed that martial law and civil law could coexist in the state of Kentucky. "But in what treatise on international law is the assumption substantiated?" Hall asked the court.

The president of the United States could not extend martial law over the entire country, or even over an entire region, unless he was conducting a military operation in each area. "Lines of bayonets and blockading squadrons" would mark those boundaries, leaving any territory outside these battle lines under civil law.

Hall argued that it was no good to consider all individuals essentially soldiers in this civil war, because even in the courts of England, military officers could not hold prisoners outside the sphere of battle. Nor could those prisoners be denied due process because they were under the protection of civil law.

An Indiana case had confirmed his interpretation. Hall read the stirring decision on the consequences of a violation of these rights: "If those sacred rights, among which are the liberty of speech, of the press, and freedom of elections—which are the three great bulwarks of free institutions—are to be stricken down and permanently destroyed by armed force; or if that force is not to be used to restore the just authority of our once glorious Government, but merely to establish, by wading through seas of blood, a single consolidated Government, having for its corner-stone certain chimerical ideas of philanthropy, fraternity, and equality, social and political, of all races of men without respect to color," that force was not worthy of being maintained. A nation could not justify itself by ideas alone. It could be great only through its actions.

Hall took his seat, handing the proceedings to his colleague.

New York State Attorney General Cochrane then rose to augment Hall's argument for the prosecution. He declared that "every American citizen was interested in the decision of this question, for it entered into the structure of liberties and hope for the future."[37]

After reviewing Dix's actions, Cochrane focused on the preciousness of freedom of speech. Lincoln had sworn his oath: "to protect and support the Constitution of the United States." Congress, according to the Constitution, could pass no laws that restrained the freedom of the press, nor laws which deprived people of life, liberty, or property without due process of law. The Constitution barred the president, in the fiercest, most precise language, from infringing on those rights. Therefore, the president had no constitutional justification for his actions.

The defense's argument, Cochrane surmised based on its earlier statements, would be that Congress itself had granted the president *new* powers when it passed the law allowing the act suspending habeas corpus.

Cochrane, however, refused that argument. The new law itself was treasonable to civil rights and scornful of liberty. He ran through the history of martial law from its beginning to the present day to show that "the act of Mr. Lincoln, under which General Dix justified himself, was unjustifiable," in past legal precedent or under the Constitution.

But what if Lincoln's actions stemmed from his role, not as president, but as commander in chief? Cochrane cited numerous texts showing that martial law could not exist without the *proclamation* of martial law, and, to quote the Duke of Wellington, martial law was no law at all. It only became necessary when courts failed to function due to an invasion or military battle in the vicinity.

Cochrane closed with caution: "Let us beware, lest while our armies are contending there at the front, here where the tables of law are exposed, here in the very forum of the law—an abyss shall be opened into which shall hurl or are hurling all the best rights and liberties of the republic." He wondered aloud, "How shall such an abyss be closed?" His response: "Why, by hurling into its midst that odious military necessity and the plea for martial law."[38]

The last speaker that day was Evarts, arguably the era's most famous lawyer and there to bolster the defense's position. In 1861, the newspapers had covered his arguments in the Lemmon Slave Case daily. Now the audience wanted to hear how he would approach Dix's defense, which was, in essence, a defense of the president. Evarts began by declaring that the suspension of the writ of habeas corpus conferred upon the president ample power to do whatever he thought necessary for the preservation of the country in time of war. In such a crisis, all powers had to be gathered to sustain the government.

"We have been but dull scholars in the sad years since the Rebellion broke out," Evarts said in his clear, ringing voice, "if we have not learned that the subject of enjoying liberties under a just and equal government, supported by a powerful nation that upholds and believes in it, is a very different matter from defending that free and equal Government against a hostile power that does not believe in it or love it, and seeks to overthrow it." He quoted an old expression, "The laws are unchanged in war but cannot be heard for its din."[39]

He cited a recent U.S. Supreme Court five-to-four decision in Lincoln's favor in the Prize Cases, which established whether Lincoln had violated the

Constitution in 1861 when he ordered a blockade of Southern ports prior to an official declaration of war. The ruling examined whether the executive automatically gained war powers at a time of conflict, or if Congress needed to assign those powers. Five judges, he reminded the court, had said Lincoln possessed war powers automatically.

When on July 15, 1861, Congress accepted that we were officially at war, Evarts said, the "executive became invigorated with the power of the nation."

It was ludicrous, he said, to suggest that if Congress granted the president the right to suspend habeas corpus, the president could not rely on his subordinates to execute it. Congress, when giving him the authority, did not intend for the president to only enjoy that authority to the extent that he himself could personally make the arrests. To think the law only extended the length of the president's arms was ridiculous.

To conclude, Evart asserted that establishing the intent to cause harm was the only way to establish guilt for a crime, then argued that all acts allegedly perpetrated by Dix lacked criminal intent. The judge might, at best, consider them trespass.

With this final concession to a possible misdemeanor, Evarts retook his seat and the case closed.

Judge Russell announced that he would deliver his decision on August 1.

By the next day, Lincoln, in the nation's capital and edged by bombarded buildings burning, sent out an anxious telegram: "By latest account the enemy is moving on Washington . . . I hope neither Baltimore nor Washington will be sacked." With all able men already at the front, D.C. lay vulnerable. That same day, Lincoln telegraphed to Grant that "we have absolutely no force here fit to go to the field." It was possible that before Russell's verdict came in, the federal government might fall to Confederate soldiers.

12

THE GOLD KEY

[New York, N.Y. – August 9, 1864]

After the lawyers packed up their papers and exited the courtroom into the greenery of Park Row, Hall's speech on the echoes between Howard's proclamation and Lincoln's announcements of the past few days remained unaddressed.

Lincoln had called the proclamation a "forgery" and deemed it "wicked and traitorous." Seward had said that the president had neither issued a proclamation nor *proposed* issuing such a proclamation. But if that were true—that the proclamation had been concocted whole cloth from the imagination of a reckless reporter—was it not extraordinary that this reporter had invented a military draft for multiple hundreds of thousands of men dated the exact same day as Lincoln's unsent order for multiple hundreds of thousands of men?

Lincoln's first act upon hearing of its publication also aroused suspicions. First, he had checked to see that the message hadn't gone out over the telegraph line based in the War Department, a telegraph line only a short walk from the White House and controlled by his own administration. His action suggested that he first thought someone close to him had sent out the "bogus" proclamation.

Once satisfied that the message hadn't been released over the War Department line, Lincoln's second act was to cut the transmission from the D.C. office of the Independent Telegraph. Eckert, his trusted telegraph operator, and a group of soldiers had been sent to that office to seize and search its records, suggesting that Lincoln so firmly suspected that someone from the White House compound or from D.C. had wired the proclamation or the information within it that, if it hadn't gone over the War Department line, surely it must have gone over the other main telegraph line in D.C.

For many hours, the president and his administration held on to this theory. When, at the end of the long, arduous day of May 18, Stanton told Dix he could release Marble and Prime from the order of arrest, he, too, shared the same belief. As he had written in his telegram from Washington, D.C.: "The officer in charge of the investigation, respecting the forged proclamation, reports that he is led to believe it originated in this city, and that the New York publishers were not privy to it." So nearly twenty hours after the proclamation first landed in the newspaper offices in New York, investigators in Washington still believed it came from D.C. Why?

The only explanation appeared to be that, as Cox had written Marble, the proclamation was "based in fact."

Lincoln and Secretary of War Edwin Stanton both knew that the supposed "bogus proclamation" had grounding. On May 17, the same date written on the bogus version, Lincoln had signed an order for three hundred thousand volunteers to register by July 1 or a draft would follow. For some reason, he had stuck the text away and not sent it.

When Chase asked Lincoln by telegram on the morning of the eighteenth if the proclamation in the newspapers was real, Lincoln admitted he had signed a similar call, thus bringing Chase into the ring of informed staffers.

I signed a very modest paper last night for the Sec. of War, about draft-
ing 300.000 in July, as I remember . . .[1]

Chase had reason to worry: he planned to sell gold abroad the next day
and the dire message would affect world markets.[2] Even early in the investigation, newspapers noted the potential financial gain on Wall Street.

So on May 17, Lincoln and Stanton had worked together on that draft
order for three hundred thousand men.[3] This toil, the unsent order, was a
three-paragraph handwritten and signed statement, essentially a boilerplate.

Order for Draft of 300,000 Men
Executive Mansion,
Washington, D. C. May 17. 1864.
To increase the active and reserved force of the Army, Navy, & Marine
Corps of the United States, a call is hereby made, & a draft ordered for
three hundred thousand men to serve for the period of—[left blank]
unless sooner discharged.

The proportional quotas for the different wards, towns, town-
ships, precincts, or election districts, or counties, will be made known
through the Provost Marshal General's Bureau, & account will be
taken of the credits & deficiencies on former quotas.

The 1st. day of July 1864 is designated as the time up to which the
numbers required from each ward of a city, town, &c, may be raised
by voluntary enlistment, & drafts will be made in each ward of city,
town, &c, which shall not have filled the quota assigned to it within
the time designated, for the number required to fill said quotas. The
drafts will be commenced as soon after the 1st. of July as practicable.
ABRAHAM LINCOLN.[4]

Despite Lincoln's vociferous denials of the "bogus proclamation" on
May 18, including Seward's specific claim that the president had neither

issued nor *proposed* issuing such a proclamation, word that the broad denial was a lie began to circulate the same day. The *Daily News* reported that the public—and markets—had regained some calm based on assurances that the proclamation was bogus, only to find themselves terrorized again before the end of the day. "The subsequent announcement which followed, from Washington, that the President will shortly make a call for 300,000 men about the first of next month, revived the excitement, and the subject was the theme of conversation throughout the city and its environ."

Indeed, Navy Secretary Welles reported that Seward came by his office that day and spoke of the "forged proclamation . . . calling for a draft of 300,000 men."[5] In fact, Howard's proclamation called for four hundred thousand. The order that Lincoln signed on May 17 called for three hundred thousand. Seward must have been thinking of the real order, still secret to most, as he sat before Welles denying the bogus proclamation.

As to the idea of a day of fasting, humiliation, and prayer, the Reverend Byron Sunderland, the chaplain of the Senate, wrote to Lincoln on May 4, requesting, with some emphasis, that Lincoln appoint a day of fasting and prayer, "Ought you not as a believer in God and Head of a mighty nation . . . on the eve of what might prove to be decisive events in the impending campaign," set such a day. When, in 1863, Congress had requested Lincoln appoint a day of humiliation and prayer, he had complied a few weeks later.

So, spurred by Sunderland, who had even directed Lincoln's attention to "events in the impending campaign," had Lincoln, in fact, a few weeks later written a longer version of the draft order, a proclamation incorporating the chaplain's request and the call for soldiers, then after preparing it, decided not to release it? Howard had said in his confession that he had "dictated" but "did not write" the proclamation. Had he made that distinction because Mallison had served as the transcriber? Allegedly, they had worked together on making the copies the night that the delivery boy ran the manifold pages from door to door. But some version of the proclamation existed before he and Mallison collaborated; Howard had showed a similar proclamation to

Kent in the week before the proclamation appeared in print. Kent had said the version Howard showed him contained a call for three hundred thousand men, the exact same number Lincoln had authorized in his order of May 17. Had there been a true Lincoln version leaked to Howard, which he embellished and used to create his own version?

Lincoln called Howard's bogus proclamation "false and spurious" and said that the newspapers had published the proclamation "wickedly and traitorously" and their actions were of a "treasonable nature . . . designed to give aid and comfort to the enemy." None of that was actually true. The newspapers were not acting "wickedly and traitorously." Lincoln had already heard the newspaper editors' side of the story through Dix by the time he issued that statement. But he made a leap to designate them as guilty and traitorous without a hearing before a judge, nor any proof that they had traitorous intent. For what purpose? What was Lincoln's intent in falsely branding them this way? He seemed to be going overboard to make an untrue statement about the newspapers with the intent to cover up the truth in the proclamation—that he had signed an order for three hundred thousand men on the exact same day as the proclamation went out calling for four hundred thousand men. He seemed to have suspected someone leaked the document—based on all the first actions from D.C. of checking the wires from the capital, shutting down the telegraph there—but he was pretending the papers invented it.

This would certainly not be the first leak of real information from Washington.

Not only did Lincoln, Hay, and Stoddard write anonymously from the White House, the whole Washington establishment sold war information to stockbrokers for pay or to profit themselves. Journalist Kinahan Cornwallis wrote in his 1879 account of the Civil War Gold Room: "As news-getters these [gold traders] were like hawks in search of prey . . . The so-called Washington party was composed not only of the private bankers, and nearly all the bank officers, in the city, but of many influential members of both houses of Congress, lobbyists, clerks, and others, in the Government offices, with facilities for obtaining early war news, and a large floating population of army contractors, and speculators who had taken up their residence there for the purpose of getting early intelligence of important events, whence they telegraphed their orders to their brokers in Wall street. Every man in the War Department, and the Executive Mansion, who was so situated as to be able to communicate valuable information in advance of the newspaper dispatches, was approached by the gold operators, and in most instances an arrangement existed between the former and the latter, for mutual profit."

Washington reporters, in particular, telegraphed news to the Gold Room, paid either by salary to the firm or individual investor that they "kept posted"; others used the information for their own buys.[6]

And Mary Todd herself, of course, stood accused of leaking material to the press. She had escaped investigation back in 1862, due to the intervention of her husband. But diary entries penned by a dear friend of the president's, which had originally been censored from publication and came to light 132 years after they were written, added to the likelihood of her complicity. Orville Hickman Browning, a fellow Illinois attorney and U.S. senator, recorded that in 1862, another confidant of Mrs. Lincoln's, Thomas Stackpole, came to his office to say that the gardener Watt ought to be given a position far from Mary Todd's reach, that he had taught her how to fix the accounting books to bleed money from public spending for her private use. He went further: "The President's message to Congress last December had been furnished to [Henry] Wyckoff by her, and not by Watt as is usually supposed—that she got it of [John D.] Defrees, Sup[erintendent] of government printing, and gave it to Wycoff in the Library, where he read it—gave it back to her, and she gave it back to Defrees. He also said that the President had ordered that Wycoff should not be admitted to the White House, but that Mrs. Lincoln was now in the habit of meeting him in the Green House, Watt arranging the interviews.

"He told me many other things which were painful to hear, and which will result in the disgrace of the family at the White House, unless they are corrected."[7]

Eight years after President Lincoln's death, Browning tried to defend Mrs. Lincoln to U.S. Supreme Court Judge David Davis in a conversation about their years in D.C., saying he thought Mrs. Lincoln had been unfairly attacked when in the White House. Davis replied "that the proofs were too many and too strong against her to admit of doubt of her guilt; that she was a natural born thief; that stealing was a sort of insanity with her." Davis said that after Lincoln's assassination he'd been asked to pay a bill for three hundred pairs of kid gloves that she had bought starting on January 1, 1865, until her husband's death in April. Davis also told Browning that Mary Todd had convinced Simeon Draper to pay her $20,000 to help him get appointed as cotton agent in New York, an appointment President Lincoln approved in the fall of 1864.[8]

Mary Todd had pushed her husband multiple times to approve appointments for her questionable confidants. In 1861, she wanted *New-York Evening Post* journalist Isaac Henderson to be made a naval agent in the New York Custom House; he ultimately proved so corrupt he had to be removed.[9] That same year, she tried to get Watt a cavalry commission. In 1862, she asked Hay to divert a staff member's salary to her own coffers. "I told her to kiss mine," he wrote Lincoln's other aide, Nicolay.[10] Saddest of all, she apparently could not stop herself. Her grief bordering on madness after Willie died inspired her otherwise empathetic husband to lead her to the window and point to the insane asylum down the way, warning her that he would have to send her there if she could not control her dangerous emotions. During the war, Lincoln had confessed to his friend, the superintendent of the Old Capitol Prison, William P. Wood, that he believed Mary's poor judgments at times "are the result of partial insanity," then asked if there might be a cure. Wood advised him to administer firmness and kindness.[11]

So might Mary Todd have been involved in this leak about the draft of hundreds of thousands of men? She would need motivation. What might that have been?

Mary Todd very much approved of the war's purpose, but she loathed Grant and wanted him removed. The bogus proclamation combined a report of terrible losses so dire they required "fasting and prayer" with a call for a vast number of new men to step up to service. Only two and a half months earlier, President Lincoln had demanded five hundred thousand men, and now, in May, he needed to nearly match that figure. Lincoln had hesitated sending the draft out, but if someone else leaked it, that astounding call for bodies might cause the people to rise up as they had during the draft riots and call for Grant's ouster.

Yet another benefit of a bogus document to someone appalled by the recent body counts: a false version of the proclamation would need to be denied by Lincoln, which would delay his ability to call up the quantity of troops he truly wanted. Perhaps, in her mind, this might stall the carnage she had witnessed so closely in the miserable hospital wards. (In fact, the bogus proclamation created a tactical advantage for Lincoln. By the time he called up five hundred thousand troops on July 19, the public had grown too weary to rally outrage. "The call . . . has not created that immediate excitement it otherwise would," wrote the *Detroit Free Press*, "had it not been looked for daily during the last month or two, in fact ever since 'Howard of the Times' anticipated the great Abraham, the father of infinite 'proclamations.'")[12]

But an even more personal reason might have led Mary Todd Lincoln to participate in the leak. Like the rest of the socially mobile set during the Civil War, Mary Todd consumed luxuries well beyond her means. In general, such spending, a *New York Times* editorial argued, was as good as throwing the wealth of the country away: "If I have a thousand dollars, for which I have no immediate use, and I spend it in dinners or wines, or costly furniture or clothing, or anything else which by my use of them are destroyed, it is just as much lost to the country as if it were burnt up. If, on the contrary, I save and invest it in mines or mills, or railroads or farming, it is used to employ laborers who are actually engaged in adding to the national wealth, in producing food, or more clothing, or more copper or gold or iron."

The editorial argued that those productive uses would create supplies for the armies and more tax revenue.[13]

Mary Todd Lincoln had rung up enormous bills on fashion and decorative household items in the White House. Mrs. Elizabeth Keckley, the first lady's personal seamstress, wrote in her memoir that leading up to the election in 1864, Mrs. Lincoln had been terribly anxious that her husband would be defeated. Keckley, a trusted confidant, was often privy to Mrs. Lincoln's personal conversations. When Keckley, a former slave, reassured the First Lady that the voters knew the president to be an honest man and would choose him again, Mrs. Lincoln replied, "If he should be defeated, I do not know what would become of us all. To me, to him, there is more at stake in this election than he dreams of."[14]

Mrs. Keckley remembered expressing confusion as to why Mrs. Lincoln would say such a thing.

"Simply this," Mrs. Lincoln replied. "I have contracted large debts, of which he knows nothing, and which he will be unable to pay if he is defeated." She had made a habit of selling government posts and the travel passes issued by the Union side to Southerners to allow them to visit relatives after they swore Union loyalty. She would lose that power should she return to normal life.

"What are your debts, Mrs. Lincoln?"

"They consist chiefly of store bills. I owe altogether about twenty-seven thousand dollars; the principal portion at Stewart's, in New York. You understand, Lizabeth, that Mr. Lincoln has but little idea of the expense of a woman's wardrobe. He glances at my rich dresses, and is happy in the belief that the few hundred dollars that I obtain from him supply all my wants. I must dress in costly materials." She lamented the scrutiny she endured, particularly because she came from the West. "To keep up appearances, I must have money—more than Mr. Lincoln can spare me. He is too honest to make a penny outside of his salary; consequently I had, and still have, no alternative but to run in debt."

Mrs. Keckley asked if the president suspected Mrs. Lincoln's level of debt.

"God, no!"—this was a favorite expression of hers—"and I would not have him suspect." Mary Todd Lincoln continued, "If he knew that his wife was involved to the extent that she is, the knowledge would drive him mad. He is so sincere and straightforward himself, that he is shocked by the duplicity in others. He does not know a thing about any debts, and I value his happiness, not to speak of my own, too much to allow him to know anything. This is what troubles me so much. If he is re-elected, I can keep him in ignorance of my affairs; but if he is defeated, then the bills will be sent in, and he will know all." Mrs. Keckley said that after that remark, "something like a hysterical sob escaped her."

Keckley went on: "Mrs. Lincoln sometimes feared that the politicians would get hold of the particulars of her debts, and use them in the Presidential campaign against her husband; and when this thought occurred to her, she was almost crazy with anxiety and fear.

"When in one of these excited moods, she would fiercely exclaim—

"'The Republican politicians must pay my debts. Hundreds of them are getting immensely rich off the patronage of my husband, and it is but fair that they should help me out of my embarrassment. I will make a demand of them, and when I tell them the facts they cannot refuse to advance whatever money I require.'"

Other White House staffers had also understood Mrs. Lincoln's debts to be crushing. Starting in March, two months before the "bogus proclamation," she had begun trying to settle her bills, raising the money through unknown means.[15] She sent her confidant, the White House housekeeper, Mary Ann Cuthbert, to New York in early March and directed her actions with mysterious telegrams: "There is a letter for you at your Hotel here—will be one tomorrow morning—Write & telegraph." A few days later: "Do not leave New York, until tomorrow, Saturday evening." A few days more, on March 10, "Come back." On April 1, she sent telegrams to merchants indicating she had paid a few bills around March 15.

On April 16, she wrote a letter to a major creditor, likely A. T. Stewart, the man who ran the deluxe department stores in New York. She told him she appreciated his "patience" and asked a special favor "having been a punctual customer & always hoping to be so, a delay of the Settlement of my account with you, until the 1st of June—when I promise, that without fail, *then*, the whole account shall be settled. I deeply regret, that I am so unusually situated & trust hereafter, to settle as I purchase."[16]

Remember that to Keckley, she had estimated those bills to be the better part of $27,000, in other words, more than her husband's entire salary for the year, enough to buy approximately twenty-seven Philadelphia rowhouses, an enormous amount of money to raise in a month and a half.

On April 27, eleven days after she wrote the letter to Stewart, Mary Todd took a night train to New York City with her son Tad. She reportedly "ransacked the treasures of the Broadway goods stores" and saw Abram Wakeman, the postmaster who would later hold open the mails to the *Scotia* past the usual hour to let the *Herald* get onboard with the word that the proclamation was false.[17] Three years later, she would confirm that Wakeman had a reason to try to help her settle her debts. When after her husband's death she found herself penniless, she wrote to a broker helping her to raise money by selling her old dresses and even a used parasol cover. "Please call Hon. Abram Wakeman," she directed. "He was largely indebted to me for obtaining the lucrative office which he has held for several years [surveyor of the port of New York, which Mary Todd convinced her husband to post him to in September 1864], and from which he has amassed a very large fortune. He will assist me in my painful and humiliating situation, scarcely removed from want."[18] On the April 1864 trip to New York, she reportedly also saw Simeon Draper, the former head of the state Republican Party, who was working for the federal government selling cotton confiscated from the Confederates. In September 1864, President Lincoln gave him the post that U.S. Supreme Court Judge Davis said Mary Todd had been paid $20,000 to secure.[19]

Might they have been strategizing about playing the market? It was a common practice to attempt to manipulate the gold market by circulating true war stories. People peddled false ones as well. The *Brooklyn Eagle* commented on the practice the day after Howard was arrested: "Bogus reports, intended to effect the price of stocks, are every day set afloat in Wall street, and they are forgotten as soon as they have subserved their purpose. If all of the individuals who have made illegitimate gains out of this war were sent to Fort Lafayette, Mr. Howard would find himself to-day in the company of the most pretentious, the most truculent, and most virulent members of the party of which he was a faithful adherent."[20]

A political and economic journal, the *Independent*, urged ferocious punishments for these false reports. "We hope this latest and largest of the frauds, and its failure, will serve as a warning to the many triflers with the public mind and heart, who, during the war, have not scrupled to give wings to lies, to fabricate outrageous stories from incidents of battle, suffering, and death, for the mere purpose of affecting prices on the exchange—wounding the public heart for the advantage of a private pocket."[21]

Looking at the news as a backdrop for stock and gold manipulators, the benefits of negative news in mid-May becomes clear. Discouraging reports about the war and about the North's possibility of victory had been continuous from the beginning of the year, causing gold values to rise. Congress refused to pass a tax to improve the Union's financial state, causing yet further gold inflation since the Union seemed headed for collapse.

But then in May, gold values teetered. The Union seemed to be winning bloody but real victories.[22] If an investor could buy during the drop in gold prices, they could wait for a dire news report to bring the values up, at which point the investor could sell to net a rich profit.

So, a diehard Republican journalist (Howard) released a proclamation perhaps based on a real piece of dire information, but issued a bit earlier than Lincoln's official call for soldiers. Where did Howard get the information? On May 20, Samuel Sunset Cox had told Marble the leak might have come from Mary Todd Lincoln. Could she have leaked the info to Howard? As Louis M. Starr, historian of Civil War journalism, would later write in a list of the first lady's favored journalists, "Joseph Howard of the *Times* rivaled Wikoff as Mrs. Lincoln's confidant."[23]

Remember that Howard had been bewildered when the detectives came to his house to arrest him. He had been flabbergasted, in fact, as they outlined the testimony against him. One might wonder if he was confused because he thought he had been part of another version of the story. Had Howard, allegedly Mrs. Lincoln's confidant, received word of the pending draft from Mrs. Lincoln on her trip to New York three weeks prior? Had he shown Kent a copy of the actual proclamation draft a week before its publication; maybe it had been written by a staff member or by Lincoln himself? Mrs. Lincoln had returned home to Washington at the very end of April. According to her letter to her creditor, Stewart, she had only a month from her return to D.C. to come up with a vast sum of money. How would she do that?

Had Howard been expecting the proclamation dated the seventeenth and pushed it to the newspapers on that date? Was he expecting merely to have gotten a jump on the news, believing that the New York papers would release the proclamation first thing in the morning and that Washington would follow soon afterward with Lincoln's official release? Had he been hoping that gap in time between publication and official confirmation would allow the first bettors, such as Howard himself and Mary Todd herself, to profit off a rise in gold prices?

Perhaps, in Howard's mind, he had released a true document and only been surprised by the administration's delay, then perhaps he had been further shocked by their denial.

After detectives arrested Howard, witnesses remarked how publicly open Howard had been about the proclamation and so confident with his allusions to the wealth he would soon acquire. "Well, I'll be rich as you in a few days," he had said, when at Brooklyn City Hall, and referred to an event in the offing that would win him a fortune. He reportedly showed no signs of anxiety or depression.[24] Would he have been so cocky had he made the story up out of whole cloth? Or was he cocky because, as a reporter, he considered himself merely to have scored a massive scoop? He *knew* the president would issue the draft, and he intended to make money on it.

What if when he brought the proclamation to the broker, he was acting as an agent of Mary Todd? Perhaps she had promised her creditor Stewart that all bills would be settled by the first of June because she intended to capitalize on the market two weeks earlier.

Then, perhaps, Howard had been shocked to have gotten in so much trouble when all he had done was release the proclamation for the first lady a few hours ahead. And now, to his bewilderment, he was headed to Fort Lafayette.

All would be revealed, it seemed, when Howard stood trial for his crime.

Brokers and investors regularly begged members of the federal government to trade information for use in stock speculation. The practice was so common that twelve days after the bogus proclamation was published, a Kentucky stockbroker coaxed David Homer Bates, a telegraph operator in the War Department, to take part. Bates's journal read:

Gold went up to 190 yesterday, the highest point it has yet reached. A man named Mularkey, a oper. from Louisville, called me Saturday

& asked me to make arrangement as follows. A stock broking firm in Louisville with a heavy capital would buy & sell gold accordingly as I would direct & half the profits were to be divided between Mularkey & me. I, being in a position where I could get all the news, could tell exactly when to buy & sell. I told Mr. Mularkey that I didn't desire to be a party to any such transaction; that I had earned a good position by my faithfulness & I didn't desire to compromise my character by any such action.

He gave me to understand that I could make $50.000 by the operation, but I declined accepting it. Before he commenced the conversation he asked me to promise faithfully that it should not be divulged to his discredit. Were it not for this promise I should have him arrested. Monday, May 30, 1864.[25]

So if the proclamation was not bogus but based on real information, what explains the Lincoln administration's original vociferous disavowal that not only had the president not produced the bogus proclamation, he hadn't even *proposed* such a proclamation? Lincoln had responded to the release with the greatest rage he had ever shown. If anger is said to be an indicator of fear, what had caused his fear at that particular moment?

At that point in the war, the government's expenses totaled $2.25 million per day. Speculators in the Gold Room regularly drummed down the value of the federal dollar with their trading. On May 19, Chase had planned to sell gold on the London exchange at a price lower than market value, with the aim of lowering the international value of gold.[26] If the bogus proclamation managed to get on the European steamer on the eighteenth, Chase's sale of gold overseas would have failed because investors would sense the imminent collapse of the Union and put their holdings in the Cotton Loan instead.

Despite the efforts to hold the bogus proclamation from going overseas, reports circulated of it reaching foreign markets. Chase found that his gold

sale in London on the nineteenth proved a disaster. Gold prices only flick-
ered by five-eighths for one day and afterward began to rise again.[27] Chase
simply could not corral the world's markets by infusing one release of gold;
gold's value was universal, not like the greenback, tied to one nation whose
future seemed desperately in doubt.

Overall, the fluidity with which investors—some bent on the Union's
destruction—moved through the U.S. markets was unstoppable. A newspaper had managed to get hold of an 1863 correspondence between Confederate investors, spelling out the mechanics of their deals: they named an
accomplice who was "to borrow the greenbacks in New York, buy the gold
and ship it to England; we then draw sterling, which is sold in New York for
greenbacks, pay up what we owe, and the balance will be profit. It will go, I
think to 200. *Such speculations help us, and our government, too; and it helps
to break their currency.*"[28]

Chase tried one last extraordinary effort to defeat his nemeses, the gold
speculators. In mid-June, a bill Chase had pushed since the early spring—to
criminalize the trading of gold—became law. Gold could be sold if the seller
had the mineral on hand. But no longer could a buyer contract to purchase
gold for delivery three days in the future. The transaction and its payment
had to be completed that particular day. The rules applied to foreign buyers
as well, although the transfer of the actual gold could be extended up to ten
days. The punishment for each illegal transaction was a stiff fine or up to a
year in prison.[29]

The day the Gold Room closed on June 21, buyers who had bought
gold short faced the brutality of those who owned gold, because buyers now
needed to pay whatever price to fulfill their promises to banks for loans or
to foreign importers.[30] No central location held a list of gold prices. Buyers
needed to run from house to house, inquiring the cost, which, by June 27,
differed by a full nineteen points from lowest price to highest.

Bankers and merchants called on Congress to kill the chaos-causing
law. Resisting the reversal of his pet policy, Chase resigned. This time, his

fifth attempt to resign over the years of his tenure, Lincoln accepted: "You and I have reached a point of mutual embarrassment in our official relation which it seems can not be overcome," replied the president. On July 2, legislators introduced a bill to rescind the law and Congress unanimously approved it with no debate.

When the Gold Room reopened on July 5, the price of gold soared to 250. Savvy brokers had managed to figure out how to corner the market during the lull when the Gold Room had closed.[31] By July 11, the price went up to 285. Government bonds lost a quarter of their value in a month. A one-dollar greenback had gone from a value of fifty-five cents to forty cents. A financial journalist reported pandemonium in the Gold Room, as investors losing thousands of dollars every minute screamed, rolled their eyes, and threw their hands to the sky. The roar sounded like a storm, and now and again, a new man would run into the scrum to holler above the mayhem and then race out. The American people watched the daily horror as the price of gold went to 300.

As for the trial of Dix and his fellow officers, Judge Russell decided that the grand jury needed to fully hear the case. The actions of the military officers were disturbing enough to warrant more than the evasion of "inexpedience." The defendants, he ruled, had tried to put themselves under the protection of the 1863 act suspending habeas corpus:

> If that provision is constitutional, it assimilates the President of the United States, during the existence of the present rebellion, to an absolute monarch, and makes him incapable of doing any wrong. This is a very novel and startling doctrine to advance under a republican form of government.

Russell went on:

I have given the case a most careful consideration; on the one hand, seeking to avoid an undue interference with the agents of the Government in the performance of their duty, and, on the other, keeping before me my own obligation to uphold and enforce the laws of this State. I do not deem it proper to state in detail the view I entertain upon the legal principles so ably discussed before me by the counsel on both sides. Such an exposition of the law would be more appropriate should the case come before the court for trial. It strikes me, however, as a fit occasion to enable the great questions of time involved in it to be brought up in such a shape as to admit of their being absolutely and finally settled.

Russell noted that the Habeas Corpus Suspension Act essentially gave Lincoln authority above the Constitution that, in fact, created his office, as well as "the right, in his discretion, to obey that instrument or not."

Rejecting the idea that martial law could exist outside battle lines, the judge claimed that if any rebellion deprived citizens of their rights in another state, "then the government of every state of the Union is at the mercy of every other state." He closed with a warning: if the president can direct anything done and his order is a perfect shield, "he becomes a despot, and is no longer the chief magistrate of a free people."[32]

And with that, he passed the case on to the grand jury and demanded a firm decision.

Sympathizers of Lincoln's felt that the war's escalation had gradually forced him to a hard line on the press as a way to control all conduits of potential espionage. But his battle against freedom of speech began in the earliest days of his presidency, starting in 1861 when he ordered the seizure of all the telegraph messages in New York.

As the years continued, his administration's hostilities toward the press escalated, sometimes launched by soldiers, sometimes by Republican vandals, many of the incidents occurring in locations outside the direct attention of national reporters. A list of attacks on newspapers in 1864 appeared in the *Register of Important Events*:

Democrat, Sunbury, Penn. Mobbed January 18, 1864. Office destroyed. Property stolen.

Mahoning Sentinel, Youngstown, O. Mobbed January 28, 1864. Attempt to assassinate the editor. Office totally destroyed.

Eagle, Lancaster, Ohio. Mobbed February 3, 1864. Partially destroyed.

Crawford Democrat, Meadville, Penn. Mobbed February 5, 1864. Saved by editor's defence.

Northumberland Democrat, Penn. Destroyed by mob, February 7, 1864.

Constitution and Union, Fairfield, Iowa. Destroyed February 8, 1864.

Crisis, Columbus, Ohio. Threatened February 15, 1864. Saved by being armed.

Statesman, Columbus, Ohio. Threatened February 15, 1864. Saved by being armed.

Democrat, Laporte, Indiana. Destroyed February, 15, 1864.

Democrat, Wauscon, Ohio, destroyed Feb. 20, 1864.

Dayton Empire, Dayton, Ohio, completely destroyed March 3, 1864.

Democrat, Greenville, Durke County, Ohio, demolished March 5, 1864.

Union, Louisiana, Mo., destroyed March 6, 1864.

Advertiser, Lebanon, Penn., attacked March 15, 1864; defended successfully.

Herald, Franklin County, Indiana, demolished March 20, 1864.

Metropolitan Record, New York, circulation forbidden at the West, March 26, 1864.

St. Mary's Gazette, Leonardtown, Ind., warned April 12, 1862.

Crisis, Columbus, O., editor seized and imprisoned May 10, 1864.

Transcript, Baltimore, Md., suppressed May 18, 1864, for publishing a despatch saying the loss of the Army of the Potomac was not less than seventy thousand, and crediting it to the Associated Press.

Volksblatt, Belleville, Missouri. Destroyed a second time, May 18, 1864.

Courier, New Orleans, suppressed May 23, 1864, and editors banished for republishing the bogus proclamation received via Cairo. The order was never revoked.

Kentucky, June, 1864, all Democratic papers excluded in the State.

News, Memphis, Tenn., suppressed July 1864.

Bulletin, Baltimore, Md., suppressed July 1864.

Register, Wheeling, Va., editors seized, paper suppressed July 20, 1864.

Gazette, Parkersburg, Va., editor seized by Gen. Hunter, July 27, 1864.

Democrat, Gallatin County, Ill., editors seized and imprisoned August 19, 1864.

Picket Guard, Chester, Ill. totally destroyed August 20, 1864.

Journal, Belfast, Me., editor seized August 1864.[33]

The public awaited the verdict in *The People v. Dix*, which Pierrepont had called "a question of vast magnitude and more important than any matter that has ever been brought before any court in the history of any nation" and which Hall agreed to be "one of the most momentous questions that had ever been brought before a court of justice."

But somehow, the grand jury case was never heard again. The burning questions of the strictures on the president's power, his ability to violate the freedom of the press and violate the sanctity of personal property, remained unanswered. The newspapers appeared silent on the matter. The election loomed in November, and editors like Manton Marble had thrown all their efforts into stopping Lincoln's violations by trying to get McClellan elected to be president. Somehow, someone had made the case simply disappear. If any justice could still be served, it was left for Howard's case to go before the courts.

13

POPULAR AS THE AIR

[New York, N.Y. – August 1864]

For months now, the bon vivant of New York society, the man reportedly intimate with Mary Todd, the dear friend of Henry Ward Beecher, stewed in jail, dining now not on pork in all forms but three months of salt horse and no vegetables.[1] "Bogus Joe," as Colonel Burke had nicknamed him, endured what an inmate had described as Fort Lafayette's "dismal living death."

Howard had, during his stint, managed to win over his fellow prisoners with witty stories and constant commentary.[2] Unlike the other inmates, he had no other audience. The columns under the name Dead Beat had ensured he could not communicate with his wife or friends on the outside. No letters could be snuck in to him. But an informant told a reporter that Howard held hopes that he would be released one day, and that the magic moment would be in a month.

From the first days of Howard's imprisonment, his family members and friends, including Beecher, tried desperately to get him out. Those Dead Beat columns in the *Brooklyn Eagle* had caused deep difficulties. "It took some weeks, various fact-filled paragraphs in the *Eagle* explaining the facts, innumerable letters and visits to Washington to convince the Secretary that the *Eagle* 'Dead Beat' and his prisoner were two entirely distinct personages," the editors reported.

To one of the *Eagle*'s persistent readers, they publicly reiterated Howard's innocence. "'E.D. Springfield,' is desirous of receiving an explicit answer to the question, 'Is Mr. Howard, Jr., now in Fort Lafayette, the author of the letters which have appeared, since his arrest, in the *Eagle*, over the signature of "Dead Beat"?'" the newspaper announced in its columns. "He is not. We trust we shall be pestered no more for information on this point."[3]

But just as that matter was settled, a new letter appeared under another occasional pen name of Howard's, Corry O'Lanus, with the added letters "D. B."[4] It could not be known if Howard had outwitted his captors or another journalist had found a way to taunt the administration yet again.

For Mallison's part, he had come to make the best of his imprisonment, enjoying the sea air and the parade of mighty vessels steaming into New York Harbor through the hot days of summer. At least in the fort, he jokingly commented to fellow inmates, he knew he was safe from the dangers of urban life: exploding gas pipes or aggressive wagon traffic. He wryly noted that he only wished Lincoln would have realized the genius of accepting the proclamation as his own work because then he would already have his new round of soldiers at the front.

On the more serious side, Mallison, an avowed Democrat, contended with his warden, Burke. One night, an officer woke Mallison and brought him to Burke, who asked how many bullets he would expect would kill him, six or eight, so that the ammunition could be readied for the morning. That remark could be dismissed as drunk insanity, except that it was coming from the man responsible for executing the death sentences of deserters under General Scott in the Mexican War.

Mallison also dealt with the punitive distribution of rations—hard conditions that may have politicized him. "Under this Administration no man is safe," he later said in an interview. "Four men talking in a bar-room in the city of New York were arrested upon suspicion of being blockade runners; months have passed, and yet they remain in the dungeons of Fort Lafayette without a trial or prospect of one; they are as innocent of the crime charged as you are."[5] His main impression of the Confederate inmates, he claimed, was a deep, unwavering hatred of Abraham Lincoln.

Within days of Howard's imprisonment, his Republican friends, including Beecher, took their campaign for his freedom to Dix, who was said to be a close friend of Howard's father. They argued that other people had led Howard into the deed.[6] Their pleas swayed Dix to go see Lincoln on Howard's behalf, and, indeed, Dix reportedly met with the president on July 19.[7] According to the *Eagle*, Lincoln responded to Dix's plea for Howard's release "with a twinkle in his eye, that it would be best to wait 'until the thing had blown over.'"[8]

Howard's father and Beecher followed up with their own pilgrimage to the White House before the end of July to meet with Lincoln.[9] John D. Defrees, the superintendent of public printing, the one involved in the Watt leak of the State of the Union case, wrote an encouraging letter to Beecher after that visit. Beecher thanked him:

It would have brought tears into the good Presidents eyes to see the wife & two little girls when I read them yr letter—I feel earnestly desirous that this lesson should turn to young Howard's moral benefit. He needed some such prostration—and I am glad to perceive that the sting of his punishment, is the imputation of a treasonable intent. He was the tool of the man who turned states evidence and escaped; & Joe, had only the hope of making some money, by a stock brokers lie & had not foresight or consideration enough to perceive the relation of his act to the public welfare—You must excuse my earnestness. He has been brought up in my parish & under my eye and is the only spotted child of a large family.—[10]

Defrees forwarded Beecher's letter to John Hay on August 3:

> I don't like to trouble the President. If you can ever find him when he don't seem much engaged, please request him to read the inclosed letter.
>
> The public good does not require the further punishment of Howard—the new tool of speculating scoundrels—and his release will gratify many true friends.
>
> The President has no truer or better friend than Beecher—and I do know he may be gratified in a matter which he takes so much at heart.[11]

On August 22, the president felt convinced that Howard had done his time. He wrote to Stanton:

> I very much wish to oblige Henry Ward Beecher by releasing Howard; but I wish you to be satisfied when it is done. What say you?

Stanton scrawled on the same note: "I have no objection if you think it right—and this is the proper time."

With that, Howard's father was on his way to Fort Lafayette to pick up his son. An associate later said that "no other man but Henry Ward Beecher could have induced [Lincoln] to be guilty of pardoning Joe Howard."

Howard would later write of Beecher, "I have always looked upon him as an elder brother, a kind of father. I went to him with my boyish troubles . . . and in one stormy period of my life, when, absurd as it may seem now, there was a question of life or death in the hands of the Washington authorities, the strong arm between them and me was that of the man I had always loved and always honored."[12]

Amazingly, as Mary Prime had predicted, Howard never endured a trial. He never faced a reckoning, a full investigation of the facts, or an identification of his associates. As Mary Prime foresaw, he was simply, quietly released.

Newspapers raged about the fact that the Republican Howard's evil act had been shuffled away, while Democrats went to jail for unspecified crimes. "One great and sickening fact is too true, that the Government, having in its hands, in a time of war, a man who has struck the deepest, darkest, and most vital blow at the heart of the country, and having the evidence in its hands of his guilt, and the purely mercenary motive by which he was instigated, and having an opportunity to show to the country its sense of the magnitude of his crime, which was only less than that of high treason itself, has nevertheless been prevailed upon to open the door of the prison where the criminal was awaiting his trial, and to let him go free," wrote the *Pittsburgh Daily Post*.

They noted that the religious press had been disgusted by the "bogus" proclamation's blasphemy, falsely asking for prayer. "The country has been made the victim of false news, manufactured reports, exaggerated statements, fictitious accounts, sent by mail and by telegraph every week since the war began. These false reports are made for the purpose of affecting the price of gold and stocks. Bad men sell the life blood of their fellows to make money by fraud. . . . No crime has been perpetrated in this country awakening a wider and deeper sense of just indignation than the one now suffered to go unpunished. So intense was the feeling of public insult and wrong at the time of its commission, that if the criminal had been hung on a tree, or shot in the back by a squad of soldiers, the people would have pronounced the punishment just."[13]

Less than a month after Howard was released, his standing was good enough that he helped win Mallison's release by writing to Lincoln, even feeling so bold as to insert a smirking description of Fort Lafayette:

> I have once intruded upon your cares to thank you for your kindness in granting an order for my release from the inhospitable retreat at Fort Lafayette & to assure you of my sincere regret at my folly & its consequences; permit me to call your attention to the case once more in behalf of the young man who was placed there at the same time as myself, but who was not included in the order for release. Mr. Beecher & Gen. Dix have written to you (or telegraphed) concerning him, suggesting the proprieties of releasing Mr Mallison, who was comparatively subordinate in the affair.
>
> I regret to say that certain 'Democratic' stumpers are making a handle of his continued confinement, taking the absurd ground that he is held on account of his Democratic affiliations.
>
> Mr. Mallison has an aged Mother dependent upon him, was no deeper (nor so deep) in the foolishness for which we were sent to the Fort than I, and has felt very keenly his position & its consequences. May I not, with all respect and regard, urge you to direct his immediate discharge on the grounds as above set forth?
>
> Believing that such an order would be productive of no harm to the State, would silence opposition talk, would gratify many of your personal & political friends, & be also just,
>
> I remain,
>
> With gratitude
>
> & esteem
>
> Yours sincerely,
>
> J. Howard, Jr.[14]

Congressman Odell had appealed for Mallison's release in early September.[15] John Defrees had petitioned in mid-September. But, apparently, Howard's plea on the nineteenth carried weight with Lincoln. The next day, the president wrote to Stanton: "Let Mallison, the bogus proclamation man, be discharged."[16]

Mallison left prison on September 23. Three years later, he passed the New York state bar and after was elected as a member of the New York assembly. In that campaign, Corry O'Lanus published an endorsement of Francis O'Pake in the newspapers. In other words, under one of his occasional pen names, it was likely Howard endorsed Mallison under Mallison's pen name.

Amazingly, Howard went on to a full, heralded career. He returned to reporting for various newspapers under his own name, delivered Howard's Letter and Howard's Column to syndication. *The New York Times* rehired him, as did the *Brooklyn Eagle*. He continued to write not only under old pen names such as M. T. Jugg, but new ones, such as Monsieur X when reviewing theater productions, or Diabolus. He wrote a biography of Henry Ward Beecher and served as president of the New York Press Club. "He has become as privileged and popular as the air, and what he says in print is read by more people than the audience given to any editorial writer in the country," the Club's history attested.

A professional rebirth of that scale was surprising enough for someone involved in using the president's name and authorship to make money, for a man who scared the country and rocked the currency. But still more inexplicable was an added honor given him. The Lincoln administration did not stop its forgiveness with simply releasing the forger. As in the case of the gardener who claimed to have leaked the State of the Union address in 1861, perhaps to cover for Mary Todd Lincoln, Howard received a sinecure position—in his case, not in the U.S. Patent Office, but within the military government. He was granted an appointment as a military recorder for the Department of the East, under Dix's supervision, where he wrote articles and recorded confessions.

Putting the forger in a trusted position was startling, to say the least. The appointment also echoed the mysterious allusion in Dead Beat's first letter the day after his arrest, in which he said, "'Is there a loyal man in the Department of the East?' 'Yes, it's Dead Beat.'" At the time, that remark had been difficult to interpret. In hindsight, it raises questions. Had Howard always been working undercover for the Department of the East? The draft rioters had attacked him as a "Lincoln spy." Did they know something that the public didn't?

In November 1861, the *Philadelphia Inquirer* made a small mention that Howard had been "tendered position" as assistant adjutant general to General Willis A. Gorman, but no further tracking had surfaced.[17]

But Howard's friends appeared more interested in pushing an opposing theory for Howard's motivation in the scheme. Charles Halpine, the military officer in Dix's office who escorted Howard to Castle Garden the night of his May arrest, later wrote his assessment of the events. He used the royal "we": "We had official cognizance of the case at the headquarters of Gen. Dix, and soon became satisfied that it was no more, upon Howard's part, than a very bad blunder in the way of a practical joke,—Gen Dix proving that he agreed in this opinion, and felt some reparation due to Mr. Howard for the undeserved severity of his treatment during the early excitement of that frolic, by specially selecting the subject of our sketch to be official Recorder of the important Military Court then in session in Bleecker street.[18] Our investigation showed us, even in its early stages, that all sensational rumors to the effect that Howard was in league with speculators who sought to affect the European stock markets, were pure poppycock, or something worse; and though we had not time to finish the case, being ordered away for duty at the South, we had so completely satisfied our judgment that Howard had only been guilty of a blunder, not an intended crime, that previous to our departure strong representations were made to Gen. Dix in favor of his discharge. As Howard looked at the matter, his 'Proclamation' was regarded as a hoax, or burlesque, much after the fashion of the 'Orpheus C. Kerr,' 'Artemas Ward,' or 'Petroleum V. Nasby' fulminations,—his error being, that he selected a subject too important and too sensitive for trifling with, at a period of intense popular excitement; and that he executed his work with such disastrous fidelity as to deceive all but the very elect,—the writer, he is proud to say, never having been taken in for a moment."

Halpine's explanation, as deep within the investigation as it was, seemed hard to fathom. It would be difficult to see how the joking renditions of political news by "Kerr," "Ward," or "Nasby" matched up to Howard's somber call for four hundred thousand troops. But Halpine insisted.

Another journalist also liked this explanation. "Joe Howard declares, and I know him well, that he hadn't an idea of such a thing till five minutes before he set to work on it. The idea struck him like a flash, and in congenial company, convulsed with laughter, the precious screed was concocted and despatched on its mischievous way."[19]

If Halpine had been successful at convincing the president that the matter was a joke, that might have sufficiently absolved Howard in Lincoln's eyes. Wrote Beecher in a remembrance of Lincoln and of Stanton: "Stanton evidently got rest from his great cares through literature; but Lincoln, from the humorists. I understood them both perfectly. Stanton had poetry for his relaxation. Everybody must have somewhere to blow off."[20]

Assistant Secretary of War Dana recalled how deep this passion of Lincoln's ran, including on the fraught night of the November 1864 elections.

"All the power and influence of the War Department, then something enormous from the vast expenditure and extensive relations of the war, was employed to secure the re-election of Mr. Lincoln," Dana recalled. "The political struggle was most intense, and the interest taken in it, both in the White House and in the War Department, was almost painful . . . On November 8th, election day, I went over to the War Department about half past eight o'clock in the evening, and found the President and Mr. Stanton together in the Secretary's office. General Eckert . . . was coming in constantly with telegrams containing election returns. Mr. Stanton would read them, and the President would look at them and comment upon them. Presently there came a lull in the returns, and Mr. Lincoln called me to a place by his side.

"'Dana,' said he, 'have you ever read any of the writings of Petroleum V. Nasby?'

"'No, sir,' I said; 'I have only looked at some of them, and they seemed to be quite funny.'

"'Well,' said he, 'let me read you a specimen'; and, pulling out a thin yellow-covered pamphlet from his breast pocket, he began to read aloud. Mr. Stanton viewed these proceedings with great impatience, as I could see, but Mr. Lincoln paid no attention to that. He would read a page or a story, pause to consider a new election telegram, and then open the book again and go ahead with a new passage. Finally, Mr. Chase came in, and presently somebody else, and then the reading was interrupted.

"Mr. Stanton went to the door and beckoned me into the next room. I shall never forget the fire of his indignation at what seemed to him to be mere nonsense. The idea that when the safety of the republic was thus at issue, when the control of an empire was to be determined by a few figures brought in by the telegraph, the leader, the man most deeply concerned, not merely for himself but for his country, could turn aside to read such balderdash and to laugh at such frivolous jests was, to his mind, repugnant, even damnable. He could not understand, apparently, that it was by the relief which these jests afforded to the strain of mind under which Lincoln had so long been living, and to the natural gloom of a melancholy and desponding temperament—this was Mr. Lincoln's prevailing characteristic—that the safety and sanity of his intelligence were maintained and preserved."[21]

Originally, Lincoln declared the bogus proclamation so wicked and treasonous that the newspapers must be shut down and face a military commission. But then when the administration realized the author was Howard—a Republican, a reporter often in his presence, and a close friend of Beecher, one of Lincoln's most important supporters—his administration jailed him for a bit and let him go without trial. Not only did they let him go, they *rewarded him* with a sinecure position within the government. Had Lincoln switched his approach because he no longer needed to keep lying that the bogus proclamation was completely made up? Did his administration essentially pay Howard off for not outing the person who leaked the information to him?

In 1904, Howard's old roommate from the Lincoln inaugural train ride, Stephen Fiske, sent him a letter, enclosing a bit of memorabilia for Howard, "which I had entirely forgotten. I guess you had too." Fiske recalled, "It brings back to the old times very vividly. In spite of hard work and various misunderstandings, they were glorious times, and I should not object to living them over again."[22]

Howard's enclosed letter, dated September 8, 1864, begins as a thank-you to Fiske for coverage Fiske apparently gave Howard's Fort Lafayette plight in the newspaper, the *Leader*. Howard said he could not leave the city after getting out of prison without expressing gratitude. "In times like these which it is fair to assume tried my soul, friends are few and those will not be forgotten. Now, with an unconditional release in my hand, money in my pocket and professional advancement in my grasp, friends are plenty but they don't fool." Howard planned to head to the White Mountains for a break for a few weeks and "then to home and a work which will open the eyes of some of our friends."

Howard had obviously come into new money, and he apparently never created that eye-opening work. Contrary to the demands of justice, and not seven months after Howard got out of prison for having forged the proclamation, he traveled back to Fort Lafayette for the Department of the East to meet with Robert Cobb Kennedy, a Confederate officer, who stood accused of trying to burn down various buildings in New York City in 1864 in retaliation for the Union's scorched-earth tactics in the South. Colonel Burke, formerly Howard's warden at Fort Lafayette, accompanied Howard, writing to Dix:

"I have the honor to report that last night, about half past ten o'clock, I visited Kennedy, taking with me Mr. Howard, of the New York Times.

After some conversation relative to the matter for which [Kennedy] has been sentenced, he made the following confession. He requested that I would make no use of the confession to his detriment in case a respite or reprieve should be received."

By passing along the confession *before* Kennedy's execution, Burke was already violating Kennedy's request. It was an act that certainly would hurt Kennedy's chances of a reprieve.

Howard reported about the journey by sea, and the appearance of the fort. Then he relayed the convicted man's description of arriving in the city and of burning Barnum's Museum and three hotels.[23] In his confession to Howard, Kennedy explained that had his Confederates "all done as I did we would have had thirty-two fires and played a huge joke on the Fire Department." Kennedy continued, "I know that I am to be hung for setting fire to Barnum's Museum, but that was only a joke. I had no idea of doing it. I had been drinking and went in there with a friend, and, just to scare the people, I emptied a bottle of phosphorous on the floor. We knew it wouldn't set fire to the wood."

And so it was Howard's report—he of the fake Scotch cap, the "bogus" proclamation—that was submitted as the last statement of a man sentenced to the gallows. A day later, the morning of the hanging, Howard reported about Kennedy cutting his hair to send a lock home to his family and crying while he waited for the scissors. After the executioner recorded Kennedy's weight and height for the noose, Kennedy asked to see Howard one more time. "I want people of the North to know that I'm no fiend and did not wage war on women and children except as a matter of necessity and retaliation."

Howard promised he would print those words, with nothing left out. Kennedy asked Howard to send his pipe to his mother. But Kennedy still disputed the charges against him—which had been bolstered by Howard's version of the alleged confession—even yelling out to the officer reading the condemnations as they prepared him for the gallows, "That's a lie, a damned lie, a damned lie!"

Kennedy sang a brief song in his black hood, and less than a half hour later, they lowered his corpse to the ground.

The *Journal of Commerce* weighed in a few months later when the confession was used as evidence in the trial of others: "Many persons will recollect that after the execution of Kennedy, in New-York on 25th March, an unsigned and unauthenticated story was published purporting to be a confession which he made the night before his death. This pretended confession was, however, discredited at the time, and finally understood to have been a bogus affair, gotten up by an ingenious reporter. It was however, of so little importance that it was quite forgotten . . . had not the judge advocate seized on it as good evidence before a military commission. Had he been practicing in a court of justice he might have found it difficult to get such matter before the jury. He would have needed a witness to the fact of the confession at least, and it might have been questioned whether it was not also necessary that it should have some relevance to the guilt of the accused."[24]

The *Journal of Commerce* included a court transcript of a government official being questioned about the confession, when it was used in this other trial. The official admitted that he had not witnessed the confession. To be used as evidence, he would need to verify its accuracy. "The judge advocate failed to call Colonel Burke . . . if he had called him, he would not have verified the pretended confession." Yet it was read into the record.

"And so it appears that the channel by which this 'evidence' first reached the public was Joseph Howard, Jr."

The paper refreshed readers' memories as to the reporter's past. "We never received an apology from any one for the treatment we received, but Joseph Howard., Jr. after a brief incarceration, was promoted to government employment as a reward of his skill in getting two newspaper offices into the hands of the military authorities, and at length turns up, in company with the colonel-commandant at Fort Lafayette, passing the night with a prisoner of state condemned to death; and a few weeks later the result of his night's work, in the hands of Judge-Advocate Holt, becomes testimony for the life or death of others.

"We state the facts for history."

Two years later, Howard would give a speech to the Young Men's Society for Ethical Culture: "The reporter he deemed the all-important element of a good newspaper, and to be a good reporter the four required qualities were: Good address, a knowledge of human nature, industry, and loyalty. The power of the press and its opportunity are greater to-day, he thought, than ever in directing public opinion and bringing relief to the wronged and oppressed."[25]

He did not list honesty or integrity as required qualities. In the years to come, Howard did demonstrate loyalty. The usually chatty man never confessed who had leaked him the announcement of the upcoming draft.

In the later part of October 1864, the *Sunday Mercury* boldly reported that Mrs. Lincoln's debts—word of which had crept into the newspapers during the Watt investigation—were being settled. Newspapers had commented in the past about her spending and shopping habits, but this exposed her far more. "The numerous creditors of Mr. Lincoln, Mrs. Lincoln, and the little Lincolns were both astonished and gladdened last week by a notification that their bills would be cashed if presented at the desk of Messrs. A.T. Stewart & Co.

"These bills amounted in gross to almost twenty thousand dollars, and have been standing since the beginning of Uncle Abe's term of office. They were commonly regarded as bad debts, and might have remained uncanceled forever had not the SUNDAY MERCURY made a hint to that effect. Some of the creditors had sold out the bills at a heavy discount, all had piled them away lugubriously.

"The notification was served by a special agent, who came to New York for the purpose. About twelve thousand dollars, it is said, was paid up on

Wednesday and Thursday, including every variety of liability—gloves, cloth-ing, etc., etc. A bill from a ready-made clothing-house for a hundred and twenty odd dollars covered Old Abe's good suit, worn out some time ago.

"The promptness with which these bills have been cashed since the ap-pearance of an intimation in these columns, shows advertisers the force and content of our circulation. All the Lincolns read the SUNDAY MERCURY, the President's lady is particularly partial to it, and her custom is worth something—if one has mind to wait four years for liquidation."[26]

Proving that indeed, she paid particular attention to the lively *Sunday Mer-cury*, that very day, Mary Todd wrote to Wakeman, the ally and confidant she had met on her trip to New York in late April and to whom she had delivered her husband's approval on the government post he sought. He knew the inner workings of her debts and her efforts to secretly pay them:

> My dear Mr. Wakeman—
> I have been much amused in looking over the *Sunday Mercury* to
> see that some kind Merchant, has been so generous towards us!

She was clearly referring to A. T. Stewart, mentioned in the article, the one whom she had owed the better part of $27,000 in April and whom she had promised to pay in full in June, after some kind of windfall.

> When will their vile fabrications cease: Not until they find Mr L re-
> elected. This is the reason, that makes their falsehoods so desperate!
> Please say *not a word*, to *anyone* not even W[eed] about the 5th Avenue
> business. I write in *great* haste—
> Your friend
> M.L.

Mary Todd Lincoln had traveled to New York on June 19, on unnamed business, and checked into the Fifth Avenue Hotel.

Years later, Howard would write about Stewart: "In private life he was not particularly esteemed. He was selfish and avaricious and thoughtless."[27] If Howard had tried to help Mary Todd Lincoln out of her debts to Stewart, he would have seen this firsthand.

After her husband was assassinated in April 1865, just under eleven months after the bogus proclamation, Mary Todd Lincoln met with her sister Elizabeth. Even then, Mary Todd was haunted by a conversation she and her husband had had in the spring of 1864. Anxious and miserable about her debts, she had hoped and prayed that he would be reelected so that he would never know her financial distress. "I could have gone down on my knees," she told her sister, "and asked for votes for him."

She told her sister that her husband had tried to calm her. "Mary," he scolded her, "I am afraid you will be punished for this overwhelming anxiety. If I am to be elected it will be all right, if not you must bear the disappointment."[28]

A believer in mystics and omens, Mary Todd felt power in his words about punishment. Perhaps his assassination had been that punishment he had referred to from the Fates or from on high, for her blistering anxiety— which she had revealed was caused by her mounting unpaid bills.

If Mary Todd passed the information in the bogus proclamation to Howard, as Sunset Cox suggested to Manton Marble, how would she have done so? More than once, Mary Todd had been suspected of moving information out of the White House to the press or to the enemy. Stoddard, charged among other duties with opening her mail, later countered claims that Mary Todd passed secrets to the Confederates with jokes about the method: "The mails are not a channel for treachery, since every letter to Mrs. Lincoln is opened and read upstairs. The telegraphic wires are under War Office censorship, of a peculiarly rigid kind, and there is no private wire to the White House. The servants, downstairs, are known to be intensely loyal, and would neither carry nor bring a communication of the Arnold-Andre kind. There is, therefore, but one entirely reasonable solution of the problem of how Mr. Jefferson Davis, or his next of kin, can receive army plans from Mrs. Lincoln, after she has obtained them . . . The Confederate spies work their way through the lines easily enough, fort after fort, till they reach the Potomac down yonder.[29]

"The Long Bridge is closed to them, and so is the Georgetown Bridge, but they cross at night in rowboats, or by swimming, and they come up through the grounds, like so many ghosts, and they put a ladder up to this window, and Mrs. Lincoln hands them out the plans.

"Where do they get the ladder?

"Well, now, you tell, if you know. They may borrow it of Jacob. But there is no other way for the alleged treasonable communication to be carried on."

For all the joking, in actuality, Mary Todd had multiple ways of getting information out secretly. After all, she had racked up massive debts without her husband knowing, a practice that she carried on by sending various aides and household helpers on missions to pick up goods and negotiate. In 1865, she sent messages in her own handwriting to various merchants and brokers, signing off as "Mary Ann Cuthbert." There is no reason to believe that such practices began that year.

And she had identified people perfectly capable of helping her. For all his teasing, Stoddard, the man who opened her mail, showed expertise at sneaking information out. Years later, he admitted he played the gold market based on information he received from within the White House and was unashamed of the fact. "Speculation in stocks and gold, especially the latter, was all the while running insanely wild in New York and other financial centers," he remembered of those Civil War years, "and I formed an idea that it was almost true patriotism to be what was called a 'bear' in gold.[30] I therefore went in, a little at first and then deeper. I had good correspondents, was not by any means a bad judge of the changing situations and their effects upon the markets. On the whole I succeeded pretty well, rarely making any important losses, except in stocks," meaning he profited on gold trading. "I had not the least idea that there was anything wrong in it for a fellow in my position, and made no secret whatever of my transactions . . .

"But about my speculations. Strange as it may seem, there were those who did not like me. Many of them. I was too positive to be popular."

He recalled, "One of these parties took it into his head that he could give me a dig over the shoulders of Wall Street.[31] He even took the trouble to attend a Red Room reception and at an hour when I was not within hearing he made a singular addition to his other compliments to Mrs. Lincoln.

"'Madam,' he smilingly said to her. 'I have to congratulate you. I am told that your favorite secretary has made a half million of dollars in his gold speculations. What do you think of that?'

"'Has he, indeed?' she responded, 'I wish he may make a million!'

"She told me about it herself, next morning, and I am inclined to think that the wily party heard something else. His real purpose was only too thinly concealed by his polite grin.

"The fact was that all sorts of men were dipping into the great gambling river of Wall Street. My own dippings were made alongside with those of senators and statesmen, not one of whom thought of concealment or supposed that he was doing anything which his position forbade him to do. We were all under the excitement of a tremendous fever to which none of us had ever before been subjected."

Stoddard organized the Fourth of July parade in 1864, intending to choreograph the most joyous and memorable celebration yet. He succeeded. Just before the parade, he decided to go short on gold. July 5 happened to be the first day the Gold Room opened after Chase's Gold Bill was repealed. "The best of it all was that good news from Gettysburg and Vicksburg came tumbling in upon that celebration, to make it cheerful," wrote Stoddard, "and that the price of gold was tumbling at a rate that made my dinner bill of small account."

He claimed that "there was no manner of secrecy about my varied speculations. President Lincoln laughed at them."[32] But perhaps Lincoln did care. By July 8, four days after Stoddard's grand achievement for the government and his windfall for himself, he was in New York, dropping a note at Manton Marble's office: "Dear Old Copperhead, I have called to see you on my way to a new field of duty. I am going as heretofore to do my utmost for Uncle Sam and Abraham Lincoln . . . Yours in all but politics, W. O. Stoddard, U.S. Marshal of Arkansas."

As Stoddard said later, he had to get away from "enemies" jealous of his successes.

Will Prime continued with the *Journal of Commerce* for many years, but lost his Mary eight years after the proclamation's publication. As her health failed, he carried her up the stairs to her bedroom daily. There she stared at the ceiling and understood his devotion, as he had etched her initials on all four corners of the room. After she died, he never married again.

Back in 1864, he had written to her:

> I have taken all your letters out & arranged them in order & read them over and I am going to have them bound in one solid book to be a precious memorial for myself while I live & for historic times when the story of our love can be the property of others. For time & death make our love no longer the possession of ourselves only, but even our most secret emotions pass into the world's history and become valuable in the great sum of the story of men & nations.[33]

At least two distinctive versions of the Civil War unfolded over the years: one full with horror, and another for those who lived in a mostly glittery society, far from the frontlines. Hundreds of thousands of men lost their lives in battle, struggled to survive as wounded, or were never heard from again. Slaves whose survival and freedom lay at stake were beaten and hunted. Reporters perished sending their view of the carnage home. The black men lynched during the draft riots hung from the lamp posts of New York City. And Lincoln, after all his cares, fell dead to the assassin's bullet at fifty-six years of age.

On the other side of the war, the gold gamblers gamed with the financial markets, wreaking misery on the working class. The rich nursed their addiction to extravagant, imported luxuries. It would be a false mourning to suggest that once upon a time Americans shared their deep woes with great sobriety and heart.

Wrote a journalist, under the penname Old Knickerbocker, in 1864:

"The war has lost its novelty; it is no longer a sensation, and the public mind runs upon trifles. People hardly give a second thought to a battle, but talk continuously about a new play. They care very little about the Message of either President Lincoln or President Davis. The late advance and retreat of the army of the Potomac neither raised enthusiasm nor caused disappointment . . . The sinking of a gunboat in Charleston harbor is a far less interesting topic of conversation than skating in the Central Park, and the capture of the Chesapeake by rebel pirates than the high price of diamonds, both black and Brazilian.

"The progress of the war is most attentively watched by those who have a pecuniary interest at stake, particularly stock and gold speculators, whose motives are purely selfish, and who would sell their country for profit . . .

"The hundreds of thousands of brave men who lie in premature graves on the nation's battle-fields are all but forgotten . . . National tragedies, unlike domestic griefs, come home to none of us. The incubus of a debt of a few hundred or thousand millions, more or less, is a matter which gives the public mind no trouble whatever.

"Meanwhile we display our freedom from care by crowding theaters, concert-halls, opera-houses, and drawing rooms, and spending our money as freely as we make it easily. And the huge hotels have their carnival, for the country seems emptying itself into the large cities, and the cry is 'still they come.' House and hotel accommodation is quite inadequate to the demand in all the great centres, especially New-York and Washington, and the tendency at all points is towards centralization.

"What will happen to us next, and how all this will end, the old Knick-erbocker, having due regard for his reputation as a seer, will not venture to prophesy. But while the sun shines, let those make hay who can. There is a dark cloud yonder."[34]

Acknowledgments

F irst, I thank Leigh Newman, the superb writer who is also a true writer's editor. I was honored that my work became the focus of her rapid-fire genius, and I have been thrilled to be in her care. My brilliant, kind agent, Anna Stein, at ICM is always the perfect counselor for my work.

Friends and family read the book in part or in full at key stages and I deeply appreciate the value of their time and insights: Ted Widmer, Will Blythe, Natalie Standiford, René Steinke, Chris Mitchell, and Alphonsus Mitchell.

As always, I marvel at the support and generosity of the world's archivists. Many assisted in large or small ways, but I particularly want to acknowledge AnnaLee Pauls and Charles Doran in the Special Collections at the Princeton University Archives; Bruce Kirby at the Library of Congress in

Washington, D.C.; Paul Harrison at the National Archives in Washington, D.C.; Tal Nadan at the New York Public Library, Manuscript Division; Ellen Keith at the Chicago History Museum Research Centre; Christopher Schnell at the Abraham Lincoln Presidential Library; Melinda Wellington at the University of Rochester Library; Krista Gray at the Illinois History and Lincoln Collections at the University of Illinois at Urbana-Champaign; Carrie Evans at the Wadsworth Atheneum Museum of Art in Connecticut; and Dennis Vetrovec in the Special Collection – Rare Books and Manuscripts, at the Cunningham Memorial Library, Indiana State University.

I also worked in or benefited from the use of the Columbia University Manuscripts Division; the Huntington Library, San Marino, California; and the New York Historical Society, Museum & Library. A deep thanks goes to my home borough Brooklyn Public Library and my beloved Leonard Branch.

As always I am grateful to Tom Tryniski for creating fultonhistory.com, an invaluable digital resource for historical newspaper research, rivaling even the Library of Congress's formidable records. He is a hero of our time for offering this free to the public.

My respect and thanks go too to all the Lincoln scholars whose work helped me better understand this Lincoln story. Many historians are listed in the endnotes, but in particular, I found the scholarship of Michael Burlingame, Harold Holzer, and Daniel Michael Epstein invaluable. So many riveting writers of the past are featured in this book, and I marvel at the initiative of Alice Barry, who took the letters of her grandaunt and granduncle that she found in a trunk and created a historical work that made the era seem so recognizable. I also thank all those anonymous talents in the newspapers of the past, whose vivid writing puts us back on those streets, in those prisons, in those newsrooms, or in Lincoln's White House.

In the production of this book, Rosemarie Ho enthusiastically helped fact-check, and Reid Sharpless and Robb Hill dug through historical records in the early stages. Ceridwen Morris contributed her significant photographic talents to my author photo. My gratitude goes to all of them.

This book has greatly benefited from the mighty talents of the team at Counterpoint: Alisha Gorder, Megan Fishmann, Lena Moses-Schmit, Katie Boland, Jordan Koluch, Donna Cheng, Yukiko Tominaga, Abbie Amadio, and Jack Shoemaker.

I also am thankful to my friends and family over the time that I have been writing this book, particularly Deb and Max Stone, Craig Lively, Ashley Prine, Andy Collins, Darren Tuozzoli, Joe Angio, Suzanne Mitchell, Diane von Furstenberg, Connie Walsh, Darcey Steinke, Michael Hudson, Rachel Mickenberg, Kenneth Krauss, Benjamin Puff, RoseMarie Terenzio, Douglas Brinkley, Carl Sferrazza Anthony, Lisa DePaulo, David Greenhouse, David Brendel, Richard Howorth, Sam Mitchell, Ed Mitchell, Lisa Govan, and Ann McGuire. Ada Calhoun has been a strong ally, from the development stages onward. She and the other founding Sob Sisters, Karen Abbott and Susannah Cahalan, went out of their way to assist this nonfiction female writer.

I thank Susannah Hunnewell Weiss, who read all of my previous books before publication, and whose courage and heart instructed this past year and all years to come.

Finally, I am grateful to Lucy and Gigi, who not only contributed their unique and specific talents to the creation of this book, but who allow me to be the daily eyewitness to their greatness.

Notes

1. The Bombshell

1. John S. C. Abbott, *The History of the Civil War in America*, vol. 2 (New York: Henry Bill, 1866), p. 492.
2. Charles A. Dana, *Recollections of the Civil War* (Lincoln: University of Nebraska Press, 1996), originally published by D. Appleton and Company (New York, 1898), p. 197.
3. Ibid., p. 199.
4. Original copy of bogus proclamation in manifold, May 17, 1864, Abraham Lincoln papers, Chicago History Museum, Chicago, Illinois.
5. Frank Moore, ed., *The Rebellion Record: A Diary of American Events*, vol. 11 (New York: D. Van Nostrand, 1868), p. 473.
6. "The Forged Proclamation," *New York Times*, May 19, 1864, col. 1, p. 8.

2. A Laughing Stock

1. "The Montgomery Convention," *New York Times*, February 12, 1861, col. 4, p. 1.

2. "The Montgomery Correction," *New York Times*, February 5, 1861, col. 3, p. 1.

3. Deschler Welch, ed., *The Theatre*, vol. 2 (New York: Theatre Publishing Company, 1887), p. 345.

4. William H. Herndon and Jesse W. Weik, *Abraham Lincoln*, vol. 2 (New York: D. Appleton & Company, 1909), quoting W. M. Dickinson, *Harper's Magazine*, June 1884, p. 159.

5. "A Turkish Journal on Abraham Lincoln's Election," *Cincinnati Daily Press*, February 2, 1861, col. 5, p. 1.

6. "The Rationale of the Enthusiasm of Mr. Lincoln's Reception," *Cincinnati Daily Press*, February 13, 1861, col. 1, p. 2.

7. [Joseph] Howard [Jr.], "The Presidential Progress," *New York Times*, February 18, 1861, col. 3, p. 2.

8. Roy P. Basler, ed., *The Collected Works of Abraham Lincoln*, vol. 4 (Brunswick, NJ: Rutgers University Press, 1953), p. 190.

9. Matthew Hale Smith, *Sunshine and Shadow in New York* (Hartford, CT: J. B. Burr & Company, 1868), p. 636.

10. [no title] *Cincinnati Daily Press*, February 13, 1861, col. 1, p. 2.

11. [Joseph] Howard [Jr.], "The Presidential Progress," *New York Times*, February 18, 1861, col. 3, p. 2.

12. "Jersey City," *New York Times*, September 3, 1860, col. 6, p. 1.

13. [Joseph] Howard [Jr.], "The New England Strikes," *New York Times*, March 21, 1860, col. 1, p. 2.

14. [Joseph] Howard [Jr.], "The Bay Strike," *New York Times*, February 29, 1860, col. 1, p. 8.

15. [Joseph] Howard, [Jr.], "The New England Strikes," *New York Times*, March 21, 1860, col. 1, p. 2.

16. Noyes L. Thomson, *The History of Plymouth Church* (New York: G. W. Carleton & Co., 1873), quoting the *World* editorial, p. 18.

17. Henry Villard, *Memoirs of Henry Villard*, vol. 1, 1835–1862 (Boston: Houghton, Mifflin and Company, 1904), p. 152.

18. Harold Holzer, *Lincoln and the Power of the Press* (New York: Simon & Schuster, 2014), p. 251.

19. John Hay, *Lincoln's Journalist: John Hay's Anonymous Writings for the Press, 1860–1864*, ed. Michael Burlingame (Carbondale: Southern Illinois University Press, 1998), p. 25.

20. Abraham Lincoln, *Collected Works of Abraham Lincoln*, vol. 1, letter printed in the *Sangamo Journal*, September 2, 1842 (Ann Arbor: University of Michigan Digital Library Production Services, 2001).

21. Lincoln, *Collected Works of Abraham Lincoln*, vol. 1, "The 'Rebecca' Letter," August 27, 1842.

22. Holzer, *Lincoln and the Power*, p. 48.

23. Lincoln, *Collected Works of Abraham Lincoln*, vol. 1, annotation 2, letter from Jas. Shield to Abraham Lincoln, September 17, 1842.

24. "A Story of Mr. Lincoln's Duel," *New York Times*, July 8, 1867, p. 8.

25. Emanuel Hertz, "The Lincoln That His Hometown Knew," *New York Times Magazine*, June 14, 1931, p. 4.

26. Holzer, *Lincoln and the Power*, p. 188.

27. Carl Sandburg, *Abraham Lincoln: The Prairie Years and the War Years* (New York: Harcourt, Brace and Company, 1954), p. 124.

28. Lincoln, *Collected Works of Abraham Lincoln*, vol. 3, "Contract with Theodore Canissius," May [30?], 1859 (Ann Arbor: University of Michigan Digital Library Production Services, 2001).

29. Holzer, *Lincoln and the Power*, p. 191.

30. Hay, *Lincoln's Journalist*, p. 21.

31. "Attempts on the Life of Mr. Lincoln," *The World* (New York, NY), February 27, 1861, picking up a story in the *Syracuse Journal* of the previous Saturday, col. 4.

32. Mrs. E. F. Ellet, *The Court Circles of the Republic, or the Beauties and Celebrities of the Nation* (Hartford, CT: Hartford Publishing Company, 1869), p. 506.

33. [Joseph] Howard [Jr.], "The Presidential Progress," *New York Times*, February 25, 1861, col. 2, p. 8.

34. Ibid.

35. "Abraham Lincoln: Joe Howard Confesses That He Fabricated the Scotch Cap and Military Cloak Story," *Chicago Daily Tribune*, September 30, 1884, col. 4, p. 9.

36. Joseph Howard Jr., "Howard's Column," *The Press* (New York, NY), February 28, 1889, col. 3, p. 1.

37. "Abraham Lincoln: Joe Howard Confesses."

38. Franklin, "Columbus Correspondence," letter to the editor, *Cincinnati Daily Enquirer*, February 26, 1861, p. 2.

39. [Joseph] Howard [Jr.], "The Incoming Administration," *New York Times*, February 26, 1861, col. 1, p. 8.

40. "Here and There," *Gettysburg Times* (Gettysburg, PA), December 11, 1956, col. 6, p. 10.

41. "Questions for Lincoln's Cabinet," *Dallas Herald* (Dallas, TX), March 27, 1861, col. 1, p. 1.

42. "Abraham in Washington: A Relic," *Anderson Intelligencer* (Anderson Court House, SC), March 7, 1861, col. 1, p. 2.

43. "Mr. Lincoln's Flight by Moonlight Alone," *Brooklyn Daily Eagle*, February 25, 1861, col. 1, p. 2.

44. "The New President of the United States: From a Fugitive Sketch," *Vanity Fair*, March 9, 1861, p. 114.

45. "Mr. Lincoln's Flight," *Vanity Fair*, March 2, 1861, p. 102.

46. Ward Hill Lamon, *Recollections of Abraham Lincoln, 1847–1865* (Chicago: A. C. McClurg and Company, 1895), p. 261.

47. "More Speeches," *Salem Weekly Advocate* (Salem, IL), February 28, 1861, col. 1, p. 2.

48. [Joseph] Howard [Jr.], "The Incoming Administration," *New York Times*, February 27, 1861, col. 5, p. 1.

3. The Crime

1. Matthew Hale Smith, *Twenty Years Among the Bulls and Bears of Wall Street* (Hartford, CT: J. B. Burr & Company, 1871), p. 445.

2. William E. Gienapp and Erica L. Gienapp, eds., *The Civil War Diary of Gideon Welles, Lincoln's Secretary of the Navy: The Original Manuscript Edition* (Champaign: University of Illinois Press, 2014), p. 331.

3. Louis M. Starr, *Bohemian Brigade: Civil War Newsmen in Action* (New York: Alfred A. Knopf, 1954), p. 310–11.

4. Francis Bicknell Carpenter, *The Inner Life of Abraham Lincoln: Six Months at the White House* (New York: Hurd and Houghton, 1868), p. 38.

5. Ibid.

6. Leaf 146, mssEC 27, Thomas T. Eckert papers, 1861–1877, vol. 2, Telegrams Received by Maj. Eckert, May 12, 1864, to June 10, 1864, tel 165, Huntington Library, San Marino, California.

7. "The Telegraph and the Presidency," *New York Times*, September 9, 1859, col. 3, p. 4.

8. Leaf 146, mssEC 27, Thomas T. Eckert papers, 1861–1877, vol. 2, Telegrams Received by Maj. Eckert, May 12, 1864, to June 10, 1864, tel 165, Huntington Library, San Marino, California.

9. Alice Scoville Barry, *Why Did President Lincoln Suppress the Journal of Commerce?* (New York: Twin Coast Newspapers, Inc., 1979), p. 3. The account was first printed in the *Journal of Commerce* and was created through family letters Barry found in a trunk. Letter from Will Prime to Mary Prime, May 16, 1864.

10. "The Peace Party," *New York Times*, February 8, 1863, col. 4, p. 1.

11. George T. McJimsey, *Genteel Partisan: Manton Marble, 1834–1917* (Ames: Iowa State University Press, 1971), p. 25.

12. Sister Mary Cortona Phelan, *Manton Marble of the New York World* (Washington, D.C.: The Catholic University of America Press, 1957), p. 27.

13. "Post Office Espionage," picked up from the *New York World*; *Daily State Sentinel* (Indianapolis, IN), July 28, 1864, col. 3, p. 2.

14. Abraham Lincoln, *Collected Works of Abraham Lincoln*, vol. 4, p. 431.

15. "Important from Washington," *New York Times*, August 9, 1862, p. 1.

16. Phelan, p. 31.

17. Thirty-Seventh Congress, Sess. III, ch. 81, 1863, p. 755.

18. S. C. Gwynne, *Hymns of the Republic: The Story of the Final Year of the American Civil War* (New York: Simon & Schuster, 2019), p. 168.

19. McJimsey, p. 48.

20. Phelan, p. 31.

21. Barry, *Why Did President Lincoln Suppress the Journal of Commerce?*, p. 2. Letter from Will Prime to Mary Prime, May 12, 1864.

22. "General McClellan's Report," *New York Times*, February 27, 1864, col. 2, p. 6.

23. Barry, p. 3. Letter from Mary Prime to Will Prime, May 17, 1864.

24. Lincoln, *Collected Works of Abraham Lincoln*, vol. 7, p. 349.

25. David Homer Bates, *Lincoln in the Telegraph Office: Recollections of the United States Military Telegraph Corps During the Civil War* (New York: Century Company, 1907), p. 135.

26. Matthew Hale Smith, *Sunshine and Shadow in New York* (Hartford, CT: J. B. Burr & Company, 1868), p. 419.

27. *American Society for Promoting National Unity* (New York: John F. Trow, Printer, 1861), p. 4.

28. "One of the Biggest Hoaxes," *Rome Daily Sentinel* (Rome, NY), Friday evening, December 13, 1907, col. 5, p. 2.

29. Smith, *Sunshine and Shadow*, p. 417.

30. Ibid.

31. "The Telegraph Lines Taken Possession of by the Government," *New York Times*, February 26, 1862, p. 6.

32. Bates, *Lincoln and the Telegraph*, p. 108.

33. Ibid., p. 118.

34. Helen Nicolay, *Lincoln's Secretary: A Biography of John G. Nicolay* (New York: Longmans, Green and Co., 1949), p. 121.

35. Benjamin Brown French, *Witness to the Young Republic* (Hanover, NH: University Press of New England, 1989), diary entry of July 20, 1861, p. 365.

36. Bates, *Lincoln and the Telegraph*, p. 138–141.

37. Allen Thorndike Rice, ed., *Reminiscences of Abraham Lincoln by Distinguished Men of His Time* (New York: J. J. Little & Co., 1886), p. 231.

38. Bates, *Lincoln and the Telegraph*, p. 41.

39. Lincoln, *Collected Works of Abraham Lincoln*, vol. 5, "To George B. McClellan," June 28, 1862, p. 291.

40. "Life On Board an Atlantic Steamship," *Brooklyn Daily Eagle*, October 12, 1865, col. 1, p. 4.

4. A Hot Day on Wall Street

1. "A Pestilence Threatened," *New York Herald,* May 19, 1864, col. 3, p. 4.

2. Louise A. Godey and Sarah J. Hale, as Alice B. Haven, "A Morning at Stewart's," *Godey's Ladies Book* (Philadelphia: L.A. Godey, 1863), vols. 66–67, p. 429–433.

3. James K. Medbery, *Men and Mysteries of Wall Street* (New York: R. Worthington, 1878), p. 247.

4. "Madame Abe Lincoln about to Change the Programme," *Daily Post* (Pittsburgh, PA), February 3, 1864, p. 2.

5. "The Poor and Our Charities," *New York Times*, January 8, 1864, p. 4.

6. James Miller, *Miller's New York As It Is, or Stranger's Guide-book to the Cities of New York, Brooklyn and Adjacent Places* (New York: James Miller, 1867), p. 60.

7. David B. Sachsman, S. Kittrell Rushing, and Roy Morris Jr., eds., *Words at

War: The Civil War and American Journalism (West Lafayette, IN: Purdue University Press, 2008), p. 204.

8. Elwin Burns Robinson, "The Press: President Lincoln's Philadelphia Organ," *The Pennsylvania Magazine of History and Biography* 65, no. 2 (April 1941), p. 160.

9. Michael Burlingame, ed., *Dispatches from Lincoln's White House: The Anonymous Civil War Journalism of Presidential Secretary William O. Stoddard* (Lincoln: University of Nebraska Press, 2002), p. xi.

10. Ibid., p. 74.

11. Louis M. Starr, *Bohemian Brigade: Civil War Newsmen in Action* (New York: Alfred A. Knopf, 1954), p. 353.

12. Matthew Hale Smith, *Sunshine and Shadow in New York* (Hartford, CT: J. B. Burr & Company, 1868), p. 44.

13. "Another Campaign Document," *New York Herald*, March 23, 1864, col. 5, p. 4.

14. Horace Greeley, "Prayer of Twenty Millions," *New-York Tribune*, August 20, 1862.

15. James Roberts Gilmore, *Personal Recollections of Abraham Lincoln and the Civil War* (Boston: L. C. Page & Company, 1898), p. 84.

16. "The Newspaper Press of America," *Temple Bar* (London), January 1863, p. 196.

17. Ibid., p. 192–193.

18. George T. McJimsey, *Genteel Partisan: Manton Marble, 1834–1917* (Ames: Iowa State University Press, 1971), p. 39.

19. Sister Mary Cortona Phelan, *Manton Marble of the New York World* (Washington, D.C.: Catholic University of America Press, 1957), p. 8; from a letter between Samuel L. Barlow and Marble, June 15, 1868.

20. Ibid., p. 24.

21. "A Millennium for Editors," *The Round Table* 4, no. 60 (October 27, 1866), col. 2, p. 206.

22. Ibid.

23. William Worthington Fowler, *Ten Years in Wall Street: Or, Revelations of Inside Life and Experience on 'Change* (Hartford, CT: Worthington, Dustin & Co., 1870), p. 46; Miller, *Miller's New York*, p. 24.

24. "Pickpockets in Wall Street," *New York Herald*, May 20, 1864, col. 3, p. 4.

25. William Worthington Fowler, *Inside Life in Wall Street, Or, How Great*

Fortunes Were Lost and Won (Hartford, CT: Dustin, Gilman & Company, 1873), p. 90.

26. "News of the Day," *New York Times*, April 29, 1864, col. 1, p. 4.
27. "Miscellaneous News," *New York Herald*, May 19, 1864, p. 4, col. 2.
28. Smith, *Sunshine and Shadow*, p. 44.
29. Ibid.
30. Medbery, *Men and Mysteries*, p. 244.
31. "Miscellaneous News," *New York Herald*, May 19, 1864, col. 2, p. 4.
32. Ibid.
33. Alice Scoville Barry, *Why Did President Lincoln Suppress the Journal of Commerce?* (New York: Twin Coast Newspapers, Inc., 1979), p. 22.
34. "A Daring Forgery," *New York Daily Tribune*, May 19, 1864, p. 1.
35. Frederic Hudson, *Journalism in the United States: From 1690–1872* (New York: Harper & Brothers Publishers, 1873), p. 375.
36. Don E. Fehrenbacher and Virginia Fehrenbacher, eds., *Recollected Words of Abraham Lincoln* (Stanford, CA: Stanford University Press, 1996), p. 161.
37. [Howard], "Affairs on the Upper Potomac," *New York Times*, October 29, 1861, p. 4.
38. Howard, "From General Stone's Division," *New York Times*, October 29, 1861, p. 5.
39. "The President at West Point," *New York Times*, June 26, 1862, p. 8.

      This article cross-references an account of Howard hearing the joke mentioned in the article, about the shark with the harpoon. Starr, *Bohemian Brigade*, p. 156:

      > But when Lincoln went up to West Point to confer with General Scott on June 24, 1862, a World man reported that "Mr. Lincoln was especially cordial in allowing reporters to proceed with him, remarking that he was not as afraid of reporters as some people are, and illustrating the fact by telling an appropriate and pertinent story." Joseph Howard Jr., the *Times* man present, said the story was "about a shark who swallowed a red-hot harpoon," but none of them reported it.

40. "The Late Gen. Kearny," *New York Times*, October 5, 1862, col. 3, p. 5.
41. "The Mob in New-York," *New York Times*, July 14, 1864, col. 4, p. 1.
42. "The Riot Renewed," *New York Daily News*, July 15, 1863, col. 4, p. 1–2.

43. "A Genuine Loyal Leaguer," *Daily Post* (Pittsburgh, PA), May 26, 1864, col. 1, p. 2.

44. "A Quarrel Among the Critics," *Brooklyn Eagle*, June 13, 1863, col. 3, p. 2.

45. "Old New York Journalists," *St. Louis Post-Dispatch*, December 28, 1881, p. 3.

46. "Republican General Committee," *Brooklyn Daily Eagle*, January 6, 1864, col. 5, p. 1.

47. Letter from Joseph Howard Jr. to Manton Marble, May 3, 1864, *Manton Marble papers*, vol. 7. Manuscript/mixed material. Library of Congress, Washington, D.C.

48. "The Howard Hoax," *Sunday Mercury*, May 22, 1864, p. 1.

5. A Warning from Washington

1. Michael Burlingame, *Abraham Lincoln, A Life*, vol. 1 (Baltimore: Johns Hopkins University Press, 2008), p. 183.

2. Michael Burlingame, *Abraham Lincoln: A Life*, vol. 2 (Baltimore: Johns Hopkins University Press, 2008), p. 36.

3. F. B. Carpenter, *Six Months at the White House with Abraham Lincoln* (New York: Hurd and Houghton, 1866), p. 30.

4. David Homer Bates, *Lincoln Stories Told by Him in the Military Office in the War Department During the Civil War* (New York: William Edwin Rudge, Inc., 1926), p. 6.

5. Charles A. Dana, *Recollections of the Civil War* (Lincoln: University of Nebraska Press, 1996), originally published by D. Appleton and Company (New York, 1898), p. 217.

6. Daniel Mark Epstein, *The Lincolns: Portrait of a Marriage*, (New York: Ballentine Books, 2008), p. 415.

7. Elizabeth Keckley, *Behind the Scenes in the Lincoln White House* (Mineola, NY: Dover Publications, Inc., 2006), p. 56.

8. Ibid., p. 55.

9. Ibid.

10. Helen Nicolay, *Lincoln's Secretary: A Biography of John G. Nicolay* (New York: Longmans, Green and Co., 1949), p. 191.

11. "Startling Developments in Prospect from Beau Hickman's Kitchen Committee," *New York Herald*, February 18, 1862, p. 4.

12. "News from Washington," *New York Times*, February 13, 1862, col. 1, p. 8.

13. Ibid.

14. Richard B. Kielbowicz, "The Telegraph, Censorship and Politics at the Outset of the Civil War," *Civil War History* 40, no. 2 (June 1994), p. 116–117.

15. "The Very Latest War News," *The Philadelphia Inquirer*, February 14, 1862, p. 1. The story of Lincoln visiting the Hill originally came from an article by E. J. Edwards recounting an anecdote that Thomas L. James, one-time postmaster general, heard from a member of the Senate committee. Some historians have disputed its accuracy because of technicalities about the titles of the men recounting the story and the "fact" that the committees did not meet in the mornings. But I found this account in the *Inquirer* saying that Lincoln attended a morning session to exonerate his family members on February 14. That would be a week before Willie's death. In other words, the core fact of his attendance at a morning meeting to exonerate his family members during this troubled time has been confirmed, making the further description likely accurate.

16. Joseph Howard Jr., "The Republican Court," *New York Times*, March 11, 1861, p. 1.

17. Louis M. Starr, *Bohemian Brigade: Civil War Newsmen in Action* (New York: Alfred A. Knopf, 1954), p. 107.

18. Justin G. Turner and Linda Levitt Turner, *Mary Todd Lincoln, Her Life and Letters* (New York: Alfred A. Knopf, 1972), p. 111.

19. "Personal Intelligence," *New York Herald* , May 2, 1864, col. 5, p. 4.

20. Elizabeth Keckley, *Behind the Scenes, Or, Thirty Years a Slave and Four Years in the White House* (New York: G. W. Carleton & Co., Publishers, 1868), p. 148–149.

21. Alice Scoville Barry, *Why Did President Lincoln Suppress the Journal of Commerce?* (New York: Twin Coast Newspapers, Inc., 1979), p. 22. Letter from William C. Prime to Mary Turnbull Prime, May 20, 1864.

22. "The Forged Proclamation," *New York Times*, May 19, 1864, col. 1, p. 8.

23. "The Forgery and the Associated Press Agency," *Pittsburgh Commercial*, May 21, 1864, col. 1, p. 2.

24. "The Forged Proclamation," *Brooklyn Daily Eagle*, May 19, 1864, col. 1, p. 2.

25. "The Proclamation Hoax," *The World*, May 24, 1864, p. 6.

26. Abbott A. Abbott, *Life of Abraham Lincoln* (New York: T.R. Dawley, 1864), p. 95.

27. "The Rebel Navy Department," *New York Times*, December 30, 1863, col. 1, p. 2.

28. *Papers Relating to Foreign Affairs, Accompanying the Annual Message of the*

President to the Second Session Thirty-Eighth Congress, Part III (Washington, D.C.: Government Printing Office, 1865), p. 31.

29. The other newspapers were the *New York Daily, Weekly Journal of Commerce, Daily and Weekly News, Daily and Weekly Day Book, The New York Freeman's Journal*, and the *Daily Eagle* and *Weekly Eagle* in Brooklyn.

30. Frederic Hudson, *Journalism in the United States: From 1690–1872* (New York: Harper & Brothers Publishers, 1873), p. 371.

31. Ibid.

32. Ibid., p. 373.

33. Ibid.

34. Harold Holzer, *Lincoln and the Power of the Press* (New York: Simon & Schuster, 2014), p. 367.

35. Allen Thorndike Rice, ed., *Reminiscences of Abraham Lincoln by Distinguished Men of His Time* (North American Publishing Company, 1886), p. 226.

36. Ibid.

37. "The President on Arbitrary Arrests," *New York Times*, June 15, 1863, col. 1, p. 8.

38. Letter from Edwin M. Stanton, United States Military Telegraph, Army of the Potomac to J. C. Kennedy, Superintendent of the Police [in] New York, March 24, 1862, reproduced on the *Journal of Commerce* website.

39. "The Bogus Proclamation in New York," *Pittsburgh Commercial*, Friday, May 20, 1864, p. 2.

40. Leaf 146, mssEC 27, Thomas T. Eckert papers, 1861–1877, vol. 2, Telegrams Received by Maj. Eckert, May 12, 1864, to June 10, 1864, tel 165, Huntington Library, San Marino, California.

41. Leaf 137, mssEC 27, Thomas T. Eckert papers, 1861–1877, vol. 2, Telegrams Received by Maj. Eckert, May 12, 1864, to June 10, 1864, tel 151 and tel 152, Huntington Library, San Marino, California.

42. Barnet Schecter, *The Devil's Own Work* (New York: Walker & Company, 2005), p. 239.

43. Harold Holzer, ed., *Lincoln's White House Secretary: The Adventurous Life of William O. Stoddard* (Carbondale: Southern Illinois University Press, 2007), p. 256.

44. John A. Dix, *A Winter in Madeira and a Summer in Spain and Florence* (New York: William Holdredge, 1851), p. 223.

45. Telegram from January 29, 1861, replicated in David McAdam, et al., *History*

of the Bench and Bar of New York, vol. 1 (New York: New York History Company, 1897), p. 308.

46. "Very Latest from General Grant," *New York Times*, May 16, 1864, p. 1; Frank Abial Flower, *Edwin McMasters Stanton: The Autocrat of Rebellion, Emancipation, and Reconstruction* (Boston: Geo. M. Smith & Co., 1905), p. 214.

47. Ulysses S. Grant, *Personal Memoirs of U. S. Grant* (London: Sampson Low, Marston & Company, 1895), p. 656.

48. "Our Own" Correspondent, "Society in Washington," *Bentley's Miscellany* (London, U.K.) 56 (January 1, 1864), p. 149.

49. Walter Stahr, *Stanton: Lincoln's War Secretary* (New York: Simon & Schuster, 2017), p. 201.

50. Rice, *Reminiscences of Abraham Lincoln*, p. 252.

51. Flower, *Edwin McMasters Stanton*, p. 212.

6. Stop the Presses

1. Frank Moore, ed., *The Rebellion Record: A Diary of American Events*, vol. 11 (New York: D. Van Norstrand, 1868), p. 472.

2. Elizabeth Keckley, *Behind the Scenes in the Lincoln White House* (Mineola, NY: Dover Publications, Inc., 2006), p. 56.

3. "The Bogus Proclamation," *New York Daily News*, May 19, 1864, col. 3, p. 1.

4. Leaf 146, mssEC 27, Thomas T. Eckert papers, 1861–1877, vol. 2, Telegrams Received by Maj. Eckert, May 12, 1864, to June 10, 1864, tel 165, Huntington Library, San Marino, California.

5. *The American Annual Cyclopedia and Register of Important Events of the Year 1864* (New York: D. Appleton & Company, 1865), p. 390.

6. Typed memorandum by Frank A. Flower to accompany an original of the Joseph Howard Proclamation sent to C. F. Gunther, M. S. Chicago Historical Society. [Frank Abial Flower was a journalist and historian working in the 1880s, as well as the first biographer of Edwin Stanton.]

7. Michael Burlingame, *The Inner World of Abraham Lincoln* (Urbana: University of Illinois Press, 1994), p. 159.

8. "Arrest of the Manager and Operators of the Independent Telegraph Company in This City," *Daily National Republican*, Washington, D.C., May 1864, p. 2.; David Homer Bates, *Lincoln in the Telegraph Office: Recollections*

of the United States Military Telegraph Corps During the Civil War (New York: Century Company, 1907), p. 236.

9. "The Bogus Proclamation," *Chicago Tribune*, May 20, 1864, p. 1.

10. Leaf 353, mssEC 27, Thomas T. Eckert papers, 1861–1877, vol. 2, Telegrams Received by Maj. Eckert, May 12, 1864, to June 10, 1864, Huntington Library, San Marino, California.

11. "Miscellaneous News," *New York Herald*, May 19, 1864, col. 2, p. 4.

12. United States Congressional Serial Set, vol. 3965 (Washington, D.C.: U.S. Government Printing Office, 1900), p. 392.

13. "The Forged Proclamation," *New York Times*, May 19, 1864, col. 1, p. 8.

14. "Death of James N. Worl," *Telegraph and Telephone Age*, August 16, 1917, p. 379.

15. David Homer Bates, *Lincoln in the Telegraph Office* (New York: The Century Co., 1907), p. 235.

16. United States Congressional Serial Set, vol. 3965, p. 391.

17. Alice Scoville Barry, *Why Did President Lincoln Suppress the Journal of Commerce?* (New York: Twin Coast Newspapers, Inc., 1979), p. 22. Letter from Mary Prime to Will Prime, Wednesday noon, May 18, 1864.

18. Ibid., p. 6.

19. United States Congressional Serial Set, vol. 3965, p. 388.

20. Ibid.

21. Bates, *Lincoln in the Telegraph Office*, p. 236.

22. United States Congressional Serial Set, vol. 3965, p. 391.

23. Barry, *Why Did President Lincoln Suppress the Journal of Commerce?*, p. 7. Telegram from Will Prime to Mary Prime, morning Wednesday, May 18, 1864; then letter from Will Prime to Mary Prime, Wednesday evening, May 18, 1864.

24. Matthew Hale Smith, *Sunshine and Shadow in New York* (Hartford, CT: J. B. Burr and Company, 1868), p. 165.

25. John A. Marshall, *The American Bastille*, 8th ed. (Philadelphia: Thomas W. Hartley, 1871), p. 517.

26. Ibid.

27. *Memoirs of John Adams Dix*, compiled by his son, Morgan Dix, vol. 2 (New York: Harper & Brothers, 1883), p. 100.

28. United States Congressional Serial Set, vol. 3965, p. 389.

29. Ibid., p. 388.

30. *Memoirs of John Adams Dix*, p. 100.

31. United States Congressional Serial Set, vol. 3965, p. 389.

32. Ibid.

33. Frederic Hudson, *Journalism in the United States: From 1690–1872* (New York: Harper & Brothers Publishers, 1873), p. 376.

34. "A Reminiscence of the Arrest and Incarceration of Five New York Telegraphers, Charged with Conspiracy Against the Government in 1864," *Telegraph Age* (New York: John B. Taltavall, Publisher, 1905), p. 56.

35. Ibid.

36. Bates, *Lincoln in the Telegraph Office*, p. 237.

37. Ibid., p. 57.

38. "The Proclamation Hoax," *The World*, May 20, 1864, p. 12.

39. "The Bogus Proclamation," *New York Daily News*, May 19, 1864.

40. "The Howard Hoax," *Sunday Mercury*, May 22, 1964, p. 1.

41. "The Proclamation Hoax," *The World*, May 24, 1864, p. 6.

42. Ibid.

43. Barry, *Why Did President Lincoln Suppress the Journal of Commerce?*, p. 7.

44. Barry, *Why Did President Lincoln Suppress the Journal of Commerce?*, p. 9. Memorandum written by Will Prime concerning the events of May 19, 1864.

45. From the *Journal of Commerce*, "The Suppression of Our Paper," *The Daily Post* (Pittsburgh, PA), May 28, 1864, col. 5, p. 1.

46. "Local Intelligence: The Arrest of General Dix," *New York Times*, July 4, 1864.

47. United States Congressional Serial Set, vol. 3965, p. 390.

7. The Hunt

1. United States Congressional Serial Set, vol. 3965 (Washington, D.C.: U.S. Government Printing Office, 1900), p. 390.

2. Ibid., p. 391.

3. "A Reminiscence of the Arrest and Incarceration of Five New York Telegraphers, Charged with Conspiracy Against the Government in 1864," *Telegraph Age* (New York: John B. Taltavall, Publisher, 1905), p. 56.

4. "One of the Biggest Hoaxes," *Rome Daily Sentinel* (Rome, NY), Friday evening, December 13, 1907, col. 5, p. 2.

5. "Reminiscences of Fort Lafayette," *New York Times*, July 31, 1864, col. 1, p. 8; "The Political Prisoners," *New York Times*, September 24, 1861, col. 5, p. 1.

6. Alice Scoville Barry, *Why Did President Lincoln Suppress the Journal of Commerce?* (New York: Twin Coast Newspapers, Inc., 1979), p. 22. Will

Prime's written account of the events, composed on Thursday morning, May 19, 1864.

7. From the *Journal of Commerce*, "The Suppression of Our Paper," *Daily Post* (Pittsburgh, PA), May 28, 1864, col. 5, p. 1.

8. "A Card from the Journal of Commerce," *New York Times*, May 19, 1864, col. 2, p. 8.

9. Barry, *Why Did President Lincoln Suppress the Journal of Commerce?*, p. 9. Will Prime's written account of the events.

10. *Journal of Commerce*, "The Suppression of Our Paper."

11. Barry, p. 9.

12. "News of the Day," *New York Daily Tribune*, May 19, 1864, col. 1, p. 4.

13. "The Difficulty Between the National and the State Executive," *Brooklyn Daily Eagle*, July 8, 1864, p. 2.

14. [no title], *New York Daily News*, May 19, 1864, p. 2.

15. "The Proclamation Hoax," *The World*, May 24, 1864, p. 6.

16. "The Howard Hoax," *Sunday Mercury*, May 22, 1864, p. 1.

17. "The Suppression of the 'Journal of Commerce' and 'World' – Very Little Excitement," *Brooklyn Eagle*, May 19, 1864, col. 4, p. 2.

18. Ibid.

19. United States Congressional Serial Set, vol. 3965, p. 393.

20. "An Infamous Forgery," *Chicago Tribune*, May 18, 1864, p. 2.

21. Leaf 159, mssEC 27, Thomas T. Eckert papers, 1861–1877, vol. 2, Telegrams Received by Maj. Eckert, May 12, 1864, to June 10, 1864, telegram from E. Sanford to Major Thomas Eckert, May 19, 1864, Huntington Library, San Marino, California.

22. Matthew Hale Smith, *Sunshine and Shadow in New York* (Hartford, CT: J. B. Burr and Company, 1868), p. 657.

23. "From Washington," *Sunday Mercury*, May 22, 1864, p. 1.

24. "Shall We Have a Free Press?" *Brooklyn Daily Eagle*, May 20, 1864, col. 1, p. 2.

25. "A Military Outrage," *New York Daily News*, May 19, 1864, p. 2.

26. [no title], *Daily Register* (Wheeling, WV), May 21, 1864, col. 1, p. 2.

27. Evan Rowland Jones, *Four Years in the Army of the Potomac: A Soldier's Recollections* (London: Tyne Publishing Company, 1881), p. 118.

28. "Hoaxes on the Newspapers and the People," *New York Herald*, May 22, 1864, p. 5.

29. "Great Astronomical Discoveries," *Nashville Republican*, September 12, 1835, p. 2.

30. "Circular Reported to Be Issued by Jefferson Davis," *Cincinnati Daily Enquirer,* May 16, 1862, p. 3.

31. "A Day of Fasting and Prayer," *Memphis Daily Appeal,* May 16, 1862, p. 2.

32. Louis M. Starr, *Bohemian Brigade: Civil War Newsmen in Action* (New York: Alfred A. Knopf, 1954), p. 240.

33. "Hoaxes of the Newspapers and of the People," *New York Herald,* May 22, 1864, col. 4, p. 4.

34. Barry, *Why Did President Lincoln Suppress the Journal of Commerce?,* p. 21; "A Card from the Journal of Commerce," *New York Times,* May 19, 1864, col. 2, p. 8.

35. "Jeff Davis vs Earl Russell: Curious Diplomatic Correspondence: Is It a Hoax?" *New York Times,* May 8, 1864, col. 3, p. 2.

36. "A Forgery; The Lyons and Davis Correspondence," *New York Times,* May 15, 1864, col. 6, p. 4.

37. "Hoaxes on the Newspapers and the People," *New York Herald,* May 22, 1864, p. 5.

38. "The Bogus Proclamation," *New York Daily News,* May 19, 1864, p. 2.

39. "The Forged Proclamation," *Weekly National Intelligencer* (Washington, D.C.), May 26, 1864, col. 1, p. 1.

40. Smith, *Sunshine and Shadow,* p. 127.

41. "The Case of Gordon," *New York Times,* February 7, 1862, col. 5, p. 1.

42. Barnet Schecter, *The Devil's Own Work* (New York: Walker & Company, 2005), p. 129.

43. "The Forged Proclamation," *New York Times,* May 20, 1864, col. 4, p. 4.

44. Ibid.

45. "Reminiscences of the Forged Proclamation Incident During the Civil War," *The Telegraph Age* (New York, NY), March 16, 1905, p. 117.

46. "The Bogus Proclamation," *Chicago Tribune,* May 21, 1864, p. 1.

47. [no title], *Daily Davenport Democrat* (Davenport, IA), May 21, 1864, col. 2, p. 4.

48. David Homer Bates, *Lincoln in the Telegraph Office: Recollections of the United States Military Telegraph Corps During the Civil War* (New York: Century Company, 1907), p. 242.

49. Leaf 201, mssEC 10, Thomas T. Eckert papers, 1861–1877, United States Military Telegraph, War Department, Received Jan. 5-July 31, 1864, Huntington Library, San Marino, California.

50. "The Howard Hoax," *Sunday Mercury*, May 22, 1864, p. 1.

51. "First of April," *Brooklyn Daily Eagle*, April 1, 1864, col. 2, p. 2.

52. "The Howard Hoax," *Sunday Mercury*, May 22, 1864, p. 1.

53. Barry, *Why Did President Lincoln Suppress the Journal of Commerce?*, p. 15.

54. Ibid., p. 17.

55. "Resumption," *Weekly National Intelligencer* (Washington, D.C.), May 26, 1864, col. 1, p. 2, reprint from the *Journal of Commerce*.

56. From an annotated copy of William C. Prime's *Boat Life in Egypt and Nubia* (1857) in the Mark Twain House, Hartford, Connecticut.

8. Clues and Missteps

1. "The Bogus Proclamation. The Arrest of Mr. Howard," picked up from *The Sun*; *Brooklyn Daily Eagle* (Brooklyn, NY), Saturday, May 21, 1864, col. 3 p. 2.

2. Ibid. The coverage of Howard's arrest by multiple newspapers is compiled in this article. See also "The Bogus Proclamation," *New York Herald*, May 21, 1864, col. 5, p. 4.

3. "The Howard Hoax," *Sunday Mercury*, May 22, 1864, p. 1.

4. Ibid.

5. "The Bogus Proclamation," *Brooklyn Daily Eagle*, p. 2.

6. "The Bogus Proclamation," *Chicago Tribune*, picking up a *New York Times* article of May 21, col. 5, p. 2.

7. Ibid.

8. "The Forged Proclamation – Arrest of the Culprit," *New York Times*, May 21, 1864, col. 6, p. 4.

9. Alice Scoville Barry, *Why Did President Lincoln Suppress the Journal of Commerce?* (New York: Twin Coast Newspapers, Inc., 1979), p. 31.

10. Letter from John A. Dix to Edwin Stanton on arrest of Joseph Howard, May 20, 1864, Abraham Lincoln papers, in folder for May 1864, Chicago History Museum, Chicago, Illinois.

11. United States Congressional Serial Set, vol. 3965 (Washington, D.C.: U.S. Government Printing Office, 1900), p. 395.

12. *Two Months in Fort Lafayette. By a Prisoner.* (New York: Printed for the Author, 1862), p. 52.

13. "The Bogus Proclamation," *New York Herald*, May 23, 1864, p. 5.

14. "An Infamous and Cruel Hoax," *Brooklyn Daily Eagle*, May 18, 1864, col. 1, p. 2.

15. John Hay, *At Lincoln's Side: John Hay's Civil War Correspondence and Selected Writings*, ed. Michael Burlingame (Carbondale: Southern Illinois University Press, 2000), p. 66.

16. Ibid., p. 68.

17. "The Bogus Proclamation," *New York Herald*, May 23, 1864, col. 2, p. 5.

18. Ibid.

19. "The Political Prisoners," *New York Times*, September 24, 1861, col. 5, p. 1.

20. "The Forged Proclamation—Arrest of the Culprit," *Pittsburgh Commercial*, May 23, 1864, p. 2.

21. "The Bogus Proclamation," *Brooklyn Daily Eagle*, May 21, 1864, p. 2.

22. Barry, *Why Did President Lincoln Suppress the Journal of Commerce?*, p. 19.

23. "The Bogus Proclamation," *New York Herald*, p. 5.

24. "Local Intelligence," *New York Times*, May 22, 1864, p. 8.

25. "The Howard Hoax," p. 1.

26. [no title], *New York Daily Tribune*, Saturday, May 21, 1864, col. 2, p. 6.

27. Barry, *Why Did President Lincoln Suppress the Journal of Commerce?*, p. 23. Letter from Will Prime to Mary Prime, May 20, 1864.

28. Barry, *Why Did President Lincoln Suppress the Journal of Commerce?*, p. 25–26.

29. Barry, *Why Did President Lincoln Suppress the Journal of Commerce?*, p. 30.

30. Manton Marble papers; letter from Samuel Sullivan Cox to Manton Marble on May 20, 1864, Library of Congress, Washington, D.C.

9. Shadow Maneuvers

1. "A Reminiscence of the Arrest and Incarceration of Five New York Telegraphers, Charged with Conspiracy Against the Government in 1864," *Telegraph Age* (New York: John B. Taltavall, 1905), p. 57, continued from page 56.

2. "The Newspaper Testimony," *The World*, July 7, 1864, col. 2, p. 3.

3. "The Forged Proclamation," *Weekly National Intelligencer* (Washington, D.C.), May 26, 1864, col. 1, p. 1.

4. Alice Scoville Barry, *Why Did President Lincoln Suppress the Journal of Commerce?* (New York: Twin Coast Newspapers, Inc., 1979), p. 26.

5. Barry, p. 29. Letter from Will Prime to Mary Prime, May 22, 1864.

6. "The Suspended Journals," *New York Times*, May 24, 1864, col. 3, p. 4.

7. Barry, p. 28.

8. "The Bogus Proclamation," *New York Daily Herald*, May 21, 1864, col. 5, p. 4. See also the "The Proclamation Hoax," *The World*, May 23, 1864, p. 1.

9. Manton Marble, "Freedom of the Press Wantonly Violated: Letter of Mr. Marble to President Lincoln" (New York: Reprinted as a pamphlet published by the Society for the Diffusion of Political Knowledge, 1864).

10. "The Suspended Journals," *New York Times*, May 24, 1864, col. 3, p. 4.

11. Ibid.

12. "Local Intelligence: The Prisoners at Fort Lafayette," *New York Times*, January 19, 1864, p. 2.

13. Frederic Hudson, *Journalism in the United States: From 1690–1872* (New York: Harper & Brothers Publishers, 1873), p. 674.

14. Bonnivard, "Letter from Canton," *Memphis Daily Appeal*, June 21, 1864, p. 1.

15. "The Bogus Proclamation and Its Author," *Brooklyn Daily Eagle*, Saturday evening, May 21, 1864, p. 2.

16. Ibid.

17. "The Draft—The Government and the Local Authorities," *Brooklyn Daily Eagle*, Saturday, May 21, 1864, p 2.

18. Roy P. Basler, ed., *The Collected Works of Abraham Lincoln*, vol. 7 (New Brunswick, NJ: Rutgers University Press, 1953), p. 347.

10. Fun Ahead

1. "Arrival of Secretary Chase in the City," *New York Herald*, April 15, 1864, col. 5, p. 1.

2. "The Golden Bear," *New York Times*, April 15, 1864, p. 4.

3. "Condition of the National Treasury," *Philadelphia Inquirer*, January 30, 1861, p. 4.

4. "Public Debt and Private Expenditure: The Peril of the Times," *New York Times*, March 17, 1864, col. 2, p. 4.

5. "Treasury Notes," *Chicago Tribune*, September 14, 1861, p. 2.

6. Kinahan Cornwallis, *The Gold Room and the New York Stock Exchange and Clearing House* (New York: A. S. Barnes & Co., 1879), p. 4.

7. Wesley C. Mitchell, "The Value of the 'Greenbacks' During the Civil War," *The Journal of the Political Economy* (University of Chicago) 6 (March 1898), p. 139.

8. Cornwallis, *The Gold Room*, p. 5–6.

9. Marc M. Reynolds, "Famous American Financiers," The Gold Speculation of

the Sixties, *Moody's Magazine* (New York: A. W. Ferrin) 8 (July–December 1909), p. 113.

10. Ibid, p. 242.

11. "The Surplus Gold in the U.S. Treasury," *Boston Herald*, February 17, 1864, p. 2.

12. "XXVIII Congress – First Session – Senate," *Cincinnati Daily Enquirer*, February 18, 1864, p. 3.

13. "Why Gold," *Detroit Free Press*, March 22, 1864, p. 2.

14. "Public Debt and Private Expenditure," *New York Times*, April 11, 1864, col. 3, p. 4.

15. "Is it Imbecility or Treachery?" *New York Times*, April 16, 1864, col. 2, p. 4.

16. "The Wall Street Gold Speculators," *New York Herald*, col. 3, p. 4.

17. "Latest from the United States: Startling Fluctuation in Gold," *Richmond Enquirer*, taken from *New York Herald*, April 25, 1864, p. 1.

18. "New York Stock Gambling," *Chicago Tribune*, April 18, 1864, col. 3; from *New York Herald*, April 15, 1864.

19. Ibid.

20. "The News," *Chicago Tribune*, April 16, 1864, p. 1.

21. Cornwallis, *The Gold Room*, p. 8.

22. "Panic in Wall Street," *The Sun*, Baltimore, April 20, 1864, p. 1.

23. Marion Mills Miller, ed., *Life and Works of Abraham Lincoln (Centenary Edition)*, vol. 5 (New York: Crescent Literature, 1907), p. 288.

24. Wesley C. Mitchell, "The Value of the 'Greenbacks' During the Civil War," *The Journal of Political Economy*, vol. 6, March 1898 (Chicago: University of Chicago Press), p. 161.

25. "Latest from the United States," *Charleston Mercury* (Charleston, SC), April 25, 1864, p. 1, picked up from *New York Herald* on April 15, 1864.

26. Mitchell, "The Value of Greenbacks During the Civil War," *Journal of Political Economy*, p. 161–162.

27. "The Bogus Proclamation," *Daily National Republican*, May 19, 1864, 2nd ed., col. 4, p. 2.

28. "Life in Fort Lafayette," *New York Times*, May 26, 1864, p. 9.

29. "The Political Prisoners," *New York Times*, September 24, 1861, col. 5, p. 1.

30. "Life in Fort Lafayette," *New York Times*, May 26, 1864, p. 9.

31. "The Bogus Proclamation. The Arrest of Mr. Howard," *Brooklyn Daily Eagle*, Saturday evening, May 21, 1864, p. 2.

32. "Our New York Correspondence," *Philadelphia Inquirer*, May 24, 1864, front page.

33. "The Bogus Proclamation and Its Author," *Brooklyn Daily Eagle*, May 21, 1864, col. 1, p. 2.

34. "The Bogus Proclamation," *New York Herald*, May 21, 1864, col. 5, p. 4.

35. "The Unconstitutional Acts of the Present Government," *The Knickerbocker Monthly; A National Magazine* (New York: Lewis Gaylord Clark) 61, no. 2, p. 157.

36. Edson Baldwin Olds, "Arbitrary arrests: Speech of Hon. Edson B. Olds, for which he was arrested, and his reception speeches on his return from the Bastille." 1863.

37. Frank Key Howard, *Fourteen Months in American Bastiles* (Baltimore: Kelly, Hedian & Piet, 1863), p. 54.

38. "The Suppression of Newspapers," *The Independent*, May 26, 1864; vol. 16, no. 808 (New York, Boston); S. W. Benedict, p. 4.

39. Ibid.

40. Charles A. Dana, *Recollections of the Civil War* (Lincoln: University of Nebraska Press, 1996), originally published by D. Appleton and Company (New York, 1898), pg. 217. Letter to Hon. C. A. Dana from W. T. Sherman, November 10, 1864.

41. Alice Scoville Barry, *Why Did President Lincoln Suppress the Journal of Commerce?* (New York: Twin Coast Newspapers, Inc., 1979), p. 10.

42. Barry, *Why Did President Lincoln Suppress the Journal of Commerce?*, p. 31.

43. Barry, p. 32.

44. *Journal of the Senate of the State of New York at their Eighty-Sixth Session* (Albany, NY: Comstock & Cassidy Printers, 1863), p. 19.

45. Ibid.

46. Letter from Manton Marble to Mr. Cassidy, July [?], 1864, p. 9. Manton Marble papers. Manuscript/mixed material. Library of Congress, Washington, D.C.

47. "The Seizure of the Press," *New York Times*, May 25, 1864, col. 1, p. 5.

48. "City Items: Governor Seymour in the City," *New York Daily Tribune*, May 24, 1864, p. 8.

49. "Seymour's Nonsense," *New York Times*, May 25, 1864, col. 4, p. 4.

50. "Blunderer Again," *Commercial Advertiser* (Oswego, NY), May 31, 1864, reprint of *New York Daily News* quote.

51. "The Bogus Proclamation," *New York Daily News*, May 24, 1864.

52. Ibid.

53. "A Clear Case," *Detroit Free Press*, May 26, 1864, p. 2.

54. "Our New York Correspondence," *Philadelphia Inquirer*, May 30, 1864, front page.

11. A Presidency on Trial

1. "The 'Dead Beat' Redivivus," *Brooklyn Daily Eagle*, May 21, 1864, col. 4, p. 2.
2. William E. Gienapp and Erica L. Gienapp, eds., *The Civil War Diary of Gideon Welles* (Urbana: University of Illinois Press, 2014), entry from May 20, 1864, p. 414.
3. "The Bogus Proclamation," *New York Daily News*, May 23, 1864, front page.
4. Telegram to Major General Dix from Joseph A. Hardie, May 27, 1864; letters received by the Office of the Adjutant General Main Series. Washington, D.C.: National Archives and Records Service, General Services Administration.
5. Lt. Colonel Martin Burke to Captain A. P. Fiske, May 29, 1864; letters received by the Office of the Adjutant General Main Series. Washington, D.C.: National Archives and Records Service, General Services Administration.
6. Abraham Lincoln, *Abraham Lincoln Papers: Series 1. General Correspondence. 1833 to 1916*: Abraham Lincoln to William H. Seward, Saturday, Introduces A. D. Russell, October 26, 1861. Manuscript/mixed material, Library of Congress.
7. "Conflict Between State and Federal Laws," *The Sunday Mercury*, June 16, 1864, p. 2.
8. Collection 452, Ac 4811: 82–84, Wilson Barstow papers, 1861–1864, Illinois History and Lincoln Collections, Illinois Library, Urbana, Illinois; Wilson Barstow letter to sister Elizabeth, June 18, 1864.
9. "News of the Day," *New York Daily Tribune*, June 25, 1864, col. 1, p. 4; "The Arguelles Case in Court," *New York Herald*, June 25, col. 1, p. 6, continued from p. 5.
10. "The Stoppage of the World and Journal of Commerce. Letter from Governor Seymour to District-Attorney Hall, of New-York," *New York Times*, June 29, 1864, col. 3, p. 1.
11. "Editorial Article 2—No Title," *Louisville Daily Journal*, August 31, 1864, p. 2.
12. "Post Office Espionage," reprinted from *The World* and *Daily State Sentinel* (Indianapolis, IN), July 28, 1864, p. 2.
13. Letter from John A. Dix to Edwin Stanton, June 30, 1864, record group 94, Entry 159GG, General's papers, Box 9, Davis-Duffee, U.S. National Archives, Washington, D.C.

14. A. Oakey Hall, "Opening Private Letters," *Cincinnati Daily Enquirer*, July 15, 1864, col. 6, p. 3.

15. "Arrest of General Dix," *New York Herald*, July 2, 1864, p. 8.

16. "Local Intelligence. The Arrest of Gen. Dix," *New York Times*, July 4, 1864, col. 4, p. 2.

17. Ibid.

18. Abraham Lincoln, *Abraham Lincoln papers: Series 1. General Correspondence. 1833 to 1916*: Edwards Pierrepont to Edwin M. Stanton, Sunday, Military Arrests, July 3, 1864. Manuscript/mixed material, Library of Congress, Washington, D.C.

19. Gienapp and Gienapp, *Civil War Diary*, p. 439.

20. Ibid.

21. "Chase and Arbitrary Arrests," picked up from *New-York Tribune*, *The Daily Post*, Pittsburgh, Pennsylvania, June 1, 1864, col. 6, p. 3.

22. "Our New York Correspondence," *Philadelphia Inquirer*, July 7, 1864, col. 3, p. 8.

23. "The Arrest of Gen. Dix," *New York Times*, July 7, 1864, col. 2, p. 8.

24. "Article 36—No Title: To The Public," *The American Annual Cyclopedia and Register of Important Events of the Year (1861–1873)*, vol. 4 (New York: D. Appleton & Company, 1875), p. 390.

25. "Arrest of Gen. Dix," *New-York Daily Tribune*, July 8, 1864, col. 4, p. 7.

26. "The Arrest of Gen. Dix," *New York Herald*, July 7, 1864, col. 2, p. 1.

27. "The Arrest of General Dix," *New York Herald*, July 10, 1864, col. 1, p. 8.

28. "Proclamation for a Day of Humiliation and Prayer," *New York Times*, July 8, 1864, col. 1, p. 8.

29. A. Oakey Hall, "Mr. Justice Story, with Some Reminiscent Reflections," *International Monthly Magazine of Literature, Science and Art (1850–1852)*, February 1 (New York: Stringer & Townsend, 1852), p. 17.

30. Manton Marble, "Freedom of the press wantonly violated: letter of Mr. Marble to President Lincoln" (New York: Reprinted as a pamphlet published by the Society for the Diffusion of Political Knowledge, 1864).

31. "The Suppression of New York Newspapers," *Pittsburgh Commercial*, July 9, 1864, col. 3, p. 1.

32. Multiple sources were used to describe the proceedings, but most helpful were "The Newspaper Suppressions," *New York Times*, July 10, 1864, col. 3,

p. 8, and *The American Annual Cyclopedia and Register of Important Events of the Year 1864* (New York: D. Appleton & Company, 1865), p. 391.

33. "The Newspaper Suppressions," *New York Times*, July 10, 1864, col. 3, p. 8.
34. Ibid.
35. "The President Will Make Another Call for 500,000 More Men," *Cincinnati Daily Enquirer*, July 4, 1864, p. 3.
36. *The American Annual Cyclopedia and Register of Important Events of the Year 1864* (New York: D. Appleton & Company, 1865), p. 392.
37. "The Arrest of General Dix," *New York Herald*, July 10, 1864, col. 2, p. 8.
38. Ibid., col. 3, p. 8.
39. "The Newspaper Suppressions," *New York Times*, July 10, 1864, col. 3, p. 8.

12. The Gold Key

1. Roy P. Basler, ed., *The Collected Works of Abraham Lincoln*, vol. 7 (New Brunswick, NJ: Rutgers University Press, 1953), p. 347.
2. "Finance and Trade," *Pittsburgh Commercial*, May 27, 1864, col. 1, p. 4.
3. Walter Stahr, *Stanton: Lincoln's War Secretary* (New York: Simon & Schuster, 2017), p. 345.
4. Balser, *Collected Works*, p. 347. .
5. William E. Gienapp and Erica L. Gienapp, eds., *The Civil War Diaries of Gideon Welles* (Urbana: University of Illinois Press, 2014), p. 412.
6. Kinahan Cornwallis, *The Gold Room and the New York Stock Exchange and Clearing House* (New York: A. S. Barnes, 1879), p. 4.
7. John Hay, *At Lincoln's Side: John Hay's Civil War Correspondence and Selected Writings*, ed. Michael Burlingame (Carbondale: Southern Illinois University Press, 2000), p. 186.
8. Ibid., p. 187.
9. Ibid., p. 189.
10. Ibid., p. xxv.
11. Ruth Painter Randall, *Mary Lincoln: Biography of a Marriage* (Boston: Little, Brown & Company, 1953), p. 316.
12. "Local Intelligence," *Detroit Free Press*, July 20, 1864, p. 1.
13. "Debt and Expenditure," *New York Times*, April 11, 1864, p. 4.
14. Elizabeth Keckley, *Behind the Scenes, Or, Thirty Years a Slave and Four Years in the White House* (Mineola, NY: Dover Publications, 2006), p. 149–150.

15. Daniel Mark Epstein, *The Lincolns: Portrait of a Marriage* (New York: Ballentine Books, 2008), p. 42.

16. Epstein, *The Lincolns*, p. 427.

17. "Personal Intelligence," *New York Herald*, May 2, 1864, col. 5, p. 4.

18. Justin B. Turner and Linda Levitt Turner, eds., *Mary Todd Lincoln: Her Life and Letters* (New York: Alfred A. Knopf, 1972), p. 435; quoted in Hay, *At Lincoln's Side*, p. 189.

19. Epstein, *The Lincolns*, p. 428.

20. "The Bogus Proclamation and its Author," *Brooklyn Daily Eagle*, Saturday evening, May 21, 1864, p. 2.

21. "The Suppression of Newspapers," *The Independent*, May 26, 1864; vol. 16, no. 808; S. W. Benedict, New York, Boston, p. 4.

22. Wesley C. Mitchell, "The Value of the 'Greenbacks' During the Civil War," *The Journal of the Political Economy* (University of Chicago) 6 (March 1898), p. 159.

23. Louis M. Starr, *Bohemian Brigade: Civil War Newsmen in Action* (New York: Alfred A. Knopf, 1954), p. 107.

24. "The Proclamation Hoax," *The World*, May 20, 1864, p. 6.

25. David Homer Bates, *The Telegraph Goes to War, The Personal Diary of David Homer Bates*, ed. Donald E. Markle (Hamilton, NY: Edmonston, 2003), p. 96.

26. Mitchell, "Value of the 'Greenbacks,'" p. 161.

27. Ibid., p. 162.

28. All of the correspondence in *Philadelphia Inquirer*, January 18, 1864.

29. Cornwallis, *The Gold Room*, p. 8.

30. Medbery, *Men and Mysteries of Wall Street* (New York: R. Worthington, 1878), p. 250.

31. Medbery, *Men and Mysteries*, p. 250.

32. "The Arrest of Gen. John Dix," *New York Herald*, August 7, 1864.

33. *The American Annual Cyclopedia and Register of Important Events of the Year 1864* (New York: D. Appleton & Company, 1865), p. 394.

13. Popular as the Air

1. John A. Marshall, *The American Bastille*, 8th ed. (Philadelphia: Thomas W. Hartley, 1871) p. 11.

2. *Batavian*, August 6, 1864, vol. 41, no. 30, p. 1.

3. "City News and Gossip," *Brooklyn Daily Eagle*, June 6, 1864, p. 3.

4. "Our 'Dead Beat'," *Brooklyn Eagle*, June 25, 1864, p 2.

5. "Personal," *Rome Sentinel* (Rome, NY), Ocober 5, 1864, col. 1.

6. "Chase and the Arbitrary Arrests," *Daily Post* (Pittsburgh, PA), June 1, 1864, p. 3.

7. "Jos. Howard Jr., Dead at Home in Manhattan," *Brooklyn Daily Eagle*, April 1, 1908, col. 1, p. 5.

8. Ibid.

9. "Gene Intelligence," *The Pittsburgh Commercial*, July 27, 1864, p. 2.

10. Abraham Lincoln. *Abraham Lincoln papers: Series 1. General Correspondence. 1833 to 1916*: Henry Ward Beecher to John D. Defrees, Tuesday, Case of Joseph Howard Jr. August 2, 1864. Manuscript/mixed material.

11. Abraham Lincoln. *Abraham Lincoln papers: Series 1. General Correspondence. 1833 to 1916*: John D. Defrees to John Hay, Wednesday, Cover letter. August 3, 1864. Manuscript/mixed material.

12. "Howard's Letter," reprint of *Globe*, July 5, 1885 column. *Boston Daily Globe*, April 19, 1908, p. 36.

13. "The President and the Forger," picked up from *Philadelphia Age*, *The Daily Post* (Pittsburgh, PA), September 10, 1864, p. 1.

14. Abraham Lincoln. *Abraham Lincoln papers: Series 1. General Correspondence. 1833 to 1916*: Joseph Howard Jr. to Abraham Lincoln, Monday, September 19, 1864. Release of Francis Mallison. Manuscript/mixed material.

15. Abraham Lincoln. *Abraham Lincoln papers: Series 1. General Correspondence. 1833 to 1916*: Moses F. Odell to Abraham Lincoln, Thursday, Release of Francis Mallison. September 8, 1864. Manuscript/mixed material.

16. *The Collected Works of Abraham Lincoln*, vol. 3, ed. Roy P. Basler (Rutgers, NJ: Rutgers University Press, 1953), p. 13, DNA WR RG 94, Adjutant General, Letters received September 20, 1864, p. 1064.

17. "Washington News and Gossip," *Philadelphia Inquirer*, November 26, 1861, front page.

18. [Chas. G. Halpine], "Brooklyn 'Evening Press' and Joseph Howard," *New York Citizen*, June 29, 1867, p. 4.

19. "New York Letter," *Daily Free Press and Times*, November 3, 1880, col. 2, p. 2.

20. Allen Thorndike Rice, ed., *Reminiscences of Abraham Lincoln by Distinguished Men of His Time* (New York: J. J. Little & Co., 1886), p. 253; "Brooklyn 'Evening Press' and Joseph Howard, Jr.," *New York Citizen*, June 29, 1867, p. 4.

21. Charles A. Dana, *Recollections of the Civil War* (Lincoln, NE: University of

Nebraska Press, 1996), originally published by D. Appleton and Company (New York, 1898), p. 261.

22. Letter from Stephen Fiske to Joseph Howard, November 22, 1904, with attached letter of Howard to Fiske, September 8, 1864; Joseph Howard Scrapbooks, Joseph Howard Scrapbook of Clippings, Correspondence, and Photographs, vol. 5, AM 14721, General mss., Special Collections, Princeton University Library, Princeton, New Jersey.

23. "The Hotel Burners," *New York Herald*, March 27, 1865, p. 8.

24. "Beauties of Military Commissions," from *Journal of Commerce*, July 24, 1865, *The World*, July 25, 1865, p. 8.

25. "Lecture by Joseph Howard, Jr.," *New York Times*, December 16, 1888, p. 6.

26. "The White House Cashier in Town," *Sunday Mercury*, October 23, 1864, p. 3.

27. [no title], *Rochester Democrat and Chronicle*, November 7, 1886, p. 5.

28. Thompson Gains Onstot, *Pioneers of Menard and Mason Counties: Made Up of Personal Reminiscences of an Early Life in Menard County, which We Gathered in a Salem Life from 1830 to 1840, and a Petersburg Life from 1840 to 1850; Including Personal Reminiscences of Abraham Lincoln and Peter Cartright* (Mason County, IL: T. G. Onstot, 1902), p. 37.

29. William O. Stoddard, *Inside the White House in War Times* (New York: Charles L. Webster & Co., 1890), p. 174.

30. Harold Holzer, ed., *Lincoln's White House Secretary: The Adventurous Life of William O. Stoddard* (Carbondale: Southern Illinois University Press, 2007), p. 273.

31. In William O. Stoddard's manuscript, *Recollections of a Checkered Lifetime*, held at the Lincoln Financial Foundation Collection in Fort Wayne, Indiana, he continues the speculation anecdote by relating the Mary Todd Lincoln story recounted here, p. 372.

32. Holzer, *Lincoln's White House Secretary*, p. 241.

33. Alice Scoville Barry, *Why Did President Lincoln Suppress the Journal of Commerce?* (New York: Twin Coast Newspapers, Inc., 1979), p. 27.

34. "Editor's Table: The Old Knickerbocker to His Readers," *The American Monthly Knickerbocker* (New York: Lewis Gaylord Clark) 63, no. 1, p. 82.

Index

ELIZABETH MITCHELL is the author of nonfiction books covering politics, sports, and history, including her most recent acclaimed saga, *Liberty's Torch: The Great Adventure to Build the Statue of Liberty*. Her novella-length work, *The Fearless Mrs. Goodwin*, was a *New York Times* and Amazon nonfiction bestseller. Formerly the executive editor of *George*, the nation's largest political magazine, she has worked as an investigative reporter and features writer. She makes her home in Brooklyn, New York.